PORSCHE

SPORTS RACING PROTOTYPES
1963–1971

PORSCHE

PORSCHE

SPORTS RACING PROTOTYPES 1963–1971

Johnny Tipler

THE CROWOOD PRESS

LISSAC
252

CONTENTS

FOREWORD

By Gijs van Lennep

Gijs van Lennep is an ambassador for Porsche, snapped here at Classics at the Castle with a 991 50th Anniversary model.

First of all, I would like to say how pleased I am to endorse Johnny Tipler's book about the era of motor racing when Porsche was in the ascendant, which was also the period when I was building my racing career – the bulk of which was spent driving Porsches – and which culminated in two wins at the Le Mans 24-Hours in 1971 in a 917 and 1976 in a 936.

My racing career even took off in a car that was distantly related to Porsche: I started competing in a tuned-up Volkswagen Beetle at Zandvoort, which is within earshot of my home at Aerdenhout in the Netherlands. I scored my first win in 1965 in a Porsche 904, which sets the scene nicely for the content of this book.

I raced examples of all the models covered in the book, including the 904 Carrera GTS, the 906, the 908 Spyder and the 917, and each one was a milestone on Porsche's trajectory to the top of the endurance racing pyramid. I enjoyed several successes in the 906, 908/2 and various 911s, and I won the inaugural Porsche Cup in 1970, organised on the initiative of Ferry Porsche and awarded to the world's best privateer driver. Also in 1970, I drove the 917 KH owned by the Finnish driver Antti Aarnio Wihuri, alongside David Piper. At Le Mans, we dropped out on lap 112 when I had a tyre blowout at 320km/h, from which I luckily emerged totally unscathed. Nevertheless, the 917 was a fantastic racing car, and I like to say that it handled like a very powerful go-kart! I'm told that no one else drove 917s more than I did, and in the 1971 Le Mans, I drove one of the Martini Racing Team's 917 KHs together with Helmut Marko. We hardly had any brakes for the last five hours, but stopping for fresh pads and so on would have cost us the lead. While most drivers went off for a doze during their downtime, during one of my breaks from driving, I tucked into a hearty steak dinner. That may have been a bit unorthodox, but we were young and didn't know any better. In fact, in that race, we set a speed and distance record for the 24-hours, and the distance one wasn't broken for 39 years.

I first met Johnny around 1973 when I was driving one of Frank Williams' Iso-Marlboro F1 cars and he was doing John Player Team Lotus PR, promoting JPS cigarettes in the Formula 1 paddocks and press offices during the Grands Prix. Subsequently, our paths have crossed many times, such as when I drove a 356 in La Carrera Panamericana, a 550 Spyder in the Mille Miglia, and a 917 Can-Am car at the Zandvoort Historic Grand Prix, and he was there too, covering those events as a journalist. We've had plenty of fun at Abbeville racetrack over the years, too, where our mutual friend, RS collector Johan Dirickx, lets me put some of his rare 911 RSs through their paces around the circuit.

So, I'm very happy to be contributing to this book about the 1960s Porsche race cars, a subject that I have always been passionate about, and as a marque ambassador, I continue to endorse the brand at events such as the 2023 Rennsport Reunion at Laguna Seca. All being well, you will read about more of my racing exploits further on in the book!

TIMELINE

1963 Type 904 coupé introduced for the 1964 racing season.

1964 Type 904 GTS competes in the International World Championship for Makes, winning mountainous Sicilian Targa Florio epic.

1965 Types 904/6 and 904/8 coupés introduced, powered by flat-4 Carrera and ex-718 F1 flat-8 engines. Lightweight open-top *Känguru* prefigures Types 906, 910 and 909 Bergspyder hillclimb cars.

1966 Type 906 coupé launched, with 2.0-litre flat-6 engine; eligible for FIA Group 4 and Group 6 categories. Designed by Helmuth Bott and Hans Mezger; long- and short-tail versions raced. Targa Florio is biggest win. Aerodynamically-improved Type 910 introduced, current for the following two seasons. Type 910 Bergspyder entered in European Hillclimb Championship.

1967 Type 907 coupé with 2.2-litre flat-6 engine launched at Le Mans, heralding Porsche's concerted attack on the World Sportscar Championship. New Type 711 3.0-litre flat-8 engine introduced. Type 910 wins Targa Florio.

1968 Type 908/1 coupé introduced, using 3.0-litre flat-8. Type 908 Bergspyder wins European Hillclimb Championship. Type 907 wins Targa Florio.

1969 Type 908/2 Flounder introduced with open-top Spyder bodywork, powered by 3.0-litre flat-8. Another Targa Florio victory. Mentored by Ferdinand Piëch, Type 917 introduced, powered by 4.5-litre flat-12 engine, using both long- and short-tail rear bodywork. Type 917 PA Spyder races in Can-Am series. Porsche wins FIA World Championship for Makes (World Sportscar Championship) in 1969, 1970 and 1971.

1970 Type 908/3 introduced, featuring compact Spyder shell and 3.0-litre flat-8 engine; victory in Targa Florio. Porsche competition programme divided between JW-Automotive and Porsche Konstruktionen. Type 917 victorious in Le Mans 24-Hours. Flat 12 engine capacity increases to 4.9- and 5.0-litres.

1971 Competition programme run by JW Automotive and Martini International Racing teams. Types 908/3 and 917 win eight out of eleven rounds of the FIA World Sportscar Championship – also known as the World Championship for Makes.

INTRODUCTION

What is so significant about these seemingly random eight years between 1963 and 1971? Almost six decades ago, they represented the era when Porsche methodically worked its way up the endurance racing ladder from class winner to outright victor. We take the company's success pretty much for granted now, in the showroom as well as on track. The period that the book focuses on reveals the skills, determination, ambition and prowess that consolidated the marque's already burgeoning reputation.

In many ways, they were the halcyon days of long-distance endurance motor racing, during which Porsche embodied the rise of the up-and-coming manufacturer, progressing inexorably from reliable class-winners throughout the 1950s and 1960s to outright victors – a platform they consolidated and never rescinded. This does not imply that they were in any way also-rans in the lead-up since anyone running a Porsche, whether factory or privateer, was a serious contender at any level of the sport from the word go.

Like Colin Chapman of Lotus Cars, Porsche started off as a car maker in 1948, and the two makes often vied for victory in the sports car classes over the following decade. While Lotus focused mainly on producing and running single-seater racing cars from 1958, Porsche concentrated on sports racing cars, dipping into F1 and F2 with the Types 718/2 and 804 between 1959 and 1962, though majoring on the 718 RSK Spyder, RS61 and Type 695 2000 GS Abarth in sports-GT racing. It is interesting to draw a parallel between the two marques since both manufactured road-going sports and GT cars and, of course, Team Lotus won

The work's 907s of Gerhard Mitter/Lodovico Scarfiotti, Jo Siffert/Hans Herrmann and Vic Elford/Jochen Neerpasch roar away from the startline to begin 1968's BOAC 500 enduro.

the F1 World Title four times during this period in which we are exploring Porsche's rise to the top. Like Enzo Ferrari, Lotus founder Colin Chapman built production cars to subsidise the company's racing activities, while Porsche raced in order to market its sports car production. It is no disrespect to Lotus to remark that the 75-year-long histories of both companies suggest that Porsche constructed the better business model. Chapman had no time for rules: he comprehended them and found ways to exploit loopholes – the 'unfair advantage', as he put it. Porsche, on the other hand, played with a straight bat. So, while Team Lotus was often the trailblazer in the rarefied field of F1 and single-seater racing cars, the sports-racing prototype arena in which Porsche competed was dominated by Ferrari, who was challenged over much of the 1960s – and beaten – by the corporate might of Ford. The eponymous Hollywood movie casts this needle match rather well. And as the titans wore each other down, Porsche capitalised on their rivalry and had eclipsed them by 1970.

I have been infatuated with Porsches since I was a child, initiated by an incident in the early 1960s involving my father spinning backwards into a hedge in his friend's 356, fortunately without incurring injury or significant damage to the car. One could keep track of Porsche's performances on track and in rallies via the motor racing magazines and a neat annual publication entitled *Castrol Achievements*. That's why I have always been fascinated by the epoch that encapsulates the subject matter covered here.

I have interspersed the specification of the cars with their performances in accounts of the World Championship races they participated in, mostly chronologically, dovetailing interviews with some of Porsche's top drivers who helped define this fabulous epoch. The book focuses on the six distinct Porsche models that raced during this period. Obviously, and inevitably, there were overlaps, for instance as Porsche tried out a new model whilst the existing one was still being campaigned, but, more or less, each car falls conveniently into each year.

Between 1963 and 1971, Porsche created and honed a series of racing cars in its Zuffenhausen factory and Weissach competitions department to run in the International Sports Car Championship Prototype classes. These cars are synonymous with the Le Mans 24-Hours and the rest of the FIA-regulated thirteen-round World Sportscar Championship races held during that period, split between the International Manufacturers' Championship and the International Sports Car Championship. The category is known today as the World Endurance Championship; these races lasted 24 hours, twelve hours, or six hours, or they were otherwise categorised by distance, usually run over 1,000km or 500km, or indeed 500 miles. According to the FIA calendar, events took place annually at various European tracks, including Le Mans, Nürburgring, Monza, Spa-Francorchamps and Brands Hatch, among others, and in the USA at Daytona and Sebring.

With the 917 KH (#023, pictured at the factory in 1970) Porsche finally achieved its ambition of winning the Le Mans 24-Hours.

Here in the Brands Hatch paddock, the 2.2-litre 907 LH of Hans Herrmann and Jochen Neerpasch came 4th in the 1967 BOAC 500.

THE WORLD SPORTSCAR CHAMPIONSHIP

The World Sportscar Championship that Porsche zealously contested virtually throughout was an endurance race series, running under several different guises from 1953 to 1993. The series' official name changed from time to time, variously to the Sportscar World Championship, the World Endurance Championship, the World Championship for Makes – or Manufacturers – and the World Sports Prototypes Championship.

The first era dates from 1953 to 1961, with six or so races each season in which sports prototypes and GT cars competed, exemplified by works entries from Ferrari, Maserati, Mercedes-Benz, Aston Martin and Jaguar, though the latter only ran at Le Mans. The 2023 movie *Ferrari,* starring Adam Driver and Penélope Cruz, encapsulates extremely well the drama of the duel between Ferrari and Maserati in 1957.

From 1962 to 1965, the FIA grouped GT cars into three categories with separate classifications, while hillclimbs and sprints expanded the championship calendar to fifteen races a year. The points system did not paint an accurate overall picture of the most significant results, so from 1966, the FIA reverted to a programme of between six and ten races, with events including the Le Mans and Daytona 24-Hours and the Targa Florio, Monza, and Nürburgring 1,000kms counting towards the Groups 4 and 5 sports-prototype championship. The crucial year of the Homeric contest between Ford and Ferrari was 1966, captured with varying degrees

Long-distance endurance races such as the Le Mans 24-Hours inevitably include nocturnal running, demonstrated by this 917 at the 2012 Classic event.

The Type 910 #28 driven by Jo Siffert and Hans Herrmann in the 1967 Nürburgring 1,000Kms failed to finish due to a dropped valve.

KEY EVENTS

Le Mans 24-Hours, 1953–
Mille Miglia, 1953–57
Nürburgring 1,000kms, 1953–
RAC Tourist Trophy, Dundrod/Goodwood/Oulton Park, 1953–69
Sebring 12-Hours, 1953–
La Carrera Panamericana, 1953–54
Targa Florio, 1955–73
Monza 1,000kms, 1963–2008
Spa-Francorchamps 1,000kms, 1963–
Reims 12-Hours, 1964–65
Buenos Aires 1,000kms, 1954–72
Zeltweg-Österreichring 1,000kms, 1966–76
BOAC 500 miles/1,000km Brands Hatch, 1967–71
Norisring 200 Miles, 1984–88
Watkins Glen 6 Hours, 1968–71, 1973–80

of veracity in the eponymous 2019 movie. The no less significant supporting cast included Porsche, Lola, Chevron, Matra, Alpine, Alfa Romeo, Chaparral and Howmet, not forgetting the AC 'Daytona' Cobras, Ford-Cosworth F3L and the odd Maserati. There was also a separate classification for GT cars between 1968 and 1975, though the swingeing rule change for 1972 that outlawed the 5.0-litre sports cars such as the Porsche 917 and Ferrari 512S saw Porsche withdraw officially, with Ferrari dropping out in 1973 and Matra in 1974.

In 1976, a separate championship for GT and new Group 5 silhouette cars was introduced, ushering in the 911 Carrera RSR Turbo-based Porsche 935 that became almost ubiquitous over the following eight or nine years. Prototypes were readmitted in 1979, followed by the Group C category, which was synonymous with the FIA's World Endurance Championship from 1982 to 1985, the World Sports-Prototype Championship from 1986 to 1990, and the World Sportscar Championship from 1991 to 1992. Several international manufacturers built Group C cars, including Porsche, Ford, Lancia, Jaguar, Nissan, Mazda, Toyota, Aston Martin and Peugeot. The most successful marque contesting the World Sportscar Championship was Porsche, who gained the most titles, followed by Ferrari.

PORSCHE LINE-UP

Over this halcyon period, the Porsche models involved in the action ranged from the Types 904 GTS (1963–66), the 906 – also known as the Carrera Six – (1966–67), the 907 (1967), the 908 (1968–71), the 909 Bergspyder (1968), the 910 (1967–69) and the 917 (1969–71). I consider it to be the era of the most aesthetically attractive sports racing cars, too – swooping curvaceous shapes unadorned for the most part by aerodynamic extravagances apart from modest splitters, spoilers and gurney flaps.

Different models of Porsche were demonstrated at the 2012 Solitude Revival, including this 908/1 coupé, 910 and 917.

The 904 GTS

This was a radical departure from Porsche's previous construction methodology, being entirely fibreglass-bodied on a traditional steel ladder-type chassis (rather than a multi-tubular spaceframe), powered by the 4-cylinder flat-4 2000cc 718/RS competition engine. A small number received the 6-cylinder unit introduced with the 911 road car in 1964 – still billed as the 901 in 1964. As well as the factory race team, the 904 was mostly raced by private entrants such as Dutch VW importer Ben Pon. Probably 108 units were built, including two flat-8 prototypes that utilised the 8-cylinder engine from the Type 718 Grand Prix cars.

The 904 also marked the passing of Porsche's 1955 4-cylinder Carrera engine that had brought so much success in cars such as the 550 Spyder, RS60 and RS61 and 356 Carrera Abarth. Its successors all employed 6-, 8- and 12-cylinder engines.

The 906

The 906 was also known as the Carrera Six, and was Porsche's last road-legal racing car. On road-based events, such as the Tour de France Auto and Sicilian Targa Florio, it fulfilled both roles. Works drivers Willy Mairesse and Herbert Müller won the 1966 Targa Florio outright in a 906.

The 906, with its mid-mounted 2.0-litre flat-6 engine, was built on an elaborate multi-tubular spaceframe chassis, reverting to earlier practice. Like the 904, it was clad in a relatively crudely-made glassfibre body, although unlike the 904, the 906's broader, flatter shape stemmed from wind-tunnel tests. For 1966, Porsche was looking to participate in the new Group 4 category for competition sports cars whilst continuing to produce the prototypes that honed the breed, which meant producing a minimum of 50 identical machines, so again, the 906 served both purposes. In total, 65 examples were made.

The 906 – Carrera Six – was the last racing car that Porsche made that could be legally driven on the public road.

The 907

Based on its contemporary 910's chassis, the 907 featured more aerodynamic bodywork, characterised by its long, rounded windscreen and perspex cover like the 906's over the 2.2-litre flat-8 engine. Launched at the 1967 Daytona 24-Hours, the three longtail 907s crossed the finishing line together (in a dramatically staged finish), taking the first three places. Probably 21 cars were made. As much as any other, this result established that Porsche now had the measure of the rival titans Ford and Ferrari (see 2019 film *Ford v Ferrari*).

Virtually siblings under the skin, the 907 KH of 1967 (left) and 908 LH of 1968 (with its complex rear aerofoils) were fundamental in raising Porsche to a higher level in the World Sportscar Championship stakes.

A trio of 907 LHs cross the finish line together in a staged dead heat at the end of the 1968 Daytona 24-Hours. The actual winners were Vic Elford and Jochen Neerpasch in number 54.

The 908

For 1968, the FIA introduced rule changes for Group 6 prototype-sports cars, limiting engine displacement to 3.0-litres, and Porsche designed the 908 accordingly. The new 908's air-cooled 3.0-litre flat-8 produced 350bhp at 8,400rpm. The 908 was originally configured as a coupé, almost identical to the 907, and now with the driver's seat located on the right-hand side, since most race circuits ran clockwise, and having the driver's weight on the right aided cornering stability. From 1969 on, the 908 was mainly raced as the 908/2, a lighter, open-top Spyder, known as a 'Flounder' due to its flat-fish form. The much more compact 908/3 was introduced in 1970 to complement the heavier Porsche 917 on twisty tracks that favoured nimble cars, like the Targa Florio and the Nürburgring. Probably 31 cars were made.

The 909

Known as the Bergspyder, the Type 909 consisted of just two pared-to-the-bone lightweight Spyders, used exclusively in two rounds of the 1968 European Hill-Climb Championship. They were underdeveloped, but paved the way for the 908/3.

The 910

Launched in 1967, Porsche made 22 units of the 910 coupé, powered by the 220bhp 2.0-litre (1991cc) flat-6, and thirteen cars were fitted with the 260bhp flat-8 in 2195cc and 1981cc format, of which seven were coupés and six were spyders. The 910 used the same complex steel tube-frame chassis as the 906, similarly clad in glass-fibre bodywork bonded to the triangulated tubes at strategic points. The principal differences included the pioneering (for Porsche) centre-lock 13in wheels, shod with correspondingly lower profile tyres, allowing a much sleeker, co-ordinated body shape. For the 1967 Targa Florio, six 910s were dispatched – three flat-6s and three flat-8s, all fuel injected – and they took the first three places.

Two vastly different incarnations of the 908 posed at Classics at the Castle: the 1969 long-tail '*Lang Heck*' in the foreground and the compact 1971 Martini Team 908/3 beyond.

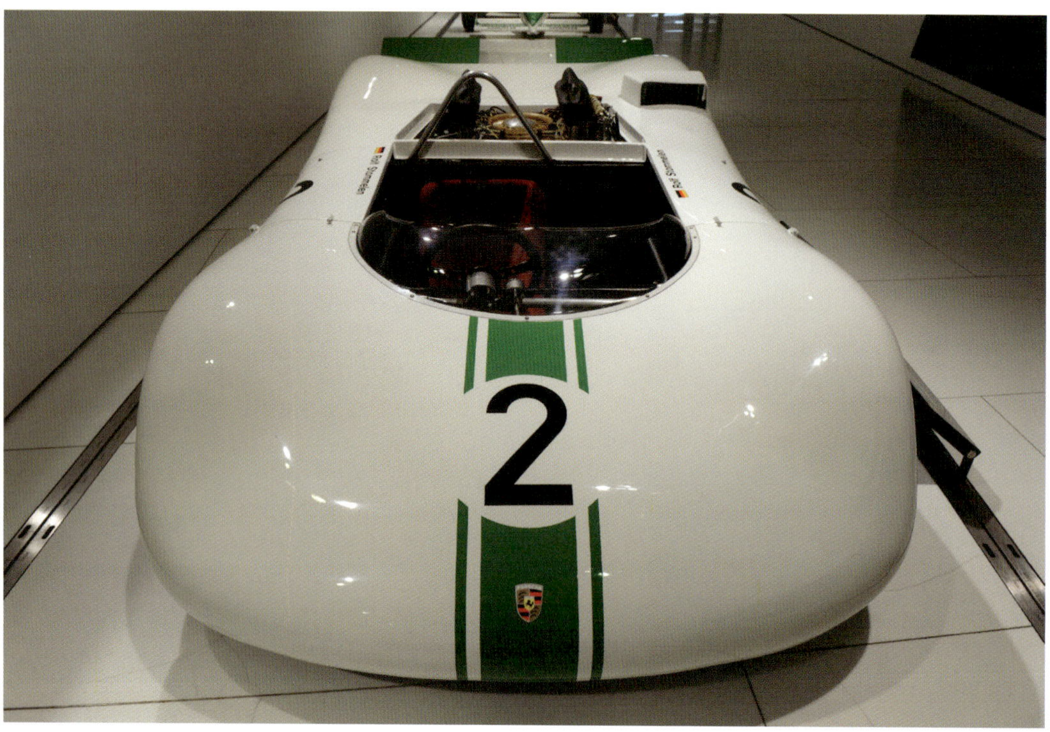

One of the disciplines that Porsche excelled in was mountain climbing, and lightweight versions were built to contest the European Hillclimb Championship during the 1960s, including the one-off 909 Bergspyder.

The 910 #017 of Vic Elford and Lucien Bianchi traverses Brands Hatch's South Bank Bend during the 1967 BOAC 500. It retired with faulty valve gear.

The 917

Porsche won the 1969 World Sportscar Championship – the International Championship for Makes – with outright victories in the 1,000km races at Brands Hatch, Monza, Spa and the Nürburgring, as well as the Targa Florio. But they had yet to win the coveted Le Mans 24-Hours trophy outright; the car intended to achieve this was the 917.

The 917 was constructed to FIA Group 4 regulations, powered by a flat-12-cylinder engine that was progressively enlarged from 4.5-litres to 5.0-litres. At first, it proved unwieldy on track, but swiftly went on to dominate sports car racing in 1970 and 1971. Drivers Richard Attwood and Hans Herrmann drove their 917 to victory in the 1970 Le Mans 24-Hours, breaking the duck as far as Porsche was concerned in that particular iconic event.

Photographed in the underground car park at the Porsche Museum at Zuffenhausen, this 917 KH is liveried as chassis #023, the car that won the 1970 Le Mans 24-Hours.

Donington Circuit's Kraner Curves section provides a thrilling prospect for the author at the wheel of the 917, as recounted later in the book.

Peter Vögele drives 917 #025 at Classic Le Mans 2018. The car was originally sold to Dominique Martin's Zitro Racing Team in 1970, and ran in the 1971 Buenos Aires 1,000 Kms placing 10th, the Monza 1,000Kms finishing 9th, and also at Spa and the 1971 Le Mans, co-driven by Gérard Pillon.

FIA GT and European Le Mans Series Champion Marc Lieb drives the 1,000bhp twin-turbo 917/30 on Weissach's Can-Am circuit, formerly raced by Herbert Müller in the European Interserie Championship in 1974.

RULING THE ROOST

When the FIA rules changed for 1972, the 917 and its contemporary Ferrari 512S were sidelined in favour of 3.0-litre prototypes; Porsche had been running 3.0-litre 908 prototypes since 1968, but the new breed would be powered by Formula 1 engines, and Porsche declined to get involved. So, while Ferrari fielded the 312P, Porsche took a breather to develop turbocharged racing versions of the 911, Gijs van Lennep and Herbert Müller winning Le Mans in 1974 with the 911 Carrera RSR Turbo. However, Porsche had already developed the open-top 917 PA Spyder for Can-Am racing in North America, culminating in the mighty twin-turbo 917/30 Spyder that won the Can-Am title in 1972 and 1973. It was so crushingly invincible that all the opposition fell away, and the category was abandoned. The 917 Spyder also won the Can-Am equivalent European-based Interserie championship every year from 1969 to 1975. Sixty-five cars were built.

A brief historical perspective. Previous Porsche racing cars from the early 1960s were the RS60 and RS61, with Porsche on a steady roll since it began racing with the 550 Spyder in 1953. Equally significantly, the firm's roots go way back to Professor Ferdinand Porsche's successful racing car designs for Mercedes-Benz and Auto Union in the 1920s and 1930s, prior to him setting up his own company in 1948 with his son Dr Ferry Porsche. It was the latter who oversaw the rise of the marque to successful international status during the 1950s and 1960s, with talented lieutenants including Huschke von Hanstein, Hans Mezger, Helmuth Bott, Peter Falk and (successor) Ferdinand Piëch masterminding the engineering that steered Porsche to the top of the charts in world-class endurance racing. It is quite a fantastic saga of racing car evolution in a particularly dangerous yet swashbuckling era, with Porsche gaining supremacy over deadly rivals Ferrari and Ford.

From regular and reliable class-winners in the early- to mid-1960s, Porsche evolved into outright winners in events like the Sicilian Targa Florio road race, an arduous 80-mile lap of largely mountain backroads that suited the size, handling and power-to-weight ratio of Porsche race cars. As we will see in more detail later on, the Targa Florio became something of a Porsche speciality, with eleven victories

Gijs van Lennep and Jacky Ickx shared the winning Type 936 #002 at the 1976 Le Mans 24-Hours, the third such victory for the Belgian and the second for the Dutchman.

spread from 1959, 1960, 1963, 1964, and every year thereafter from 1966 to 1970, as well as the final race in 1973 for good measure. Porsche also logged nine 2nd places and twelve 3rds, slightly better than runners-up Alfa Romeo, and much better than Ferrari. In this respect, the Targa Florio is a better yardstick of Porsche's excellence in the sporting arena than the much vaunted Le Mans 24-Hours, in which it was successful in respect of class wins during the 1950s and 1960s, but did not win outright until 1970.

Porsche won the Daytona 24-Hours in 1968 with the 907, and the Targa Florio in 1968 with the 908, at last conquering Le Mans outright in 1970 with the 917. These are the bare bones, steps on the ladder: over the course of six chapters, the book broadly charts the introduction, evolution and race career of each specific model.

The 917 became defunct when the rules were changed by the FIA for 1972, after which Porsche adapted its road-going 911 2.7RS into the 911 Carrera RSR Turbo, 934 and 935, which also became outright Le Mans winners. That makes the period between 1964 and 1971 very much a standalone era, witnessing the rise of Porsche from a regular and reliable class winner to the out-and-out victor. Porsche's success on the racetrack was, thereafter, a given. By 1976, the 917's spiritual successor, the 936, was the Le Mans and World Championship winner, followed by the virtually unbeatable 956 and 962 in the Group C series of the 1980s.

CHAPTER 1

THE PORSCHE 904 CARRERA GTS 1963–66

The 904/6 of Ralf Kelleners and Afschin Fatemi comes perilously close to the wall at La Source hairpin during the 2016 Spa Six Hours.

Porsche set out to design a completely new car in 1963 to maintain their stronghold in the under 2.0-litre GT racing class. The 904's inception was partly in response to the introduction of the Alfa Romeo GTZ (Tubolare Zagato) and Abarth's 1600 OT (Omologata Turismo), designed specifically to contest the FIA GT class. For homologation purposes, they needed to build at least 100 units of the new car in twelve months, and, as far as Porsche was concerned, the new model would have to be a road-going model because, in those days, they would be unlikely to sell 100 full-on race cars. As a road-going model, it still conformed to Group 3 Appendix J rules. The firm's Formula 1 programme was sacrificed to free up resources to design and develop the 904, on the assumption that the development costs of the GT racer would be recouped by sales. Porsche's engineers started with a clean sheet for the 904 because the tubular spaceframe construction employed in the construction of the Type 718 and RS60/61 Spyders would be too expensive and time-consuming in the creation of what was going to be a production car. The 718's mid-engined layout was carried over so that the Fuhrmann four-cam 'Carrera' flat-4 unit was mounted between the cockpit and rear axle on a steel ladder-frame chassis, and clad with fibreglass (GRP) body panels. Ferry 'Butzi' Porsche, grandson of founder Prof Ferdinand Porsche and designer of the 911, was responsible for the styling of the plastic body. He included some of the styling cues and the windscreen of the 718 in the design, and the fabrication of the body panels was outsourced to aircraft manufacturer Heinkel, who moulded two bodies a day, while Porsche managed a single chassis a day. Heinkel's methodology involved spraying chopped fibreglass into moulds rather than the laying-up by hand method employed by manufacturers such as Lotus (pre-VARI) and TVR at the time. The 904's upper and lower bodyshell panels were bonded and bolted onto the ladder chassis, a configuration that proved to be more rigid than the previous spaceframe chassis.

The 1967cc 904 GTS flat-4 is cradled amidships, in this case with an oil tank to the right and petrol tank at the rear.

Five 904 GTSs under construction in the Porsche Zuffenhausen factory – testing took place on the newly completed Weissach track – featuring ladder chassis, engine cradles and flat-4 motor, with fibreglass bodies bonded and bolted to the chassis.

The original plan was to install the brand new 2.0-litre flat-6 engine, designed for the forthcoming 901/911, but it was not ready when Porsche needed to present the car for homologation, so the 1966cc Type 587/3 180bhp quad-cam 356 Carrera 2 engine was used instead, allied to the road car's new five-speed gearbox. The suspension consisted of

Front brake disc, caliper, wishbone and damper of a 904/6.

The Stanley Gold 904/6 demonstrates the Kamm Tail aspect of its styling, which contributed to its aerodynamic shape.

coil springs and dampers rather than trailing arm front and swing-axle rear suspension, with unequal-length A-arms at the front. Brakes were 275mm (10.8in) discs at the front and 285mm (11.2in) at the rear.

Three 904 prototypes were constructed and tested during the autumn of 1963, and the car was unveiled in late November. Within the factory, it was referred to by its '904' type number, but at launch, it was marketed as the 'Carrera GTS'. Their confidence was not misplaced: a fortnight after introduction, only 20 of the 90 units slated for public consumption were unsold. Production started soon afterwards in the new 901/11 plant, and by April 1964 the 904 was homologated as a Grand Turismo racing car. January 1964's *Motor Sport* magazine published a front three-quarter shot of the 904, with this extended caption:

> *The Porsche Type 904 GT coupe, which is for sale to racing customers, has a fibre-glass body bonded to a steel box-sectioned chassis. It has a 'Manx-tail' end to the body, and the rear window is vertical, sunk into the smooth contours of the sides. Grilles behind the doors take in air for the Weber carburettors and for the cooling fan. Disc brakes and bolt-on wheels are used, while the slot in the nose takes in air for the oil cooler.*

Porsche's 904 project was also a radical departure from the series of Carreras developed in the past, the engine in the new car being in front of the rear axle, as on a Porsche Spyder, instead of behind the axle. The Porsche 904 bore no resemblance to any previous production models, and they probably built 114 altogether. *Autosport* revealed the specification of the new 904, commenting on the innovative trend for placing the powertrain of competition Grand Touring cars amidships:

> *Ferrari has adapted the much better mid-engine position, which is in front of the rear axle but behind the driving compartment, which is standard Grand Prix layout. And while Porsche did this with their experimental GT coupé using the 8-cylinder engine, the production GT cars were full rear-engine layout. The new Porsche is designated the Type 904, not to be confused with the Type 901, which is the touring 6-cylinder that appeared recently at all the motor shows…*

(and, of course, became known as the 911).

The new 904 was a complete break from Porsche tradition in its construction, with a chassis frame comprised of two deep-section box members, suitably cross-braced, whereas previous Porsche coupés – the 356s – were of monocoque construction, made from thin sheet steel or sheet aluminium. The 904 suspension consists of double wishbone and coil-spring front suspension, rack and pinion steering, and double wishbone and coil-spring rear suspension, all of which are descended from the F1 and F2 Grand Prix 787 and 718 Porsche 8-cylinder cars. The air-cooled 2.0-litre Carrera 4-cylinder engine is mounted ahead of the rear axle, with transmission via a 5-speed Porsche gearbox, and the drive is taken to the independently-sprung rear wheels through one-piece driveshafts, having inboard universal joints that not only swivel in all planes, but also extend in and out on short links, giving friction-free movement to the rear end. These new universal joints achieved by mechanical means the same effect as Lotus arrived at with the rubber-ring 'doughnut' universal joints used on their 1960s racing cars.

Six-cylinder engine and transmission of the 904/6 are cradled off the rear of the ladder chassis, which also provide pick-up points for the rear suspension.

The 904 coupé body is made of fibreglass, in two longitudinal halves – top and bottom – and bonded and bolted to the chassis frame, the whole tail hingeing upwards to give access to the engine and gearbox. The 4-cylinder engine has a 92 x 74 mm bore and stroke, giving 1966cc, and develops 180bhp at 7,000rpm, using Weber carburettors and a 9.8:1 compression ratio. Porsche insisted, correctly as it turned out, that it was not an 'airport racer', but an all-around GT car that could run in the Targa Florio and on smooth circuits or in rallies of the Tour de France type.

THE 904 IN RACING

The race record took off at the 1964 Sebring 12-Hours, where drivers Lake Underwood and Briggs Cunningham's 904 finished 9th overall and 1st in the prototype class. It was the beginning of a highly successful racing career, including overall victory in the Targa Florio for unfancied veterans Colin Davis and Antonio Pucci, and many class victories in the WSC 1,000km endurance races and the Le Mans 24-Hours, while rally successes included Eugen Böhringer and Rolf Wütherich (who was the ill-fated James Dean's 550 Spyder co-driver) finishing 2nd in the snow-bound 1965 Rallye Monte Carlo.

During 1964, Porsche continued to develop the 904 and provide customers with uprated components to keep the cars on the pace. Two factory race cars were fitted with a 2.0-litre version of the F1 718's flat-8 engine, and later in 1964, the flat-6 appeared, although these unhomologated cars ran as prototypes.

Taking the Targa Florio as a good benchmark for judging a car's overall prowess – not to mention that of its drivers – Porsche's victory in 1964 carries as much weight as Ferrari's Le Mans win the same year. Horses for courses at this point in time. As *Motor Sport* magazine's Denis Jenkinson reported in its June 1964 edition, 'a production competition GT car had won, and undoubtedly vindicated Porsche's policy of development through racing'.

Historically, Porsche won their class virtually every year since they first ran at Le Mans – *La Sarthe* – in 1951, and the 904 GTS was no exception, coming 4th and 5th overall in 1965, and winning the imponderable Index of Performance and Index of Thermal Efficiency categories. We are shortly going to take a close look at the car that was the Targa Florio victor, one of the original works' 904 GTSs making its European debut at the Sicilian enduro on 26 April 1964. Driven by veterans Colin Davis (an ex-pat British racer who lived in Rapallo) and Baron Antonio Pucci from Palermo, for five laps each of the 72km Piccolo Madonie circuit, chassis 904-006 (race number 86) outlasted both its prototype siblings around the sinuous mountain course, not to mention the host of Alfas, works Ferraris, debutant GT40 and sundry Cobras. After Davis set the fastest lap at 41m 10.5s, Pucci put the car into the lead on its 7th lap, and they were followed home by a second works' 904 GTS driven by Herbert Linge and Gianni Balzarini. As *Motor Sport*'s Denis Jenkinson said in his report of June 1964:

In the Porsche pits there was an air of satisfaction, for though the works prototypes had broken down, they had a production GT car in the lead with an older model in second place and another 904 model in fourth place, while the eight-cylinder car of Barth and Maglioli had been repaired and was running again, but too far behind to hope to get anywhere.

This was regarded as an outstanding success, since the 904 was essentially the company's first customer racing car, and (apart from Sebring) they had proved it was a winner from the outset.

Also on the Porsche driver roster were a couple of Formula 1 stars: Jo Bonnier and 1962 F1 World Champion Graham Hill. This compelling duo had raced for Porsche since 1960 in Hill's case, and 1961 in Bonnier's. But, having practised as assiduously as only Hill could, he did not get a go in the 1964 Targa, Bonnier having retired the car on the second lap.

Midway through the 1964 season, *Motor Sport*'s Jenkinson took stock:

Herbert Linge drove the 1981cc flat-8 powered 904/8 at the Norisring street circuit on 5 July 1964.

Antonio Pucci and Colin Davis on their way to winning the 1965 Targa Florio. The photo gives an idea of the arduous nature of the circuit's terrain.

The 904 GTS was an effective rally car, pictured here at the 7th International Porsche Ski-Treffen Winter Rally at Zürs-Arlberg, Austria, in 1964.

At one time a GT car was a practical and usable road car that could be raced, but development and the rules has caused the appearance of the Porsche 904 and the Ferrari 250 LM, which are splendid racing cars but not everyday GT cars, although there are people who use a 904 as a road car. It has also developed very fast and powerful racing coupés that are getting into the hands of inexperienced drivers, as witness the number of crashed 904 Porsches this season, and had there been a hundred Ferrari LM models available there would have been a lot more crashes – not because there is anything wrong with these cars, far from it, but they are very fast racing machines and there are not more than 20 or 30 drivers in Europe capable of handling them to their limit.

And he would know what he was talking about, having navigated Stirling Moss to victory on the 1955 Mille Miglia.

At Le Mans 1964, the headliners were the Ferrari 3.3-litre 275P prototypes – the mid-engined cars appearing for the first time – and 250 GTOs, vying with the AC Cobras for outright supremacy. The prototype class up to 2000cc was a predictable victory for the lone 8-cylinder Porsche of Jo Bonnier and Richie Ginther. After the throttle-sticking troubles had been sorted out and a moment of alarm when Bonnier thought the rear suspension was falling off, the car ran well, albeit two laps behind the overall winner. A further four 904 GTSs occupied the top ten positions.

The 904 GTS of Antonio Pucci/Colin Davis won the 1965 Targa Florio, with Gianni Balzarini/Herbert Linge 2nd in another 904 GTS.

F1 stars Graham Hill and Jo Bonnier brought this 904/8 home in 4th place in the 1965 Targa Florio. The 904/8 Känguru is just visible behind it.

Dutch Porsche concessionaire Ben Pon steps between a quartet of works' 904 GTSs in the Nürburgring paddock during the 1965 1,000Kms meeting. Pon and Koch finished 25th.

THE 904 GTS SPEC

Introduced in December 1963, the 904 GTS consisted of a pressed steel frame made up of rectangular section longitudinal beams and cross-bracings. A new departure from aluminium panels was the lightweight, curvaceous fibreglass body made for Porsche by Heinkel: very pretty, even though the bottom half did not quite line up with the top half, which left a peculiar lip along the length of the hull. The 1967cc 587 Carrera flat-4 engine developed 180bhp @ 7,000rpm and was mounted amidships ahead of the axle, while a new gearbox was located behind the axle, allied to a single-plate clutch and ZF limited slip diff. The suspension consisted of unequal-length wishbones at the front with wishbones and twin forward-facing radius rods and coil springs at the rear. Larger ducts for cooling the bigger rear brakes mark out the 904/6, and it was superseded in 1966 by the 906, or Carrera 6. Bluntly, the 1964 launch of the 911, whose completely new 6-cylinder engine and modified MacPherson Strut front suspension represented a clean break with Porsche tradition, rendered the 904 obsolete. By 1966, it had been swept away by Porsche cousin Ferdinand Piëch and his Carrera 6. Meanwhile, the 904 Carrera GTS enjoys a unique place in the manufacturer's history as the last competition car to be fitted with the four-cam, 4-cylinder Carrera engine.

The fuel tank and on-board fire system are located in the nose of the 904/6.

The 904/6's rear suspension involves reversed upper wishbones, upper and lower longitudinal radius arms, coil-over dampers, and an anti-roll bar.

Interestingly, there was much debate about top speeds achieved by the fastest Ferrari and Lola-Ford prototypes: a radar beam positioned on the Mulsanne Straight – long before chicanes were installed – indicated that Richie Ginther's Lola had hit 340km/h – 211mph – by virtue of slipstreaming three works Ferraris.

The 904 GTS entered by August Veuillet and driven by Robert Buchet and Guy Ligier came 7th overall at Le Mans 1964.

TYPE 904 CARRERA GTS MAJOR SUCCESSES

1964
1st, Targa Florio
3rd, Nürburgring 1,000kms
7th, 8th, 10th, 11th, 12th, Le Mans 24-Hours
1st, Reims 12-Hours
1st, Tulip Rally
1st, Alpine Rally
1st, European Hillclimb Championship, GT & Sports classes
1965
1st, Rossfeld Hillclimb
1st, Gaisberg Hillclimb
1st, European Hillclimb Championship, GT class
2nd, Monte Carlo Rally
2nd, 3rd, 4th, 5th, Targa Florio
4th, 5th, Le Mans 24-Hours

CLIMB EVERY MOUNTAIN

Meanwhile, Porsche was invincible in hillclimbing – mountain-climbing, or *Berg-Rennen*, as it is known in Europe. At Rossfeld – close to Hitler's Berchtesgaden eyrie – Edgar Barth won Round 1 of the European championship in an 8-cylinder Elva-Porsche, with Herbert Müller second in an 8-cylinder 904. Heini Walter set a new 2.0-litre GT record in a 904. I have driven this course in a 991 Turbo, and it is, to my mind, more thrilling than lapping a racetrack, partly because of the topography and fathomless drop-offs, and the demands of negotiating numerous hairpin corners.

Here is *Autosport*'s take on the uphill series:

> *At the time of going to press, three further events have taken place in the European Hillclimb championship, these being Mont Ventoux in France on June 14th, Gaisberg, Austria, on June 28th, and Trento-Bondone in Italy on July 12th,*

making with the Rossfeld meeting a total of four rounds out of this series of seven.

Mont Ventoux was the longest event in the championship curriculum, measuring 22 kilometres or 13 miles, and incorporated the most gruelling road surfaces imaginable. Current champion Edgar Barth, who won the first event with a flat-8-engined 2.0-litre Elva Porsche, switched to last year's championship-winning flat-8 Porsche prototype, and he had little difficulty in winning the championship class from Anton Fischaber's Lotus-BMW. Gaisberg, like Rossfeld, required competitors to score on an aggregate of two runs. Barth once more set the pace and scored his hat-trick, and Müller, with the hurriedly prepared Elva-Porsche, was placed second. The meeting was full of incidents, most of which could be blamed on poor crowd control.

When I drove the Gaisberg climb in 2019 in a Porsche 718 Cayman with Antony Fraser, there were no such problems, though the hilltop restaurant was very popular with hikers as well as car and bike fans, and parking at the summit was difficult. On the other hand, we had the Zistelalm Hotel, mid-way up the climb, virtually to ourselves. Back then, Barth's best time of 4m 11.54s for the 8.5km hill course constituted a new outright record. The sinuous 17.5-km Trento-Bondone climb in northern Italy was the scene of Barth's fourth consecutive win, which clinched for him the 1964 European title, with three further qualifying events. His time of 12m 17.8s bettered his old record by 0.08 of a second.

Two further events, Cesena-Sestrière on 26 July and Schauinsland-Freiburg on 9th August, came next. Edgar Barth, who had already assured himself of the title for the second successive year by winning Trento-Bondone, continued to dominate the championship with

Rolf Stommelen was 3rd of three 904 GTSs on the wet Gaisberg Hillclimb on 19 September 1965, with Michel Weber 1st and Sepp Greger 2nd. The author, and photographer Antony Fraser, fondly remember staying at the Zistelalm Hotel when reprising the route in 2019 aboard a 718 Cayman.

Michel Weber's 904 GTS recorded 4th fastest time up the Trento Bondone hillclimb on 10 July 1966, behind Mitter's 906, Herrmann's 910 and Greger's 906.

The 904 of Michel Weber being fettled in readiness for the 1966 Schauinsland-Freiburg Hillclimb, in which he came 4th. Mitter's 910 coupé was the winner.

his works-entered 2.0-litre 904 prototype, and won at Cesana in a new record time of 5m 33.1s. Second place went once more to the young Swiss driver Herbert Müller in the Scuderia Filipinetti 2.0-litre flat-8 Elva-Porsche, over five seconds behind the winner. At the penultimate round, Freiburg-Schauinsland, Barth kept up the pressure to notch up his sixth successive championship win, ascending in a new record time of 6m 40.66s for the 11.2km course. This is another key European hillclimb I have driven a few times, courtesy of local Porsche spares specialists FVD Brombacher – father and daughter Willy and Franziska – variously in a 997 GT3 4.0, a 992 GTS and a 996 GT2. We never reached the summit in one go, always irresistibly tempted to stop at the halfway-house Sternwald restaurant. Record-breaking was never the goal.

THE 1964 SEASON

For the Reims 12-Hours race on 5 July 1964, the Porsche factory entered a lone 8-cylinder version of the 904 GTS coupé for Edgar Barth and Colin Davis and a full series production 904 for Gerhard Koch and Gerhard Mitter,

A pit stop for JT's 986S on the former Reims Grand Prix circuit, once home to the International 12-Hour endurance race, whilst covering the Rallye Monte-Carlo Historique with photographer Alex Denham.

and there were eight further 904 models in the hands of private owners. The event had last been held in 1958, when it had been run for GT cars. Now, prototypes augmented the entry list, effectively a half-distance Le Mans. The main concern was the after-dark start, with the traditional Le Mans-style sprint across the track for drivers to leap aboard their cars. The 904/8s were quickest away, and very quickly, a new average lap speed was posted of 203km/h – 126mph – in the dark, with two virtual hairpin bends to cope with on the road circuit. I expect most of us have paused there for the obligatory selfie beside the renovated pits, and to marvel at the speeds potentially attainable on those long, straight public roads.

Herbert Linge's 904/8 exhibits a bit of lean as it rounds a hairpin on the Norisring street circuit, Nuremberg, 5 July 1964.

Anyway, behind the Ferrari LMs, Lola-Fords and AC Cobras, the 904s began moving into the higher places as faster cars retired. In the final outcome, Porsche placed 5th, 6th, 7th, and 10th, and we note the name van Lennep at 15th, sharing a 904 with van Zalinge entered by Racing Team Holland.

The wonderfully expansive Tour de France Automobile was, at the time, a round of the FIA World Sportscar Championship. The Tour Auto was organised annually by the Automobile Club of Nice, with the participation of the French Shell Oil company and many other firms, including Dunlop Tyres. The idea of the event was very simple: a few French racing circuits were selected, together with an equal number of hill climbs, and then ten days were taken up driving around between them, with every other night being spent in a hotel at one of the selected towns. This may sound like a very relaxing way to go rallying, but anyone who has competed in this event will be quick to disabuse you of that fallacy. The actual amount of rest that the drivers and navigators got was minimal, and the event was no less of a strain on the competing cars, demonstrated by the high proportion of retirements.

Between 1960 and 1962, the number of starters remained constant at 116, while the number of finishers fell from 48 to 46, and in 1963, only 31 survived out of 122 starters. This was serious stuff, making the modern pastiche – the Tour Auto Optic for classic cars run by Peter Auto, who also run Classic Le Mans among other historic events – look something of a jolly. An enjoyable one, nevertheless. With certain reservations: I lost my driving licence covering it one year in a press Boxster 987 S, caught doing 160mph (258km/h) on a stretch of brand new autoroute in the Dordogne while leapfrogging a stage or two for the benefit of my colleague Antony Fraser (who needed to be ahead of the rally retinue in order to take photographs as the cars swept by). Having brusquely confiscated my licence at the next *péage*, the arresting officer demanded to see Antony's so he could lawfully take the Porsche's wheel. He was unable to produce it, the document being at the time in the care of the Yorkshire Constabulary. Fortuitously, the discovery of a letter from Porsche in the glove box identifying us as legitimate custodians of the vehicle enabled us to

Like the Alpine A110 behind it, the 904 GTS is a great handling car on a tarmac stage event like the French Tour Auto, seen here at the Souillac start in 2008.

Stanley Gold's 904/6 going neck-and-neck with an Alfa Romeo Giulia TZ2 during the Plateau 4 race at the 2012 Le Mans Classic: both models are well matched in performance and handling.

proceed to the Albi racetrack and beyond, to Clermont-Ferrand's Charade circuit.

Four decades earlier, in the GT category, the Porsche 904 GTSs were up against Alfa Romeo GTZs and sundry MGBs, Spitfires, Renault Alpines and Renée-Bonnet Djets. The works Porsche 904s of Robert Bouchet/Herbert Linge and Gunther Klass/Rolf Wütherich were never seriously challenged, and they took the win in the GT category, with 904 GTSs occupying 3rd through to 6th places in the leading classifications.

The 1964 season closed with the Linas-Montlhéry 1,000kms on the spectacular partly-banked circuit just south of Paris. It marked the first appearance of a Porsche 904/6 GTS, being a 904 GTS with a 6-cylinder engine replacing the original 4-cylinder Carrera engine. Outwardly, the new car was basically a production 904 fibreglass coupé, and the flat-6 engine was of the type being fitted to the new production touring Porsche, still known as the 901. This explains partly why the 904 GTS was originally designed with so much room in the engine compartment, because when you hinge up the tail of a 904, the 4-cylinder Carrera engine looks a bit lost in a fore-and-aft direction. The air-cooled flat-6 engine fits in very nicely.

Overhead view of the 904 GTS with engine cover partially hinged backwards, revealing the 1967cc flat-4 engine.

STANLEY GOLD'S 904 #006

The Gold/Junne 904/6 in the Le Mans pitlane during the 2012 Classic event.

With Le Mans' control tower, hospitality suites and startline pits garage architecture towering above, the Gold/Junne 904/6 proceeds along the pitlane.

Among the marvellous machinery at Classic Le Mans in 2010 was a former factory 904 GTS race car, which just happened to have that 1964 Targa Florio win to its credit, and owner Stanley Gold gave chapter and verse on its life and times. The event was a veritable Porsche fest, with fans and factory thronging to celebrate the 40th anniversary of the marque's first win at La Sarthe.

After its 1964 Targa triumph, 904 GTS #006 was entered next at the Nürburgring for the 1964 1,000kms at the end of May. When a practice crash wrecked a work's 904 prototype, the Targa winner was instated, and a driver shuffle placed Herbert Linge and Gerhard Mitter at the wheel. In amongst the works Ferrari GTs for much of the race, they were eventually put out of the running by a broken oil pipe, though the Pon/Koch 904 GTS came 3rd overall, the similar Siffert/Schiller car came 8th, and Stirling Moss's Lucky Casner/David Hobbs SMART 904 GTS was 9th. (SMART = Stirling Moss Automobile Racing Team) And, of course, they mopped up the 2.0-litre GT class.

Several six-pot 904/6s ran in-period, and the Porsche factory team's line-up also included a pair of 2.0-litre 904/8s that ran at Le Mans in 1964; the Type 771 flat-8 engine was a legacy of the 1963 W-RS 718 sports-prototype and the Type 753 that powered the Type 787 (804) F1 car in 1962. A pair of 2.0-litre flat-6s and a 2.0 flat-8 also contested the 24-Hours in 1965. Stanley reckons the flat-6 only adds 100lbs to the all-up weight of the car, which is not enough to mean that they must tweak the suspension to compensate. There is a price to pay for the extra performance, though: 'The purists hate us!' lamented Stanley. 'But it's not so much that we did it to win, cos that's not what I'm all about; it was really for durability.' Indeed, the correct flat-four can always be reinstated. Other mechanical changes have been less radical. For Le Mans, with its ultra-long straights, his mechanics fit higher gears, for instance.

The 904 GTS does not demand any special driving techniques. 'You just need to be careful about the wind,' warns Stanley. 'Le Mans favours this particular car, but historically, there were a few cars that got put up in the trees. It's one of the places where manufacturers began to understand the need for spoilers.'

Aerodynamics rapidly moved forward from mere streamlining. The 906 featured a lower-set nose with vestigial fins on either side, and by 1968, the 908 coupés had rear wings. But in 1966, the spaceframe-chassis, 6-cylinder 906 (Carrera Six) was Porsche's racing standard-bearer, and the sun had set on the 904's front-line career. It is special, then, to see 904 GTSs at historic events; there are usually one or two at the Nürburgring Old Timer and Silverstone Classic. But the Le Mans Classic elicited an unprecedented eight 904s, one with 1988 24-Hours winner Jan Lammers aboard, an impressive sight lined up side by side under the awning of the paddock garage.

The 904/6 of Stanley Gold/Yves Junne leaves the Pits during the 2012 Le Mans Classic.

The penultimate Porsche 904/6 constructed, chassis 006 was given select outings by the works team during the 1965 season. The best result was 2nd by Gerhard Mitter during the Course de Côte hillclimb on the legendary Mont Ventoux. During the 1980s, it was completely restored to its original configuration by Gunnar Racing. In the following years, the 904/6 has been used extensively and we see it here in action during the 2010 Le Mans Classic.

Le Mans Classic

There is nothing quite like Classic Le Mans; bigger than Goodwood Revival, Silverstone Classic or even the Nürburgring Old Timer, the Sarthe's 13.5km circuit length also allows for a sprawling paddock, numerous car club gatherings and spectator camping, plus the facilities on hand for the 24-Hours enduro give it greater clout. Its biennial formula of splitting entries into grids of six eras of competition, with over 70 cars in each, gives each 'plateau' three races, including a night session, with at least one driver change per race. It's a petrolhead's paradise, ensuring racing virtually right around the clock for the full 24 hours' duration.

Among the bevvy of 904 GTSs running in Grid 4 was Stanley Gold's ex-works car from 1964–65. In many ways, he typifies the historic racing fraternity: a racing car buff who puts his money where his mouth is, he pits a car with impeccable provenance amongst the mêlée of priceless machinery, and there is a relaxed assurance about his car and his achievements with it.

A line of 904s in the paddock's tented enclave in readiness for 2012's Classic Le Mans.

Several 908/6s run at Classic Le Mans in Plateau 4, such as this one in 2012.

A 904 running in the 2018 Le Mans Classic approaches the Ford Chicane.

So, 904 GTS #006 was pensioned off to Ganser of Munich, whence it was shipped to California, passing through several hands before ending up with Abarth aficionado Scott Gauthier in Arizona. It is here that chassis 904-006's second competition career took off.

Chatting to Stanley Gold in the Le Mans Classic paddock, he describes how the car came into his hands:

> *Ten years ago, I had a 695 Abarth-Carrera and Scott Gauthier owned the 904 GTS – after a long period of negotiation I traded him the Abarth Carrera for the 904. In terms of economics, I'm not sure he didn't get the better break, but I've had more fun! For starters, there's a little more room in the 904 and, given my girth, that's good for me. It's actually quicker too.*

This 904/6 #006 was in good shape, so Stanley began competing with it in 2000, notching up five or six races. Then trouble struck.

> *I took it on a rally in Arizona in 2001 and was racing for the lead with a girl in a Porsche Carrera. She saw that I was catching her and she hit a bridge where the road surface wasn't level, and dumped a whole street full of oil. I started skidding and put the car into a guardrail at 80mph, and it did extensive damage.*

Happily not to Stanley. Most of the repairs, including the 904's fibreglass body, were handled by classic Porsche restoration experts Gunnar Racing in West Palm Beach, Florida. It was mended in time for 2002 Classic Le Mans, and after Stanley won his 'grid', the Gunnar Racing website proudly proclaimed: 'to show we know what we are doing, this car just won the Le Mans Classic'.

Stanley has campaigned all five Le Mans Classics with the 904 GTS, and was a member of the Index of Performance-winning team in 2002, though it broke a cylinderhead stud and was a non-starter in 2004. There was a return to form in 2006 when once more car and driver shared the spoils of victory. Stanley raced it again in 2008, though the other team cars failed to perform as well as the 904 GTS. 'And of course we won the trophy this year,' he reminds me, 'so you picked the right car to write about – it's a three-time winner of the Le Mans Classic!'

Love Affair

Stanley loves it to bits: 'I've put a lot of miles on this car, and I like it a lot. It's nimble, easy to drive, there's good vision in terms of the mirrors and knowing where everybody is, and it responds very well. It's very stable and it's a delight to drive.' And he knows whereof he speaks. Stanley's a serious player on the historic scene – we first met when I was covering La Carrera Panamericana in Mexico in 2006, and he and regular co-driver Yves Junne were racing a 911. He has also run the 904 GTS up the hill at the Goodwood Festival of Speed, finished 31st out of 300 entries in a three-hour endurance race on the Nürburgring Nordschleife, circulated France twice on La Tour Auto, raced at Laguna Seca several times and appeared at Daytona's RennSport Reunion.

Mechanics work on the 904/6 of Stanley Gold and Yves Junne in the paddock enclave during the 2012 Le Mans Classic.

Driver change for Stanley Gold and Yves Junne aboard their 904/6 during the 2012 Classic Le Mans.

The 904/6 of Stanley Gold, Yves Junne and Andy Prill rounds La Source Hairpin during the Spa Six Hours.

Historic racing car specialist Lee Maxted-Page turns into Bruxelles Corner in his 904 GTS during the 2011 Spa Six Hours.

Irvine Laidlaw's distinctive 904/6 on the grid during the 2010 Nürburgring Old Timer meeting.

Rear-three-quarter view of the 904 GTS in the paddock area during the 2008 Solitude Revival.

The former Walt Disney board member's interest in Porsches began in 1989 when the 'gas guzzler' tax was introduced in the United States, penalising high fuel consumers. Between Christmas and New Year 1990, Stanley treated himself to a 964 to avoid the new charges. 'It was a nice car,' he says, 'but pretty soon I realised that the guys who were having the most fun were the ones with the old cars.' In no time at all, the desire to restore a 356 consumed him, and that project occupied the next eight years. Attending Monterey Historics in 1998, he fell in love with the 904 GTS and resolved to forsake concours for the track. He took lessons in race driving, and by 2000 he had started his alternative career.

In spring 2010, there was a major sea change as far as Stanley's 904 GTS was concerned: a 2.0-litre flat-6 engine was fitted. As Stanley explained:

> *We're going to run it at Spa in the Six Hours in September, and we were worried about putting that many hours on the four-cam Carrera engine, so we put the six-cylinder engine in. The chassis is well set up to take a six, but to say it was easy would be unfair to my mechanic, who spent a lot of time making it work.*

The correct flat-4 can always be reinstated. Other mechanical changes have been less radical. For Le Mans with its ultra-long straights his mechanics fit higher gears, for instance.

> *No question, we fit tall gears for long straightaway running. You can get 148–150mph going down Mulsanne, especially the first part where you come flying out of Tertre Rouge. The wind can be a factor there too. It didn't happen so much this time because the weather was warm and stable, but several years ago there was a crosswind and the car was starting to get light, so I lifted just so that we could finish the race!*

It is special, then, to see 904 GTSs at historic events; there are usually one or two at the Nürburgring Old Timer and Silverstone Classic. But Le Mans Classic elicited an unprecedented eight 904s (one with 1988 winner Jan Lammers aboard), an impressive sight lined up side by side under the awning of the paddock garage. Their pert, flowing lines are not challenging like the leviathan 917 or a wham-bam 935; but they are one of the most aesthetically coherent Porsche designs.

TARGA TITAN

904 GTS, chassis 904 #006, main achievements in period:

26 April 1964	Targa Florio Drivers: Baron Antonio Pucci/ Colin Davis 1st overall
31 May 1964	Nürburgring 1,000kms Drivers: Gerhard Mitter/Herbert Linge 12th overall
20–21 June 1964	Le Mans 24 Hour Race Drivers: Gerhard Koch/Heinz Schiller 3rd in GT class up to 2000 cc 10th overall
11–21 Sept. 1964	Tour de France Rally Drivers: Herbert Müller/Michel Weber DNF – Crash
16–23 Jan. 1965	Monte Carlo Rally Drivers: Eugen Böhringer/ Rolf Wütherich 2nd overall

The 904/6 #006 finished 4th overall in the 1965 Le Mans 24-Hours, and 1st in the Index of Performance listing; this was normally the province of the Alpine-Renaults, which were absent in 1965.

INDEX WINNERS

Historically, Porsche had won their class virtually every year since they first ran at La Sarthe in 1951, and the 904 GTS was no exception, coming 4th and 5th overall in 1965 and winning the Index of Performance and Index of Thermal Efficiency. Speaking of which, Stanley Gold's 904 GTS, chassis 006, was a member of the Index of Performance winning team at this weekend's Classic Le Mans. Fifty-six years ago, his car was the Targa Florio victor, having been one of the original works' 904 GTSs making its European debut at the Sicilian enduro on 26 April 1964. Driven by Colin Davis, an ex-pat British racer who lived in Rapallo, and Baron Antonio Pucci from Palermo, for five laps each of the 72km Piccolo Madonie circuit, chassis 904-006 (race number 86) outlasted both its prototype siblings around the sinuous mountain course, not to mention the host of Alfas, works Ferraris, debutant GT40 and sundry Cobras. After Davis set fastest lap at 41m 10.5s, Pucci put the car in the lead on its 7th lap, and they were followed home by a second works 904 driven by Herbert Linge and Gianni Balzarini. This was regarded as an outstanding success, since the 904 was essentially the company's first customer racing car, and (Sebring excepted) they had proved it was a winner from the outset.

Stanley Gold's 904 GTS #006 also ran at Le Mans in 1964, driven by Heinz Schiller and Gerhard Koch to 10th place and the third out of five 904 GTSs entered to finish – theirs was the only works car, the others privateers. This further endorsed the flat-4 model's reliability, though the pair of 1981cc flat-8 prototypes failed to finish; even so they were a demonstration of the engine capacity trajectory Porsche was aiming at. Schiller and Koch's 904 GTS covered 4,227.5km (2,626.8 miles) at an average 176.1km/h (109.4mph).

TOUR DE FRANCE

The works 904 GTSs also ran in the 1964 Tour de France Automobile, which was a counter in the FIA's World Championship for Makes that year. The ten-day Tour included on-track stages at Le Mans, Pau, Clermont-Ferrand (Charade), Reims and Rouen circuits, the strenuous 2,000-mile itinerary also interspersed with hill-climbs. The Stanley Gold 904 GTS 006 was driven by Herbert Müller and Michel Weber, and though it crashed out, other 904 GTSs occupied 3rd through 6th places in the GT results.

Despite a high attrition rate at the Nordschleife in 1965 when several 904s crashed, due largely to driver error, the 904 GTS also functioned perfectly well as a rally car, as demonstrated by Eugen Böhringer – a driver normally associated with Mercedes-Benz – and co-driver Rolf Wütherich – who, as riding mechanic, had survived James Dean's fatal crash in 1955 in the ill-fated *Little Bastard* 550 Spyder – by placing 904 GTS 006 2nd overall in January 1965's Monte Carlo Rally.

Despite being an out-and-out racing car rather than a front-wheel-drive rally saloon like the winning Mini-Cooper and the pursuant Saab 96s and Citroën DSs, Böhringer slid the 904 GTS through blizzards and thick snow over the Col-de-Turini to check-in 2nd overall, with no penalties incurred on the mountain stages. *Autosport* commented:

> *The idea of long-distance racing being for GT cars and prototype GT cars was quite a good one when it was introduced, but the prototypes seem to be getting away from the accepted standards of a GT car of late. The mid-engined GT car has not proved to be the saleable proposition that the old-fashioned front-engined GT car was. The only exception to this rule is the Porsche 904 GTS, and the recent performance by Böhringer in finishing 2nd in the Monte Carlo Rally in one of these mid-engined*

Porsche racing manager Peter Falk and Rolf Wütherich (left) with the 904 GTS that the former James Dean mechanic co-drove with Eugen Böhringer on the 1964 Monte Carlo Rally.

GT coupés has rather squashed any idea that it is only a racing GT coupé. However, Böhringer is an exceptional man, and Porsche is an exceptional factory. But I cannot foresee us all using mid-engine GT cars for GT motoring as distinct from racing.

Of the rally itself, *Autocar*'s commentator John Davenport had this to say – and it is worth quoting because Porsche's excursions into rallying had been, up until now, the province of the 356 coupé.

The performance of the Porsche 904 and its crew is really amazing, considering the weather and the snow conditions en route, for nearly all the other cars – considered from the point of view of the marque rather than individual performances – that did well on this rally were front-wheel drive saloon cars rather than out-and-out racing cars.

There were six Saabs amongst the 35 finishers, as well as six Citroëns, four Mini Coopers and two Austin 1800s. However, in addition to the Porsche 904 of Böhringer, there were several other GT cars among the finishers, and apart from the two Sunbeam Tigers and three Spitfires, another Porsche, but this time a 911, driven by Herbert Linge and Peter Falk, was also amongst the select few at the finish. After that, the 904 GTS enjoyed another season running as a top-line GT and prototype.

A 904 GTS passes the iconic Seehaus building during the 2008 Solitude Revival meeting.

THE 1965 SEASON

The World Championship for Makes kicked off with the Sebring 12-Hours, staged on Florida's notoriously bumpy airfield circuit. We are now in the realm of American V8-powered prototypes, and the winning car was a Chaparral-Chevrolet with a Ford GT40 in 2nd. Out of a 66-car entry, Porsche 904 GTSs finished 5th and 6th – Underwood/Klaas and Pon/Buzzetta, with Linge and Mitter 9th in the debutant 906.

The Targa Florio was held on 9 May, ten laps of the 72km road circuit, and in its class, Porsche was largely up against Abarth and Alfa Romeo GTA and GTZ opposition, though Ferrari had dispatched a 275GT P2 in search of an outright win. In the 1600cc to 3.0-litre class were three work's Porsche 904s, a flat-8 coupé driven by Jo Bonnier and Graham Hill, a similar coupé with a flat-6 engine driven by Maglioli and Linge, and a new car driven by Colin Davis and Gerhard Mitter.

This was a 904 chassis, but instead of having the familiar fibreglass coupé body, it was fitted with unconventional open bodywork, very abbreviated fore and aft, with humps over the wheels. Nicknamed the *Känguru*, it had a flat-8 engine in the same chassis wheelbase as the coupé, but because it had very little overhang front and rear, it looked relatively short and somewhat peculiar. It was to have been driven by Bonnier and Hill, but they both gave it a try and stepped away, opining that it was practically undriveable because it leapt about all over the road. However, Colin Davis and Gerhard Mitter drove it and thought it was acceptable, so the team was happy. In the results, the winner was the Ferrari P2 of Vaccarella and Bandini, with Davis and Mitter 2nd in the unloved *Känguru*, Maglioli and Linge 3rd, Bonnier and Hill 4th, and Klass and Pucci 5th in a 904 GTS. The Formula 1 duo might have placed higher, but Bonnier was delayed by throttle cable trouble. Perhaps more auspiciously, the success of the open-top 904 *Känguru* was the harbinger of 1968's 909 Bergspyder, not to mention the fabulously successful open-topped 908/2 and 908/3 series that would follow.

Dutch Porsche concessionaire Ben Pon finished 3rd overall and won the 1600 to 2.0-litre class in the Spa-Francorchamps 500kms – billed as the Grand Prix de Spa, unlapped by the leading Ferrari 275LMs of Willy Mairesse and David Piper. Next, Pon and co-driver Rob Slotemaker came 4th in the Monza 1,000kms, behind two Ferraris – a 275LM (Parkes/Guichet) and 330P2 (Surtees/Scarfiotti) – and a Ford GT40 (McLaren and Miles) – witness the start of the Ford vs Ferrari duel epitomised in the eponymous Hollywood blockbuster. This prompted motoring journalist Denis Jenkinson to have a mild rant about the class system:

> *In the GT racing championships, there is rather a silly situation arising in which Porsche are not getting the full credit they deserve. GT racing is divided into three categories and three separate championships for classes 1, 2 and 3, which are 1000 to 1300cc, 1300 to 2000cc and over 2000cc.*

In the past, the results were almost foregone conclusions in being Abarth, Porsche and Ferrari, and in any race in which all three categories took part, the class winners would invariably finish in order of engine size in the overall results. This year – 1965 – with Ferrari falling out with the CSI and giving very little support to GT racing or to private owners, it was left in the big category to the Alan Mann-entered Shelby Cobra Coupé, and they were content to go comparatively slowly, certain of winning their class and gaining maximum points for the championship. Competition in category two was very strong between various private Porsche teams and the works-supported cars, so it happened quite often that a private 2.0-litre Porsche beat the Cobras in the overall race results but got no more benefit as regards championship results. If there were an overall GT championship, then Porsche would be leading. But as it is, Porsche was merely leading their class, and Cobras were leading their class, both playing according to the rules and doing all that was required of them.

Gerhard Mitter drove the 904/8 Känguru at the Norisring on 4 July 1965 – a lightweight hillclimb special on a street circuit.

The Mefco Racing Team 904 GTS of Martin Hone and John Morris is trailered into the Brands Hatch paddock ahead of the 1967 BOAC 500.

A 904 GTS in the assembly area during the 2021 Goodwood Speedweek Meeting, surrounded by formidable opposition in the shapes of Cobras and Stingrays.

RING CYCLE

The Nürburgring 1,000kms was held on 23 May, and in the GT category, Porsche was expected to dominate. However, a Ferrari Dino 166 – dubbed a two-seater Grand Prix car – driven by Bandini and Vaccarella stole the show initially. In the Porsche camp, all was far from well, for the team was upset by the death of one of its stalwarts, Edgar Barth (father of Jürgen), on the eve of the race after a long illness, and in practice, the open 8-cylinder Spyder that went so well in the Targa Florio had gone off the road for no apparent reason and been wrecked. Bonnier and Rindt were driving the 8-cylinder coupe, and although they finished 3rd, it had not been an easy run because the carburetion was adrift, causing the engine to cut out on snap throttle openings. Davis and Mitter drove a 6-cylinder 904/6 coupe, as did Nöcker and Klass and Maglioli and Linge. These racing versions of the 911's flat-6 were blessed with two spark plugs per cylinder. A group of five 904 GTS Coupés made up the 2.0-litre GT class, with Ben Pon and Gerhard Koch driving a factory car. They were well ahead and creeping up the scoreboard, when a gearbox mounting broke, which delayed them, and although they were able to continue, it was only at reduced speed, so a private 904 GTS of Anton Fischaber/Udo Schutz won the class.

The Ford versus Ferrari battle got into its stride at Le Mans in 1965. Ferrari fielded ten prototypes and one GT, while Ford had six prototype GT40s and five Daytona Cobra coupés. During the ensuing 24 hours, the giants tore themselves apart, leaving the unexpected victory to Jochen Rindt and Masten Gregory in a 275LM Ferrari. Herbert Linge and Peter Nöcker came 4th in their flat-8 904 #001, winning the Index of Performance, with Koch and Fischaber 5th in another 8-cylinder 904 #091.

The Reims 12-Hours was held on 3 and 4 July, attracting a meagre 22 cars. It was a contest between Ferrari and AC Cobras at the front, and an 11.00pm start time lent a nocturnal frisson to the event, but, given the high-speed nature of the road circuit, mechanical fragility meant only thirteen cars finished. The highest Porsche finisher was the 904 of Mike d'Udy and Paul Hawkins in 6th place.

Running in the Prototype class, Herbert Linge and Peter Nöcker finished 4th overall in the 1965 Le Mans 24-Hours in their 904/6.

CHAPTER 2

THE PORSCHE 906 'CARRERA SIX' 1966–67

Armin Zumtobel exits the Mercedes Arena section on the Nürburgring F1 circuit during a round of the World Sportscar Masters Championship, held during the 2007 Old Timer meeting.

With 65 units built, the 906 – also known as the Carrera Six – was Porsche's last street-legal racing car. On events such as Tour Auto and Targa Florio, indeed, it doubled as a road car, too.

The Carrera 6 succeeded the 904, yet it also heralded a completely new era. With the 904, Porsche had effectively retained its iron grip on the under-2.0-litre GT class. As the potential for further development remained, why the change? For a start, Ferrari threatened to break Porsche's grip with the rapid new V6 Dino. Second, a return to triangulated tubular spaceframe technology was desirable, because it had been discovered that repairing the 904's chassis and body was problematic, and the old bonding technique had created problems with chassis rigidity. Third, the need to build a combination road-race car, which had dictated the design of the 904's box section chassis frame no longer applied, due to another shift in the regulations. The GT regs for 1966 now required 50 and not 100 units to be manufactured, a sales quota that Porsche's marketing men were confident could be reached with purpose-built racing cars. Equally significant was the arrival on the scene of another of Professor Porsche's grandsons, 28-year-old Ferdinand Piëch, who'd been appointed the new head of Porsche R&D and had his sights set on achieving overall supremacy in endurance racing. Time to move on. The new Carrera 6's flat-6 engine was derived from the newly introduced production 911, and would henceforth power numerous racing Porsches.

The mechanical orientation of the Carrera 6, including its mid-engined configuration, followed the 904 layout. Unlike its predecessor, however, the 906's radical new body shape (cd: 0.35) was designed in the wind tunnel. After the 906's debut at Daytona in early 1966, finishing 6th overall and winning the 2.0-litre prototype class, it was an immediate success. The first showdown with Ferrari's new Dino was at Sebring seven weeks later, and the Carrera 6 won: the Dino might have been quicker, but the Carrera 6 was tougher.

It feels fast: the 1990cc 210bhp flat-6 enabled the 906 to reach 60mph in 4.3sec and 0–100mph in 9.3sec, with a top speed of 170mph.

The orange air trunking rather dominates the 906 engine bay, while the fibreglass cladding the forward-facing fan and carburettor trumpets provides a contrast of texture.

Racing at close quarters, a 906 and Alpine A210 negotiate the Ford Chicane during their Plateau 5 race at Classic Le Mans 2012.

HIT THE ROAD!

Following on from the ladder-frame 904, the Carrera 6, with its mid-mounted flat-6, was built on a multi-tubular space-frame chassis, reverting to earlier practice.

Like the 904, it was clad in a crude (as far as the inner finish was concerned) glass-fibre body, though unlike the 904, the 906's broader, flatter shape stemmed from wind-tunnel tests. In 1966, Porsche was looking to participate in the new Group 4 category for competition sports cars, whilst

Viewed in profile, from nose to tail the 906 is a harmonious blend of swooping curves and purposeful fitments.

Its Type 901/20 casings cast in Elektron magnesium alloy, the 906's 2.0-litre flat-6 is snugly mounted within the bars of the chassis' triangulated spaceframe.

continuing to produce and field the prototypes that honed the breed. That meant producing a minimum of 50 identical machines, and by April 1966, the Carrera Six 906's homologation papers were stamped.

Here's how *Motor Sport* magazine greeted the 906 in its February 1966 issue:

> *Last year, Porsche were very successful with the GTS 904 coupé, running them in their own team as well as selling them to numerous private owners who also achieved a great deal of success. More than 100 of these fibreglass coupés with the flat-four overhead cam engine were built, and it was homologated as a production GT.*

During the year, the works ran some experimental 904s fitted with flat-six engines as used in the new 911 production model, with a greater power output and more racing characteristics.

> *These were prototype cars for an entirely new model that will be built in a batch of 50 to qualify as a Group 4 sports car. Known as the Carrera 6, it has a tubular space frame chassis with independent suspension all-round by coil springs, and the 2.0-litre flat-six engine and 5-speed gearbox mounted behind the driver, clad in a fibreglass body with gullwing doors. The engine develops 210bhp at 8,000rpm, with a maximum of 8,200rpm. The bodywork is a most unusual shape, and extremely functional rather than aesthetic. It is a mere 3ft 2½ in in overall height, while the dry weight is a bit over 11cwt. The production run on this new model is expected to be completed in time for it to be homologated before the beginning of the European season, and if the speed of production of the 904 was anything to go by, the 50 Carrera Six models should present no difficulty to the Porsche factory.*

The British concessionaires, who were the Aldington brothers, intended to return to active racing with the Carrera 6, run by their own works in conjunction with the factory, and Mike d'Udy would be the owner-driver. The Aldingtons formed a new company, Porsche Cars GB Limited, to handle all Porsche activities in Britain, and would enter this Carrera 6 in suitable races. AFN Limited, who used to build and market the Frazer Nash, would also have a second Carrera 6 as a spare, and more in the pipeline, since several of the existing 904 drivers and teams had already placed orders for the Carrera 6.

Access to the 906 cabin is via upswung gullwing doors.

The first 906 to be imported into Great Britain arrives by trailer at Porsche concessionaire AFN's Isleworth premises in West London.

KAROSSERIE WEINSBERG

According to Jürgen Barth, 'the man who designed the frame of the 906 (Drawing Nr 906 401 001 00) was a Herr Müller, who drew it on 19 October 1965.' The job of making 50 elaborate spaceframe chassis was delegated to Karosseriewerk Weinsberg, while the low-slung body with its bulbous front wheel-arches to house tall 15in steel-wheels and its lift-up beetle-back engine cover, plexiglass greenhouse windows and gullwing door cockpit, was laid up by hand in moulds then sanded and painted accordingly, with little effort to finely treat the inner surfaces.

When the 906 was launched, aerodynamic addenda were in their infancy; these spoilers added to the front corners were the start of a new science.

Elements of the 906's glass-fibre body are wrapped around and bonded over the lower and mid-ship chassis tubes. The quality of the fabrication leaves much to be desired, though it obviously works; it just looks a bit amateurish, compared with what you see going on in, say, the Lotus factory, even back in the day. But then, racing cars were constructed with a different mindset and objective to production cars. On the 906 bodyshell's painted outer surface, the weave and weft of the glass-fibre matting is visible in a raking light, while inner surfaces are unfinished – as a glance inside the engine cover starkly reveals. The whole construction is very raw, and there is a slight gap between the door and the hoop of the windscreen frame.

Those small front aerofoils on each corner that look like recent aerodynamic add-ons were present pretty much from the start, though some 906's were larger than others. Taking advantage of its stock of 904 componentry, the 906 was fitted with unequal length wishbones and coil-spring damper units at the front and wishbones, twin forward-facing radius arms and coil-spring damper units at the rear, with braking by ATE-Dunlop disc brakes all round.

The 15in, five-stud steel wheels were shod with Dunlop racing tyres, 5.25/10.50-15 on the back and 4.75/10.00-15 on the front. Power was provided by a much-modified, dry-sumped 2.0-litre 911 flat-6, based on a magnesium crankcase rather than aluminium, with new cylinders, pistons, titanium conrods and valve-gear.

Two banks of three twin-choke downdraught Weber carbs surmounted the Porsche-logo'd cam-covers and the cooling fan faced forwards, directly behind the cockpit's rear bulkhead. The transmission was via a single-plate clutch and five-speed all-synchromesh gearbox. Up front, under the Dzus-fastened panel, lay the oil tank, oil cooler and clutch and brake-fluid reservoirs. Like the crankcase breather hoses at the rear, bulbous orange cooling flexi-pipes emerged python-like from the two channels in the nose of the car, where the frontal chassis tubes were embedded in the glass-fibre floorpan. The 906 weighed 580kg and delivered at least 210bhp – though on the cam it feels like much more than that.

One of the 5.25/10.50-15 Dunlop Racing Tyres cladding the 15 x 8in GA rear wheel of the 906.

Topped by a sextet of Weber carbs and cooling hoses, the 906 engine and transmission are cradled within the tubular spaceframe chassis.

RACE PROGRAMME

The FIA's International Trophy for Prototype Sports Cars was scheduled to have nine rounds in 1966, including Daytona, Sebring, Monza, Targa Florio, Spa-Francorchamps, Nürburgring, Le Mans, Hockenheim and Reims. The European Hill Climb Championship, which had always been a haven for Porsches, included events at Rossfeld, Mont Ventoux, Trento-Bondone, Cesana-Sestrière, Freiburg-Schauinsland, Olon-Vilars and Gaisberg.

Porsche debuted the Carrera 6 at the 1966 Daytona 24-Hours on 6 February, with Hans Herrmann and Herbert Linge placing 6th overall, behind most of the Ford GT40s and a lone Ferrari, and followed home by four 904 GTSs. *Motor Sport*'s Michael Tee commented:

> *They looked as if they could have gone on for another 24-hour session. The German team had merely poured in fuel and changed tyres and drivers, but nothing else. So, for its first race, the Carrera Six made an excellent showing.*

Next up came the Sebring 12-Hours, Florida's second World Championship event – and reflect that Britain did not have a single qualifying round, having abandoned the RAC Tourist Trophy at Dundrod in 1955, another country-lanes event above Belfast akin to the Isle of Man TT. A decade later, in 1966, you have to consider that in big-time events on the international stage, the front runners were still likely to be the big-engined 7.0-litre Ford GT40s, Ferrari P2s, the odd Chapparal and Corvette, plus AC Daytona Cobras. In the next speed bracket – and with a reputation for reliability – was the Porsche squad, with regular sports cars such as MGBs, Sunbeam Alpines, Triumph TR4s and Jaguar E-types all in the running. The lone Carrera Six from Daytona was now backed up by another works car – Hans Herrmann and Jo Buzzetta, and Gerhard Mitter and Günter Klass – and three private owners. The Carreras were backed up by five 904s – two works cars and three private owners. One of those privately owned was entered and driven by Briggs Cunningham and John Fitch. The works Carrera Sixes finished 4th and 6th – Herrmann/Buzzetta and Voegele/Siffert in that order, with privateers Lake Underwood/Ed Hugus bringing theirs to the finish in 8th.

At the Le Mans Test Weekend on 2 and 3 April, the works Porsches driven by Herbert Linge and Peter Nöcker were 'sounding terrific and will certainly be running at the end of the 24 Hours if their performances at Daytona and Sebring are anything to go by', predicted Denis Jenkinson. Linge's car was fitted with fuel injection and carried a flow meter in the

A pair of long-tail 906 LHs driven by Gerhard Mitter (1st) and Hans Herrmann (3rd) on a very bare-looking Hockenheim Motodrom, round 10 of the World Sportscar Championship, on 14 August 1966. It was something of a walkover: 906s occupied the first six places, and eight out of the top ten finishers.

At the summit of Gaisberg Hillclimb on 3 September 1967, Sepp Greger in the 906 was 6th quickest, followed by the 906 of Alex Soler-Roig, while the Ferrari 250 GTB in the picture of Karl Schafranek was 31st.

Sepp Greger in 906 #027 tackles the Gaisberg Hillclimb on 4 September 1966, coming 3rd after Mitter and Herrmann in 906 #002 and #001.

Gerhard Mitter takes the start at the Gaisberg Hillclimb on 3 June 1965 in the 906/8 Bergspyder #010, setting 4th fastest time. Waiting behind him is Rolf Stommelen in the 904/GTS #102, who was 3rd fastest. Weber and Greger were 1st and 2nd, also in 904 GTSs.

Changeover days: illustrating the switchover from 904 to 906, in the paddock during the 1966 Sebring 12-Hours meeting, number 52 is the Herrmann/Buzzetta/Mitter 906, which came 4th, #54 is Gregg/Follmer 904 GTS, which finished 7th; #55 is the 904 GTS of Schutz/Glemser (DNF) and #53 is the 906 of Mitter/Klaas, DNF.

passenger seat, an indication of the general trend towards injection rather than carburettors, with Porsche at the forefront of such innovation. It also had a slimmer nose cowling, and on Sunday, they experimented with a long tail attached with screws to the standard tail in a quest for higher top speed and better aerodynamics on the Mulsanne Straight – heralding a series of long-tailed coupés that encompassed the next three models – 907, 908 and 917. A third Carrera Six present on Test Weekend was that of the French entrant August Veuillet, driven by Robert Bouchet. Known as Toto, Veuillet was the founder of Sonauto, the French Porsche concessionaire, in 1950. He was also the first to run a Porsche at Le Mans, in 1951, with Edmond Mouche co-driver, finishing 20th overall and 1st in class in a 356.

Next on the calendar was the Monza 1,000-Kms, run in heavy rain on the awe-inspiring 10km circuit that included the tricky banked oval section tacked onto the familiar race circuit, which became defunct in 1969. Considering the appalling weather conditions, everyone drove with great circumspection and incidents were few. The speed on the banked part of the track was slashed by the introduction of chicanes at the beginning of each banked turn. These were new tarmac roads, built in the infield, forcing cars down to bottom gear to negotiate the right, left, right, left- and right-hand corners before moving onto each set of banking. Even so, the Ferrari P3s and GT40s were reaching 160mph past the grandstands after their virtual standing start round the South banking. It was a win for the John Surtees/Mike Parkes Ferrari 330 P3, with two GT40s 2nd and 3rd, followed by Gerhard Mitter and Hans Herrmann Carrera Six in 4th and Jo Siffert and Vogele in another Carrera 6, with Colin Davis and Dieter Glemser in 7th in another 906. Monza has always been one of the fastest circuits, but the Carrera Sixes were able to challenge – and beat – many of the big-engined cars.

50TH TARGA FLORIO

The 50th Targa Florio was run on 8 May 1966. The annual battle against the Sicilian mountains encompassing ten laps of the Piccolo Madonie circuit was once again a Ferrari versus Porsche affair because the expected onslaught by Ford did not materialise, nor did the lone Chaparral. Ferrari entered the open 4.0-litre 330 P3 for Vaccarella and Bandini and two Dino 206 models for Parkes and Scarfiotti and Guichet and Baghetti. The Porsche team arrived in force with an impressive array of cars, transporters, a travelling workshop and a radio communications team for race control – relaying information from the Collesano pits to a refuelling depot at Brivio Polizzi, halfway around the 72km lap. All the Porsches were new Carrera Six models as regards chassis and body, but one was fitted with a 2.2-litre flat-8 engine, and two were flat-6s with Bosch fuel injection, these three running in the prototype category. Driver pairings were Hans Herrmann and Dieter Glemser (#111), Jo Bonnier and Gerhard Mitter (#143) and Günter Klaas and Colin Davis (#142). There were two factory-prepared Group 4 Carrera Six models in the sports category, driven by Antonio Pucci and Vincenzo Arena (#141) and the other 906 #128 loaned to the Scuderia Filipinetti for Willy Mairesse and Herbert Müller.

In addition to these works cars, there were five more Carrera Sixes in private hands. The green one of Mike d'Udy and Pieter De Klerk #129 was entered by Porsche Cars GB, but was transferred to the prototype class as it was brand new and had not been registered for road use, this being a stipulation of the new Group 4 rules. Unfortunately, d'Udy crashed it early in the race.

The race's half-century was celebrated by a run out on the 148km Grosso Madonie mountain circuit that was used in early iterations of the event. In official practice, eyebrows were raised when Günter Klaas in the 2.2-litre 906 beat Nino Vaccarella's time in the 4.0-litre Ferrari P3. The race was as dramatic as ever – pitting drivers and cars against the road rather than one another – akin to a big-time tarmac rally. But inevitably faster cars have to lap or accommodate

TYPE 906 'CARRERA SIX' *MAJOR SUCCESSES*

1966
6th, Daytona 24-Hours
4th, Sebring 12-Hours
1st, Targa Florio
4th, 5th, 6th, 7th, Le Mans 24-Hours
1967
6th, 7th, Le Mans 24-Hours
1st, European Hillclimb Championship, Touring Car class
1968
1st, European Hillclimb Championship, Touring Car class

slower ones. When, late in the race, Bandini in the 330 P3 was forced off by a locally-driven Ferrari GTO, the works Ferrari rolling into a tree, luckily without major harm to its driver, it was a walkover for the remaining 906s.

Müller/Mairesse took the lead, well ahead of the Dino Ferrari, Willy Mairesse driving the closing laps, going typically fast to bring the works Carrera Six home to win the 50th Targa Florio – in 7hr 16m – with Pucci and Arena 3rd behind the Dino 206S, with Claude Bourillot and Umberto Maglioli 5th in the second Scuderia Filipinetti 906 #139.

Four seasons in, the 906 was still competitive, as demonstrated by Alfio Nicolosi and Angelo Buonacorsi bringing theirs to the 1970 Targa Florio finish in 38th place, an event dominated by the 908/3.

Willi Kauhsen and Karl von Wendt finished 12th in their IGFA Team 906 #119 in the 1968 Nürburgring 1,000Kms.

Fans line the fencing to witness the 906 of Willy Mairesse and Herbert Müller as it approaches the Cerda pits on the way to winning the 1966 Targa Florio.

Hedging their bets: the 906 #119 of Gerhard Koch and Herbert Linge takes a close interest in the scenery during the 1966 Nürburgring 1,000 km, placing 10th overall.

The Nürburgring 1,000Kms staged on 5 June 1966, on the 22.8km combined Nordschleife and Sudschleife, saw a surprise win for the new 5.3-litre Chaparral-Chevrolet 2D, a sort of cat among the Ford and Ferrari pigeons produced by Texan engineer Jim Hall and Hap Sharp, driven by Jo Bonnier and 1961 F1 World Champion Phil Hill. Unusually, Chaparral used automatic transmission.

PORSCHE CARRERA SIX 906 #129

Race Record during Mike D'Udy's tenure.

8/5/1966, Targa Florio, Sicily
Drivers: Mike D'Udy/Peter de Klerk, crashed in practice, DNS.

5/11/1966, Kyalami 9-Hours *Rand Daily Mail*
Drivers: Mike D'Udy/Peter de Klerk, crashed on lap 187.

27/12/1966, Pietermaritzburg 3-hours
Drivers: Mike D'Udy/Peter de Klerk, 2nd overall, 1st in class.

20/1/1967, Killarney, Cape Town
Driver: Mike D'Udy, 3rd overall, 1st in class.

1/5/1967, Spa 1000kms
Drivers: Colin Davis/Roy Pike, DNF, ignition failure.

20/5/1967, Martini International Trophy, Silverstone
Driver: Mike D'Udy, 5th overall, 1st in class.

28/5/1967, Nürburgring 1000kms
DNS.

23/7/1967, Mugello Grand Prix
Drivers: Mike D'Udy/ David Piper, DNF, driveshaft failure.

30/7/1967, BOAC 500, Brands Hatch
Drivers: Dieter Spoerry/Rico Steinemann, 13th overall, 2nd in class.

20/8/1967, Zeltweg 500kms, Austria
Driver: Mike D'Udy, DNF, accident at 19 laps.

28/8/1967, Guards Trophy, Brands Hatch
Driver: Mike D'Udy, DNF, misfire.

14/10/1967 Silverstone
Driver: Mike D'Udy, 1st overall, DSQ.

7/4/1968 BOAC 1000kms, Brands Hatch
Drivers: Mario Cabral/Jacques Duval, 19th overall, 4th in class.

12/4/1968, Oulton Park 100 miles.
Driver: Roy Pike, 7th overall, 3rd in class.

25/4/1968, Monza 1000kms
Drivers: Robin Widdows/Brian Hart, DNS.

19/5/1968, Nürburgring 1000kms
Drivers: Robin Widdows/Brian Hart, DNS.

26/5/1968, Spa 1000kms
Drivers: Robin Widdows/Brian Hart, DNS.

27/6/1968, Silverstone 6-hours
Driver: Hugh Dibley, 15th overall, 4th in class.

10/8/1968, RAC Birthday Cup, Croft, Yorks.
Driver: Terry Hunter, 8th overall, 2nd in class.

17/8/1968, Oulton Park
Driver: Terry Hunter, 12th overall, 2nd in class.

2/9/1968, Brands Hatch
Driver: Terry Hunter, DNF.

10/8/1969 Thruxton, Kodak Trophy
Driver: Terry Hunter, 8th overall, 1st in class.

9/1969 on, Various SCCA events, USA
Driver: Carl Armstrong.

The Porsche team were out in force with a 2.2-litre 8-cylinder car that had run in the Targa Florio, three Carrera Sixes with fuel-injected engines, and a standard Carrera Six. Team chief Huschke von Hanstein had assembled a miscellaneous collection of drivers and spent time during practice pairing them off in suitable cars. After struggling with varying lap times, mechanical sympathy, different personalities, reliability factors and so on, he settled for Jochen Rindt and Nino Vaccarella in the 8-cylinder car, Hans Herrmann and Dieter Glemser, Udo Schutz and Günter Klass, Bob Bondurant and Paul Hawkins in the fuel-injected 906s, and Jean-Pierre Beltoise and Peter Nöcker in the standard Carrera Six.

Apart from the possibility of an outright victory with the 8-cylinder car, which Rindt took round in 8m 44.4s to claim third fastest time overall, Porsche were intent on a class win, as there were just three Dino Ferrari 206s against them. Another curiosity was a 904 GTS with a camera mounted in the nose, relaying film to a helicopter overhead. It was driven by journalist Paul Frère, who qualified the car 26th on the grid out of 77 starters. Despite it being something of a race of attrition, with cars continuously dropping out, the Porsches were bested by two Dino Ferraris of Scarfiotti/Bandini and Rodriguez/Ginther, though Bondurant/Hawkins' 906 came 4th, and brothers Gijs and David van Lennep finished 7th in the Racing Team Holland 906.

LE MANS 1966

The Ford versus Ferrari battle for outright supremacy was really evident at Le Mans 1966, held over 18 and 19 June, and some were calling it Europe versus America. Ferrari's chances received a setback before the race when one of its star drivers, John Surtees (1964 F1 World Champion for Ferrari), had a row with Dragoni, the team manager and walked out. (Dragoni favoured Bandini and Scarfiotti and not the English motorcycle champion, while Enzo Ferrari, who did not attend races, was misinformed by Dragoni.) At any rate, the focus of attention was on the phalanx of thirteen Ford GT40s and fourteen Ferrari 330 P2s and P3s. As mentioned previously, the atmosphere is captured well in the movie *Ford v Ferrari*.

Henry Ford II was present to drop the flag to start the race, an example of Dearborn's thirst for victory. He was not disappointed. Twenty-four hours later, the works Fords of Bruce McLaren/Chris Amon and Ken Miles/Denny Hulme attempted a joint finish, crossing the line in unison. The stewards decreed that since the McLaren/Amon car had started further down the grid it had thus travelled furthest and was given the win.

Running in the Prototype class, the 906 #153 Long Tail of Jo Siffert and Colin Davis passes the pits at Le Mans 1966 on its way to finishing 4th overall, averaging 118.11mph (190.08km/h), covering 2,834 miles (4,562km).

It's Le Mans 1966, and the Gunther Klaas and Rolf Stommelen 906 #111 takes the Esses on its way to an eventual 7th place and 1st in the Sports category.

Driver change for the 906 #153 of Colin Davis and Jo Siffert which came 4th overall at Le Mans 1966. Davis clambers out of the car while Siffert and Huschke von Hanstein are on the pit wall, with drivers De Klerk and Klass looking in on the action from their adjacent pits.

Udo Schutz and Peter De Klerk came 6th overall in the 1966 Le Mans 24 Hours in their works-entered 906 LH.

It's Le Mans 1966, the Ford versus Ferrari battle is in full swing, with GT40s taking 1st, 2nd and 3rd; Porsches occupied the next four places. Here, the 906 LH of Hans Herrmann and Herbert Linge passes the Ferrari 275 GTB of Piers Courage and Roy Pike on the start-finish straight. This 906 came 5th overall, the Ferrari 8th.

So, nevertheless, it was a Ford 1-2-3, with Davis and Siffert 4th in their Carrera Six – taking the Index of Performance award, and more Carrera Sixes in 5th, 6th and 7th – Herrmann/Linge, Schutz/De Klerk, Klass/Stommelen, who won the Sports Car category. The works 906s all sported the long-tail *'lang-heck'* bodywork configuration, as captured on film by my old friend and colleague Roger Dixon.

Eventually, 65 Carrera 6s were made, including nine Bosch fuel-injected cars, designated 906E, one of which (Siffert/Davis) finished 4th at Le Mans that year and won the Index of Performance. Like its two siblings that came 5th (Herrmann/Linge) and 6th (Schutz/de Klerk), it ran the long-tail bodywork that prefigured similar versions of 907, 908 and 917 models.

The 906's legacy is that it spawned a generation of increasingly refined tube-framed Porsche racing cars. Introduced in 1967, the 910 was similarly specified to the 906 – with 2.0-litre flat-6 and 2.2-litre flat-8 engines – but in a more rounded shell and running on 13in wheels. By 1968, 28 910s had been built, qualifying it as a Competition Sports Car so it was up against more prosaic machinery. Later in 1967 came the 2.2-litre 907 prototype, a still more aerodynamic shape, swiftly succeeded by the 3.0-litre 908 prototype in coupé form and Spyder in 1969. And that was superseded by the mighty flat-12 917.

A 906 on a rural stage near Souillac in the Dordogne during the 2007 Tour Auto.

DANCING BAREFOOT

In 2010, Antony Fraser and I were guests of Adrian Hamilton, purveyor of historic racing cars and roadable exotics – and son of 1953 Le Mans winner Duncan (Jaguar C-type). Adrian was selling a 906 on behalf of its French owner from his idyllic barns near Basingstoke. It was on the market at the time for £685,000. I guess you would need to pay twice as much at the time of writing, fifteen years later. He had flagged it up as a usable classic, being road-registered with an MOT, so it would be eminently eligible for events like Tour Auto, Giro de Sicilia and Tour Britannia. As a point of reference, in 1966 the Carrera Six cost a little over £6,000. When another car, 906-101, changed hands at Monaco a few years ago, Bonham's hammer dropped at €579,500.

Barefoot 1960s popster Sandy Shaw would have been a shoe-in with the Carrera Six. To access the clutch pedal, I am obliged to emulate her on-stage trait by removing my size 10s to fit the left foot between the footwell wall and steering column, to thrust the clutch pedal deep into the 906's nose while probing its gate for dogleg first. Between that and the fact that there's nowhere for me to put my head, the 906 is a tricky drive. Away from its natural racetrack environment, keeping it 'on the cam' in traffic means dropping to 2nd or 3rd to avoid the 2.0-litre flat-6 s-s-s-spluttering. And that is after I have actually made it into the cockpit, which proves literally the first hurdle. Both legs in first over the broad sill, using the handily slanting chassis tube as a support, easing them beneath the flat-bottomed aftermarket Momo wheel, and settling into the spartan bucket seat. With the doors closed I feel cocooned, and I am immediately conscious of the lack of headroom – either they were short-arses back then or the seat was mounted even lower – though AH's mechanic Doug assures me that they are the originals, albeit refurbished. Some well-known backsides have already caressed this leatherette – for instance Rico Steinemann at the 1967 BOAC 500 for one – and he went on to be Porsche competitions chief. And also, F1/F2 engine builder extraordinaire, Brian Hart; but did they have the protection of the five-point harness that envelops my torso like a spider's web? A lap belt, maybe.

The switchgear is racecar basic, and the procedure for starting up is child's play. The red on-off key for the battery is in the front door-shut, with a fire extinguisher pull-switch above it, while on the far side of the dashboard strip are the two little pull-out ignition switches and a matching turn indicator switch next to them. The oil pressure and temperature gauge are in a tiny niche like something from a Nativity tableau, then there is the wash/wipe button, which, mercifully, I do not need, and the rev-counter in its round-arched binnacle is right in front of me. There is no speedo, and the light switches are on the left of the steering column. A fan is angled right at the driver, though I cannot work out how to operate it, and there is an air vent on top of the dash that is not connected; my ventilation comes from the two flaps in each door side-windows. The windscreen washer catheter lives in the passenger footwell. There is a fly-off hand brake as well.

Once all ignition switches are turned on, I twist the key right a notch and the fuel pump ticks away, then I turn it further and the flat-6 snarls into life. I catch the revs with the accelerator pedal and those Weber throttle slides do their work. Up-and-running, heel-and-toeing is straightforward, but I need the full travel of the clutch pedal to find 1st and reverse gears, and it demands 3,000rpm to get it rolling without hiccoughing. In fact, the clutch action is surprisingly soft; it is just a long way down. The brake pedal benefits from pumping for maximum *rallentando*, though once on the move the brakes seem fine.

This 906 benefits from an aftermarket Sparco steering wheel, with rev-counter and original switchgear ranged around the dashboard, and electrical switches positioned within the left-hand sill and door shut.

I sit very low in the creaking seat, backside inches from the blacktop, and from time to time, I am reminded of its proximity by a harsh scrape as the belly pan bottoms out. My view directly through the rainbow arch of the plastic windscreen is of the road a few feet ahead, and the front wheel arches, topped by the dinky 1960s streamlined mirrors, dominate peripheral vision like a pair of giant green bananas on either side of the car. The rearward view provided by those chrome wing mirrors is minuscule, and not much better in the inside mirror, looking back through the sepia-tinted opaque plastic of the slatted engine lid window. But with no bodywork visible straight ahead, my middle-distance forward vision is perfect for judging apexes for turn-in. There is no time to think too hard about that, though; it is mostly intuitive, as soon the next corner comes rushing up.

Crisp bark

Beguiling from the standpoint of a trackside spectator, the crisp bark of the flat-6 at high 5–6,000rpm with its gunshot staccato key changes at successive gearshifts is absolutely deafening within the cockpit. I tolerate it because I am living a dream. It is rather like having Sex Pistol Johnny Rotten screaming in your ear – only it is you controlling the duration and intensity of the sound as you work the gearbox and throttle according to the terrain. Racing drivers are not merely showing off as they drive through the paddock constantly blipping the throttle; because, if you don't, the engine stalls. This is not widely understood by the good citizens of Farnham as I negotiate the one-way system of its splendid Georgian centre, and a few bemused glances come my way.

The cramped (for a 6-footer) driving position within the 906 cockpit, and reveals the unfinished fibreglass of the roof and the fibreglass cladding the chassis tubes in the floor. The gearstick, gauges and switchgear are in close proximity to the driver, who is fully occupying the diminutive bucket seat, whilst harnessed in a six-point Willans harness.

Sensational rear three-quarter tracking shot by Antony Fraser of the 906 in action on the B-road byways.

Surely one of life's greatest pleasures is to drive the 906 as it twitches and jiffles on the backroads, with every steering input creating instant reactions.

The paradoxes do not end with the de-restriction signs.

Out on the open road, the 906 is a riot, and not just because of its omnipresent soundtrack. Diffidence has no place here. Forsaking all the niceties of my 911 road car, I remind myself this is a racer, grab it bouncer-like by the lapels and just go for it. Now it makes sense. Give it its head on the undulating country lanes, and it's a tiger. The thing is, it needs to be kept on the cam to avoid misfiring, and that means there is little time to relax between corners when I am downshifting, double-declutching and feeding it into apexes, always with a bit of power on. During rear tracking, camera man Fraser tells me it is popping flames on that crackling overrun. Magic! Given a pair of earplugs, I could do this all day.

Whilst the 906 twitches and jiffles, every steering input eliciting instant effect, bump steer is also in the recipe as the taut chassis and those tall Dunlop racing tyres paw their way over the B-road contours. I reflect that it feels more securely planted than a mid-1960s 911, as it should.

This is some workout. We pause to check if Fraser's cornering shots are focused, and I unclip the rudimentary gullwing door catch from the driver's seat and hoist the lightweight panel above my head to aerate the steaming cockpit. The Meccano bracket hinges up and clips on to support it. Not pretty, but it works. When we are done, AH's mechanics kindly remove the door altogether so I can clamber out. I am soaked with sweat, and my scalp bears creases where it bounced off the chassis tubes in the cockpit roof and the lip of the door top. Maybe I'm scarred forever – in which case, as Sandy Shaw sang, 'there's always something there to remind me'. I will never forget the thrill of driving this 906, possibly the ultimate racer for the road. Is it worth half a million pounds though? Much as it pains me to say so, since it is way out of my league, but I reckon it is. The Carrera Six is an iconic, achingly beautiful design, and 906-129 is the genuine article. Its double-edged specification allows you to do the Le Mans Classic and drive it home if you want. Provenance is the clincher, though. It never won big-time like the works' 906s, but it still participated in those battles of the giants in the late-1960s, and that is priceless.

THE HERBERT LINGE INTERVIEW

The first worker to be signed up at Porsche's Zuffenhausen plant, Herbert Linge's 40-year career with Porsche took him from factory mechanic to test driver, racer and Weissach production manager.

Born at Weissach, on the doorstep, so to speak, Linge joined Porsche as an apprentice in 1943, and in 1948 was the first mechanic hired when the firm relocated from Gmund in Austria to Stuttgart-Zuffenhausen, where he was involved in the construction of the original 356. 'It was built by a small group of twelve people,' he said. 'In Austria they made the 356 with an aluminium body but in Stuttgart we had to do it in steel, so we ended up having the bodywork made by Reutter across the street – we couldn't use the factory as there were still American soldiers billeted in it.'

Linge never worked for anyone else but Porsche and, in a nutshell, his career followed the research and development path.

> *After the war I was supposed to go to the engineering school but the returning soldiers took priority, so I worked for Porsche doing all the servicing and test driving. I had a good position already, so after three years when I had the chance to go to engineering school my boss said, 'You don't need the school anymore'.*

In 1952 he was sent to the USA to set up and develop the service network for the US franchise. Compact and amiable with a ready smile, he adapted quickly to his new home. 'It was in-at-the-deep-end,' he laughed. 'I didn't speak any English when I went there, but I quickly learned.' In the right place at the right time, he was a key player in Porsche's assault on La Carrera Panamericana, the source of the Porsche Carrera nomenclature.

> *In 1952 the concessionaires were taking their own Porsches to do the Mexican road race, and they asked for factory help. Porsche said, 'Well, Linge is in the States, he can come over to Mexico and take care of your cars,' so I looked after two cars, standard 356s. I was Count von Berkheim's co-driver, but we had a problem with the transmission. A year later I was there because Karl Kling and Hans Herrmann were driving the 550 Spyders with the 1500 Super engines – they didn't have the Fuhrmann four-cam engine at this time – but both dropped out, so I took care of Juhan's car,*

Photographed in his 911 SC Targa at the 2008 Solitude Revival, Herbert Linge's career at Porsche began in 1943 (aged 14) and he retired as Operations Manager at the Weissach Development Centre in 1987. He died in January 2024, aged 95.

Herbert Linge relives the 1954 Carrera Panamericana in a 550 Spyder at the 2008 Solitude Revival.

> *and he won against the Borgward, who were one of our main rivals at the time.*

Mexican marvel

In 1954 he was back on La Carrera Panamericana as a mechanic on the 550 Spyders, now running the four-cam engines, and he set up tyre dumps along the 2,000-mile route to provision the Porsches on the rapacious Mexican roads. Suddenly he was drafted in as a driver:

> *There was a guy called Segura from Argentina, and he'd had enough; he was exhausted and wanted to pull out.*

Huschke [competitions manager von Hanstein] said he didn't mind which Porsche got the result, any Porsche would do, whether it was privateer or factory. So, he put me in the car. In fact, he had nominated me as second driver in all the Porsches. Nobody knew he'd done that. I didn't even know!

Linge drove Fernando Segura's 356 for two days and clawed back a sizeable deficit in time and places. 'It was running 35th when I took over, and we were up to 5th by the time he'd recovered, and we were 4th in class at the finish.' Linge holds the Panamericana in high esteem: 'It was a great race. The cars were going faster and faster, and there were a lot of accidents, even after the race when ordinary people were back on the road and driving like crazy. Unfortunately, that caused the end of it.'

Elsewhere, Linge had been competing at club level in his own right, first on motorcycles, then in a VW Beetle with Porsche transmission. His performance led sharp-eyed scrutineers to place him in the prototype category, while miffed Porsche drivers complained to the factory. Taken to task by one of the head honchos, Albert Prinzing, not so much for his precocious success but for driving a Volkswagen, Linge responded that there was an easy answer – just give him a Porsche.

I had a little experience in competition, and I was doing all the test driving with our cars, and Helmut Polenski, who was European Rally Champion at the time, wanted me to co-drive him. Then Hans Herrmann chose me as his co-driver as well because I knew the car and I could repair it and drive it if necessary. So that's how I got started, and from then on, I always had a chance to drive the factory cars.

The works usually ran three or four cars at major events, one of which was fitted with an experimental engine or transmission, and that was the one that Linge generally drove.

Motor Sport's Denis Jenkinson described him as 'a hard racing driver who got on with the job.... who excelled on difficult circuits like the Nürburgring, the Solitude-ring and the Targa Florio.' Though he never actually won a high-end event he was often in the points. He much preferred endurance races to sprints and hill climbs and has an enviable record of competing in the classics: 'I drove the Nürburgring 1,000km fifteen times, the Targa Florio twelve times, and thirteen times at Le Mans, all long-distance races for Porsche. Every big race is great,' he said.

Throughout the 1950s and 1960s, Herbert Linge and Hans Herrmann were key protagonists on the Porsche works' driver roster.

It's Le Mans 1963, and Edgar Barth, team manager Huschke von Hanstein and Herbert Linge contemplate proceedings beside their 718/8 #047. They came 8th overall.

In 1963 he and Edgar Barth (Jürgen's father) came 3rd overall on the Targa in a 2.0-litre 356 Carrera GS. But although overall victory eluded him, Linge's tally of class wins over a decade-and-a-half is mighty impressive: the 1954 and 1957 Mille Miglia, 1955 and 1958 Sebring 12hrs, the 1960, 1963, 1965 and 1967 Le Mans 24hrs, 1961, 1962 and 1963 Nürburgring 1,000kms, 1962 and 1963 Targa Florio, 1963 Solitude GP, 1966 Daytona 24hrs, 1967 Paris 1,000kms (Montlhéry), 1968 Marathon de la Route (Nürburgring), and the 1969 Austrian GP (Zeltweg), by which time the new boys like Elford, Siffert and Rodriguez were in the ascendant.

Herbert Linge and Edgar Barth drove this Porsche 356 B 2000 GS 'Dreikantschaber' in the Targa Florio on 5 May 1963.

Herbert Linge demonstrates his prowess in a 904 GTS during the 2008 Solitude Revival, held on the former road circuit in the surroundings of Schloss Solitude.

Abarth with Barth

Another car with which Linge enjoyed much success was the Type 695 GS Abarth 1600, coming 1st in class no fewer than six times in 1963 with Edgar Barth. 'We were 2nd in class at Sebring, the first time out in the GT Championship but I won the German GT championship in '63 with this car.'

However, his favourite Porsche is the 904/6.

> *It was fantastic to have the 904 with a 6-cylinder engine; that really was a perfect car; you could race it, and you could drive it on the road. It's more of an all-rounder than the 906 and 907; they are race cars, but the 904 does everything. You can go on the Tour de France and 1st, 2nd and 3rd is no problem with this car. In '65, I drove with Peter Nöcker at Le Mans, and we came 4th overall behind the big Ferraris.*

They won the Index of Performance too, normally the prerogative of the Alpine-Renaults. The essence is reliability, consistency and good handling, and Linge felt the 6-cylinder was even better than the 4-cylinder: 'They were smoother and easier to drive. We had two or three 904s fitted with the 8-cylinder, but that was overpowered.' The 904/8 of Linge/Barth was clocked at 175mph on the Mulsanne Straight in 1964, though it retired with clutch failure while heading the Index of Performance table.

Linge was closely involved in the development of all engine types, from the original flat-4 to the four-cam Carrera unit, the flat-6, the flat-8 and flat-12. There is a dramatic difference between a four-cam engine and the regular flat-four, though Linge claims it is a very reliable unit, albeit quite a complex construction. 'The four-cam engine was too expensive for normal production and repair,' he said, 'so it was always going to be a race car engine. That's why, pretty soon, the 6-cylinder engine came in, because it was much cheaper to produce and repair.' He did all the testing up to and including the 917. 'I was supposed to co-drive John Woolfe in '69 when he crashed and was killed on the first lap of Le Mans,' he recalled ruefully.

Porsche had recommended that Linge take the first stint, but Woolfe, well known in UK club racing circles with a Lola T70 and GT40, was keen to debut his customer 917, with dreadful consequences. 'The 917 became a great car,' continued Linge, 'but in the beginning we didn't have a chance to test it. We could only test it a little bit at the small airport, but there you never got out of third gear. The aerodynamics needed sorting out, though the engine was perfect. So, the car was not finished, not really ready to be sold to amateur customers.' One of Linge's last missions in a racing car was sharing the 908/2 with Jonathan Williams at Le Mans in 1970. Entered by Solar Productions, this was the camera car that filmed race footage for Steve McQueen's *Le Mans* movie. Linge also doubled for the Hollywood star in a 917 during shooting later that summer, and at McQueen's insistence, there was no shirking the 230mph top speed on the Mulsanne Straight; not a problem for Linge, who had long ago written the rule book.

Linge was Porsche's chief test driver during the 1950s and 1960s, and indeed the location of Porsche's test facility at

Aerial view of Weissach Test Track and skid pan in the late 1960s, the dominion of the head of R&D, Dr Helmuth Bott, who joined Porsche in 1952 as an operations assistant, rising to become head of testing and development in 1978. He noted that the fastest driver was Willi Kauhsen with the 850bhp 917/10 Can-Am car in 1972.

Telling it like it is: veteran Porsche racer and test driver Herbert Linge takes the author down memory lane at the 2008 Solitude Revival.

Weissach is down to him. It was a step up from the early days, as he testified. 'We had to do our testing at a small airport nearby, but we could only have that occasionally. We could use Hockenheim, and we had permission to go on the local autobahn, though there were no tight corners. So, we looked as far away as the Alps.' Ah, but what about the Nordschleife? 'When you start building a car, you don't need the Nürburgring; it can be done at a smaller venue. But afterwards, when it's finished, the testing was always at the Nürburgring. No question, we would go there to measure the brakes and the handling.' There was still a need for a site close to Zuffenhausen, and Linge proposed an area of scrubland close to his Weissach home. 'Dr Porsche was pleased to see this, and he said, "OK, you talk to the Weissach people and see if we can buy the land."' His home had a clear view of the test track and development centre, where he was the production manager in R&D between 1972 and 1987, working in close company with Dr Helmuth Bott.

Although he retired from the factory in 1989 (Bott retired a year earlier), Linge hung on to his racing credentials and went back to Weissach the following year to help turn the 964 C2 into a car for the Carrera Cup series. 'I redesigned it as a racing car,' he said. 'We only had 50 cars to build, so that was quite special.'

When I interviewed him at the Solitude Revival in 2012, he showed up in his road car, a prized 1978 911 SC Targa, unusual in petrol blue. Its registration plate read BB-LW 911; the LW stands for Linge-Weissach, which is appropriate. 'I only go out with this car if it is dry because I have nobody at home who will clean it – so I have to do that myself!' He is the second owner, following a dentist in Karlsruhe who put 80,000km on it before Linge bought it in 2003. Despite its low mileage and pristine condition, he spent two-and-a-half years stripping it, taking everything apart, and rebuilding with new componentry; an interesting insight into his desire to have everything working perfectly, when most of us would be delighted to run such a car as found. 'When a car is that age you need to change the brake cylinders, gaskets and bushes,' he responded. 'I don't want to lose a brake while I'm driving.' Why an SC, when he could have bought a 3.2 Carrera for a similar price? The purist spoke:

> *The SC was the first 3.0-litre engine with mechanical injection, and it has no power steering or anything, and that's what I like. I am very pleased with it, and the funniest thing is the gas consumption, which is between ten and eleven litres per 100 kilometres.*

All credit to him that the SC comes from a period when Porsche set out to build cars that would indeed Linge(r) longer.

THE HANS HERRMANN INTERVIEW

Hans Herrmann was a crucial personality in Porsche's competition history, and he was centre stage during the 1950s and 1960s, finally retiring after giving Porsche its first Le Mans win in 1970, paired with Richard Attwood in the red 917 of the works' Austrian Salzburg Konstruktionen Racing Team. Yet curiously, it is probably the previous year's 24-Hours that he is best remembered for, the victory that nearly was. Hans, driving a 908/1 coupé with Gérard Larrousse, duelled with Jacky Ickx in a JW Gulf-Ford GT40, swapping the lead several times each lap, only to concede the win – by less than 100m after 24 hours' racing – due to ailing brakes. These, though, were twilight appearances for a man who had raced for the Mercedes-Benz Formula 1 squad more than a decade earlier.

Stocky, tanned and sprightly for his eight decades, Hans greeted Antony Fraser and me at his Sindelfingen office, where two enormous desks, walls peppered with photographs and illustrations, a scattering of model cars and objects from his car accessory business, spoke of a busy and fruitful life. A massive Mercedes-Benz S-class coupé sat in his parking bay. He is particularly keen on showing off his photo albums and his recently published biography. His racing career spanned eighteen years, from 1952, when he drove 356s and 550 Spyders, to his 1970 Le Mans win. He is a survivor as well, having endured two terrifying accidents, both in Formula 1 single-seaters, one at Monaco in a Mercedes and another at Berlin's Avus when his BRM P18 overturned – there is a well-known shot of him kneeling on the tarmac as it barrel-rolls over him. 'We were losing a lot of drivers even in the late '60s,' he recalls: '...Mitter, Mairesse, Scarfiotti, all Porsche drivers, and my wife Magdalena asked me to give up if I should win Le Mans. I had already decided to retire at the end of 1970, but the victory that year brought the moment forward. I stopped there and then.'

Hans was born in nearby Stuttgart in 1928, and from the age of eight he wanted to be a racing driver.

> *We had little models of the cars; I was Caracciola, the others were Nuvolari, Rosemeyer. In 1943, I was eligible for call-up, but my mother didn't want me to go into the military. There were reserved occupations, one of which was working as a baker, so she got me apprenticed to a bakery. Eventually though, everyone got called up, and with four friends we boarded a train bound for the Eastern front. By now it was February 1945, and everything was chaos. We hid in the train toilet for a while, then in the night we got off and walked home.*

In 1946, aged eighteen, Hans was eligible for a driving licence. He bought a 1928 BMW Dixie, an evolution of an Austin 7 that the Munich company made under licence, and made a living as a taxi driver. With a view to indulging his boyhood ambition, his third car was a Porsche 356, but before being eligible for a racing licence he was obliged to cut his teeth in a rally. He finished 6th in the Freiburg to Dromingen Rally, and promptly entered the 1952 Nürburgring Cup race. 'There were around 20 cars in the race, identical 356s. I retired. Then came the first Mille Miglia. I was 1st in class and 30th overall.'

Hans Herrmann at the 1967 Targa Florio, standing in front of 910 #006 of Maglioli/Schutz. To the right, behind the lorry, is a Porsche hillclimb star, Lodovico Scarfiotti. The 910 #012 of Herrmann/Siffert came 6th overall.

Hans Herrmann reprises his role as a Mercedes-Benz Grand Prix driver in 1954–55, demonstrating a 300 SLR at the 2008 Solitude Revival.

The Carrera suffix that's applied to select Porsche cars was adopted after the works' team's success in 1954's Mexican road race, La Carrera Panamericana, with Herbert Linge (left), Hans Herrmann, Huschke von Hanstein, Jaroslav Juhan, Fernando Segura and mechanics Werner Enz and Sigmund Muyerlein. Herrmann/Linge took the class win in their 550 Spyder, and Porsche took the Carrera name.

Posing with the 550 Coupé #001 after the 1953 Le Mans 24 Hours, Hans Herrmann, Paul Frère and team manager Huschke von Hanstein link arms, with Herrmann's co-driver Helm Glöckler to the right. Frère and von Hanstein finished 15th overall, Herrmann and Glöckler 16th.

His first Le Mans was in 1953, sharing the Porsche 550 Coupé with Helmut Glöckler. They finished 16th overall, and racing manager Huschke von Hanstein was impressed.

> *One of their drivers had a big accident in training which ended his racing career, so there was an opportunity for me. But I had not yet got enough points on my licence to do an international race, so von Hanstein and Richard von Frankenberg told the organiser, 'He is a good guy, we can vouch for him', and we were 1st in class.*

On the strength of which, Ferry Porsche asked him to drive for the factory in German championship events. At this time, Mercedes-Benz was on the verge of a comeback thanks to Rudi Uhlenhaut and Alfred Neubauer. They had two drivers already, Fangio and Kling, and they needed a third. So, they invited four drivers to the Nürburgring for two days of testing. Hans was quickest, but it raised a dilemma as he also had a contract with Porsche for 1954, which Neubauer tried to overturn. With some difficulty Hans managed to honour commitments to both manufacturers, Mercedes-Benz in Formula 1 and Porsche in sports car events.

> *It was also difficult for me because one was front-engined and the other had the engine behind, and this produced different handling characteristics. Also, the Mercedes F1 car was much more powerful.*

By 1970, Hans could look back at a racing career spanning two decades, including class wins in La Carrera Panamericana and the Targa Florio, and a Grand Prix drive with Mercedes-Benz factory team cut short by a near fatal accident at Monaco in 1955.

Hans claims his English is not good, but it is much better than he thinks. Chatting with him again at Le Mans ahead of the 40th anniversary of his victory with Richard Attwood, Hans reflected, 'My wife always wanted me to stop racing because it was very dangerous,' he said. 'She was very protective, because in ten years I lost more than twenty friends.' There wasn't exactly an ultimatum: 'she asked me as I was leaving home to drive to Le Mans, "Hans, if you win this race, will you stop?" and I said yes.' The prospects for the Anglo-German pairing did not look great. Neither spoke the other's language, so communication was by

Hans Herrmann takes the chequered flag to win the 1970 Le Mans 24-Hours, Porsche's initial outright victory at La Sarthe. Standing beside the flag waver, his co-driver Richard Attwood greets him home.

sign language and via other team members. Disenchanted with what he saw as the unnecessarily car-killing pace he and Vic had set in 1969, Richard chose veteran Hans as his team-mate. Placed in the Porsche Salzburg Konstruktionen team, they were allocated the 4.5-litre car rather than the newer, faster 5.0-litre version, and were the slowest 917 in practice. Was it better to drive for Porsche-Salzburg, the works team, or for JW Automotive? 'The two teams were like families, so it was no better to drive for one or the other.'

Wet and dry

Hans started the race, and says he asked Richard not to attempt to keep up with the leaders – for the first six hours of the race not to be in the front group so it would be calm and save time and energy as the race wore on. He had more than enough experience as he had driven it over fourteen times, and he was bringing to bear the strategy of his experience and why they won.

The car we were driving had a slightly smaller engine, 4.5-litres, but it was safer than the 5.0-litre. The 5.0-litre engine was a development of the 4.5-litre engine, and we couldn't be sure at the time; maybe they had stretched it too much, so the car we had was safer and it wasn't going to break down in the night. The engine was a bit less powerful, of course, it was maybe 8–10km/h slower down the Mulsanne Straight. We could do 384km/h during practice, but for the race we kept to only 315km/h – so, a good bit less. We didn't use the full revs because it was a 24-hour race. It was the most terrible race because the weather conditions were so changeable, going from dry to rain, dry to rain again. We were having to change the tyres from dry to wet – seven or eight times we changed the wheels because of the water on the track. The whole team did the same for each car. At the beginning of the race, we were 12th; after 3–4 hours, we were 9th, and so on… and in the last two to three hours, we were leading, but I can't remember the middle part. You are leading, but you are still worried. Are the brakes working? You're listening to the engine, and you are very careful that nothing unfortunate happens. I wasn't really relaxed because something could still happen to the car or the tyres or something. I still had in my mind the previous year's race when Gérard Larrousse and I drove the 908 and we so nearly won. In '69, during the final one and a half hours, Ickx and I passed each other a dozen times, and our brakes were not effective anymore. We did have the chance to change them, but that would have ruled out any chance of the win because we would not have been able to catch the GT40. There was a chance we could still win the race because maybe Ickx was having the same braking problems, so we decided to continue driving. The GT40 was just powerful enough to hold onto the lead and win, by 100 metres. That was close!

How did it feel when the chequered flag came down, and you knew you had won?

We were so lucky, and I felt so proud, but also, I had said to my wife that this would be my last race, and I was extremely lucky because, at the end of it all, I had survived. We used to joke that racing was dangerous then, but not the women! Today, it's different; women are dangerous, but the racing is not! After the race, there was a big party in a chateau to celebrate the win, hosted by Ferdinand Piëch, and Porsche celebrated the victory with him. I had been up for 40 hours, and I was tired after the race and all the celebrations. When I got home my wife was more than happy; my sons were then one and five years old, so she was pleased about the victory, but also because I would be retiring.

It was great, then, to hear him reprise first-hand the joy of scoring the marque's first outright Le Mans victory.

CHAPTER 3

THE PORSCHE 910 1966–68

The curvaceous frontal lines of the 910, pictured here at Chobham test track, were superior aerodynamically to the 906.

In 1967, Porsche was on a roll, consolidating its catalogue of sports racing prototypes with the gorgeous 910. The cutest of the new-generation Porsche sports racers that blossomed at the end of the 1960s, the 910 incorporates many of the preceding 906's features. 'The shape of the 910 came from Buzzi Porsche as well as the 906,' says Porsche racing and engineering legend Jürgen Barth. It was also touted as the circuit racing coupé version of the uncompromising open-top Ollon-Vilars 906 Bergspyder hillclimb car. In fact, the first three 910s – #001–#003 – received their baptism of fire at the Freiburg-Schauinsland and Gaisberg Hill Climbs on 31 July and 4 September 1966, setting fastest time of day at both venues in the hands of Gerhard Mitter and Hans Herrmann. The fact that they were quickest is a reflection on the quality of the rival entries and the talent of the drivers, but it certainly got the 910 off to a great start.

Gerhard Mitter guides the winning 910 #002 coupé up the Schauinsland-Freiburg Hillclimb on 31 July 1966.

Hans Herrmann nears the summit of the Gaisberg Hillclimb in the prototype 910 #001, coming 2nd, just half a second behind Mitter in the other 910 prototype #002, on 4 September 1966.

The European Hillclimb Championship courses were invariably set in spectacular mountainside venues; here, Gerhard Mitter runs up the Gaisberg course in 910 #002, setting fastest time of the day.

The frontal view of the 910 demonstrates that the front wings (fenders) are somewhat lower than those of the 906, with benefits to the car's aerodynamics as well as the driver's vision. Unlike the 906's gullwing doors, those of the 910 are hinged off the windscreen surround.

The 910 is based on a triangulated tube-frame chassis, like the 906, and features a pert fibreglass bodyshell, bonded strategically to the chassis frame tubes. Like the 906, the 910 has its steering-wheel on the left-hand side of the cockpit, but instead of the gullwing doors of the 906, the 910 has the doors hinged on the forward edge of the windscreen A-frame surround, and it also has a detachable roof panel. The 910 was fitted with either 6- or 8-cylinder engines. Launched in 1967, Porsche made 22 units of the 910 coupé powered by the 220bhp 2.0-litre (1991cc) flat-6, and thirteen cars were fitted with the 260bhp flat-8 in 2195cc and 1981cc format, of which seven were coupés and six were spyders. For long-distance events, it was normally equipped with the six-pot motor and the flat-8 for the Targa Florio.

Hunkered down amidships between the chassis tubes, the 2.0-litre flat-6 is a snug fit, cooling fan facing forwards behind the cockpit bulkhead and a mechanical fuel injection pump nestling between the two banks of triple trumpets flanked by enormous throttle springs.

The 910's 1990cc flat-six engine is topped by injection trumpets, throttle linkage and fuel pump.

Fibreglass trumpets guide cooling air onto the 910's transmission casing. The inner wheel arches leave a certain amount to be desired in terms of smoothness of finish.

The twin-plug engine's sparkplug caps have clips over them to keep them from popping off due to vibrations. The magnesium gearbox extends rearwards, with the lightweight breather trunking to the transmission purpose-made in rigid fibreglass. It is simple yet effective, with nothing left to chance. Everywhere you look there are triangulated chassis tubes and suspension rods.

Built on a similar complex steel tube chassis frame to the trend-setting 906 of a year earlier, the 910's front track is nearly 4in wider than the 906's, at 1,430mm (56.3in) against 1,337mm (52.6in), though the suspension is the same, with upper and lower wishbones allied to leading and trailing radius arms, variable rate coils and hydraulic dampers all round, plus adjustable anti-roll bars front and rear. Brakes are ventilated front discs, and the dual braking circuit is adjustable via a balance bar to allow a greater braking effect at the front or back.

The principal differences from the 906 are the pioneering (for Porsche) aluminium centre-lock 13in wheels shod with commensurately lower profile tyres, allowing the designer to come up with a much sleeker, co-ordinated body shape that still ranks as the purest of the genre-spanning types 904 to 917 – like the 906, the fibreglass bodywork is bonded to the chassis tubes at strategic points. As Jürgen Barth points out, 'the 910 has a slightly different tube-frame configuration from the 906, and the tubes are not identical everywhere.'

Bosch mechanical fuel injection is employed for the first time, the pump belt-driven off a camshaft. The door opening arrangement is better, with hinges on the windscreen hoop and the end of the front wing, rather than roof-hinged gullwing, though the door when open does rest on the front wing and oil filler cap.

The 910's front panel is removed to reveal the oil cooler and triangulated tubes of the chassis frame.

Having enjoyed a successful season with the 906 in 1966, the factory raced the 910 in the prototype category in 1967, Hans Herrmann and Jo Siffert coming 4th overall in the Daytona 24-Hours – amazingly on the same set of Dunlops – and Gerhard Mitter and Scooter Patrick 3rd overall at Sebring behind a pair of 7.0-litre Mk II Fords.

In profile, the 910 projects a streamlined nose and Kamm-tail aerodynamics.

Serving the fuel injection system, the 910's Bosch pump is mounted above the flat-6 motor.

Paul Hawkins and Rolf Stommelen shared the winning 910/8 #024 in the 1967 Targa Florio, with Cella/Biscaldi 2nd and Elford/Neerspach 3rd in 910/6s, a clean sweep for Porsche.

The 910 #028 of Jo Siffert and Hans Herrmann started from 3rd on the grid for the 1967 Nürburgring 1,000Kms, but dropped a valve and did not finish.

Jochen Rindt swings the 910 #027 he shared with Graham Hill around Druids Hairpin at Brand Hatch during the 1967 BOAC 500.

For the Targa Florio, six 910s were despatched – three flat-6s and three flat-8s, all fuel injected – and they scooped the first three places: Paul Hawkins and Rolf Stommelen won with a 2.2-litre 8-cylinder car, Leo Cella/Giampiero Biscaldi were 2nd and Jochen Neerpasch/Vic Elford 3rd. Aussie Paul Hawkins was a firm favourite with us young race fans, always having a friendly word when pounced on in the paddock. Vic Elford became my friend in his later years. He practised a 906 before driving a 910 in the race. 'It was my first time ever in a real race car,' he recalls, flagging up the advancement of the 910 design:

I only drove the 906 a couple of times, including my first Le Mans in 1967 and for my first practice laps at the Targa Florio. The 906 was difficult there because of the restricted tunnel vision between the big front fenders. But I soon got used to that and found it comfortable and easy to drive. The actual race was in a 910 where visibility was much better.

A point reinforced by Jürgen Barth: 'The better suspension and the better aerodynamics made the 910 easier to drive than the 906,' he says.

The 'Hanstein Army' had seven cars running at the 1967 Nürburgring 1,000kms, and with no works Fords or Ferraris present, 910s took the top four places, the first three being six-cylinder versions; Vic's was 3rd.

Run on 28 May 1967, the Nürburgring 1,000Km was won by Udo Schütz and Joe Buzzetta in their 910 #007. The roof is absent to accommodate Schütz's helmet.

A pair of works' 910s circulate in close company at Brands Hatch during the 1967 BOAC 500 race – the 910 of Graham Hill/Jochen Rindt leads the similar car of Vic Elford/Lucien Bianchi at Druids Hairpin. Both retired with valve issues.

Porsche 910 #013 is offloaded from the transporter by a mechanic (insouciantly smoking!) in the Brands Hatch paddock ahead of the 1967 BOAC 500. This, the Rindt/Schutz car, started and finished 11th, 16 laps behind the winning Chaparral. (Rindt co-drove two 910s in this race.)

Some of the leading privateer teams were quick to buy 910s, including Tony Dean, Bill Bradley and Richard Bröstrom, whose cars are parked in the Silverstone paddock ahead of the Martini Trophy 300-mile race on 17 May 1969. Amongst a top-line field that included eleven Lola T70s and five GT40s, the Dean/Bradley car finished 7th and Bröstrom 11th.

At the star-spangled inaugural BOAC 500 at Brands Hatch there were five 910s present, with top-names on the Porsche driver roster including Graham Hill and Jochen Rindt. Jo Siffert and Bruce McLaren placed 3rd in a flat-8 910 behind the winning Chaparral 2F of Mike Spence and Phil Hill, and Jackie Stewart and Chris Amon's Ferrari P4, and ahead of its successor, the 907 of Hans Herrmann and Jochen Neerpasch. At season's end, Herrmann and Schutz were 3rd in the Paris 1,000Kms at Linas-Montlhéry, splitting the big V8 Fords and V12 Ferraris.

The 910 was obviously superior to the Carrera 6 by virtue of its aerodynamics and smaller diameter wheels, so supposedly none were sold to privateers that season – to keep customers who had just shelled out for a new 906 the year before on side. However, Porsche made a point of racing only brand-new cars in World Championship events, so inevitably, a trickle of surplus cars became available as the season wore on. Come 1968, 28 examples of the 910 had been built, more than the requisite 25 units for the production sports car category, and staunch independent British racers like Tony Dean and Bill Bradley were first in the queue to get their hands on the new model.

DR HELMUTH BOTT

Ranked as one of Porsche's greatest engineers, Helmuth Bott joined Porsche in 1952 as a production assistant, then worked in the experimental department to become head of Research & Development by 1968, largely based at the Weissach test facility. Crucially, Dr Bott was instrumental in the development of most of the cars covered here, the Types 906, 910, 907, 908 and 917. Subsequently, he was responsible for the 917/30 Can-Am programme, the Group C Types 956 and 962 prototypes, and the 1.5-litre TAG turbo V6 engine project that powered the McLaren MP4 F1 cars in the mid-1980s. One of the leading progenitors of the original 911, he masterminded its transformation in 1986 into the all-wheel-drive 959 supercar.

FERDINAND PIËCH

On 1 April 1963, Ferdinand Piëch, the grandson of Prof Ferdinand Porsche, started working at Porsche. In 1966, Piëch became the head of testing, and was also the main force behind the Porsche 906.

Piëch's mission was to create ultralight racing cars, and the subsequent 907, 909 Bergspyder, 908 and 917 were his progeny. In 1968, Piëch was appointed head of development at Porsche, seeing his creation win Le Mans. On 1 March 1972, it was decreed that no Porsche family member could be involved in the management of the company. All the family members left the company for a back seat on the supervisory board leaving only Ferry Porsche active for the period needed. Ferdinand Piëch also had to leave and established his own independent engineering office. Then, on 1 August 1972, Piëch moved to Audi NSU Auto-Union AG as head of technical development.

The 906 driven by Dieter Spöerry and Rico Steinemann finished 13th in the 1967 BOAC 500 at Brands Hatch.

Peter Falk, left, chatting with Ferdinand Piëch at the finish of the 1967 Freiburg Schauinsland Hillclimb, with Gerhard Mitter in the 910 Bergspyder with which he set the fastest time of the day.

PETER FALK

In 1959 Peter Falk joined Porsche as an engineer, one of only ten employees in the test department. Five years later, he began working in pre-series and racing support, where he was instrumental in getting the 911 prepped as a viable race car. On the 1965 Monte Carlo Rally, he was Herbert Linge's co-driver in a 2.0-litre 911. 'I spoke into a thick plastic tube that went straight into Herbert's helmet,' he recalled – the precursor of the intercom system used today. The duo finished the rally 5th overall.

In the following years, racing cars from the 906 to the 917 were built under the aegis of Falk as head of the pre-series and racing department. From 1973 to 1981, he was test manager in the development of the 911, 924 and 928 series, responsible for the body, gearbox, road testing and endurance run areas.

As head of race car development and racing director in the 1980s, he was responsible for the success of the 956 and 962 Group C cars, which, with seven overall victories at Le Mans and eleven world championship titles, made this racing car project one the most successful in the company's history.

BILL BRADLEY AND THE MIDLAND RACING TEAM

In 1967 and 1968, Bill Bradley campaigned a similarly liveried white 906 with blue stripes under the Midland Racing Team banner.

However, when the 910 was released to privateers he quickly acquired two – the white one in his familiar paint scheme, and a silver-grey one, 014, which was sold to sometime Porsche works driver Joe Buzzetta in 2001. A Birmingham butcher by trade, Bradley became de-facto 910 works racer, operating from his Huntingdon workshop situated behind the Specialised Mouldings factory. Meanwhile, over in Germany, Irishman Paddy O'Grady was the team's engineer; he had been an engineering apprentice at Zuffenhausen in 1965 (seconded from BMC) where he funded his living expenses by working in the repair shop within Porsche's customer race shop. After the apprenticeship finished, he just carried on working at Zuffenhausen. Paddy recalls:

> *The factory racing department was divided from the customer racing department by a wall going right up to the roof. We didn't change rooms, we kept to ourselves, and*

Bill Bradley seemed to have got his priorities right: Porsche 906 #144 racing car, with Mini Countryman and Bedford Dormobile as support vehicles. And a hammer as a chock. He and Mike Costin came 17th in the 1967 BOAC 500 at Brands Hatch.

there was a certain amount of competition between the two departments. But often when the racing department had a lot to do, the work was passed over to the customer competition department, and that's what happened with the last three 910s. I was part of a team of six people who built those cars.

As for Bill Bradley's 906 and 910s, Paddy was allowed to work on them in the Porsche customer racing department and, if necessary, write workshop orders: 'I didn't rebuild engines at that time,' he tells me; 'they went to the engine department. I used to rebuild the gearboxes, but if we were in a terrible hurry with a crashed car, then that would be rebuilt by the factory in the customer competition department.' Things moved on when, in 1968, one of Bill Bradley's cars came in to be repaired, and Paddy suggested they set up an independent race preparation shop at Fellbach, east of Stuttgart. This was called Bill Bradley Racing, employing Paddy and Peter Bayer, who was one of the top mechanics at the time, and Paddy spent the next two or three years commuting between Stuttgart and Huntingdon, fettling cars and engineering them at races all over Europe.

Old timer

Two decades on, and Bradley out of the picture, in the early 1990s the firm changed its name to P.O. Sportwagen Technik, and Paddy O'Grady still preps his three 911s – a 2.7, a 3.2 Carrera and 964 Carrera Cup race cars for the German Old Timer series.

The first outing for 910-020 was the Monza 1,000Kms, on 25 April 1968, entered by Bill Bradley with Vic Elford co-driving, and it was quickest of the five 910s present. 'In 1968 Porsche had too many drivers,' comments Vic, 'so we each missed one race. Monza was my turn, so I drove with Bill.' At the start, Vic was well up with the works GT40s and factory 907s and 908s, but a wheel came off during Bradley's stint and he was lucky to get going again with the aid of some marshals who found the missing wheel nut. As a result, a secure 4th place receded to 9th overall. Vic drove the car several times that year, retiring at Mugello, 'because it broke', and Nuremburg's Norisring road circuit on 30 June after a collision with Frank Gardner's Lola T70. He fared better at the Solituderennen staged at Hockenheim on 21 July. Vic remembers it well. 'I had a great race. I missed some of the practice and when I was there it was wet, so I started way down at the back and had to work like a dog – without slipstreaming – to catch up to the pack. I passed them all to win the 2.0-litre category.'

After a huge scrap with Alex Soler-Roig in another 910, Vic came 4th overall behind the big bangers and ahead of a load of 910s and 906s. Up-and-coming F3 star Alan Rollinson drove 910-020 with another well-known privateer, David Prophet, at the Paris GP at Montlhéry, coming 20th overall and winning the Coupe du Salon. Then at Austria's Zeltweg airfield circuit (pre-Österreichring) Bradley and fellow 906 and 910 owner Tony Dean shared driving duties, starting the 500Kms from the back of the 4-3-4 grid. A ball joint broke on the 910's front suspension at half distance, but there was compensation on the home front where Bill Bradley was still campaigning his Carrera 6.

On 7 April, he and Eric Liddell came 12th in the BOAC 500, and by the Brands Hatch Bank Holiday meeting on 3 September, he had won the 1968 RAC Sports Car Championship for Group 4 cars.

In 1969 Bradley campaigned 910-020 on a similar basis, coming 12th and 1st in class at the Spa 1,000Kms sharing the driving with Tony Dean, 12th in the Nürburgring 1,000Kms again with Dean, and 3rd overall and 1st in class at the Vila Real 6-Hours street race in northern Portugal.

The Swiss Hart Ski Racing Team 910 #027 driven by Rico Steinemann and Dieter Spöerry came 7th overall and 1st in the 2.0-litre prototype category in the 1968 BOAC 500 at Brands Hatch.

Photographed beside the cobbled pavé of Chobham Test Track, the 910 retains its cockpit lid, fitted as standard, but removed to suit taller drivers.

At Zeltweg's 1,000Kms on 10 August, Bradley placed 11th with Swiss driver Dieter Spoerry sharing the wheel, then, moving up the results sheets, Bradley and Spoerry came 5th at Montjuïc circuit in the Barcelona 12-Hours.

In 1970 Paul Vestey and Roy Pike drove the car in the BOAC 1,000Kms at Brands Hatch, though the ignition failed. That was its last race under Bradley's tenure, though he kept it until the late 1980s, when Paddy O'Grady restored it for another contemporary racer, Mark Koenig. After four years of refurbishment, Koenig drove it in the early 1990s Group 4 race series. Fiskens sold the car for Koenig, and it did Le Mans Classic in 2002 and 2004 and, road registered, the current owner did the Tour Auto 2008.

CHOBHAM TEST TRACK

While Zuffenhausen developed its next project, the baton was passed to independent racers, and a few years ago I grabbed the chance to sample privateer Bill Bradley's 1968 example. This time, I had got my earplugs in, in anticipation of putting another unsilenced Porsche racing car through its paces. I have got my sensible Piloti race boots on as well.

Tinnitus trauma'd from the 906 I drove a few weeks previously, Achilles tendons wrenched from driving barefoot, I had come to Chobham better prepared. My benefactor was Will Stone from Kensington-based sports-racing car specialists Fiskens. He had brought along the gorgeous 910 they were selling – chassis 910-020 – and he had primed it ready for me to give it a go on the 2-mile test track. Ground-hugging in traditional Porsche racing white with its in-period blue stripes, I was appraising the 910 coupé run by privateer Bill Bradley in 1968, chassis number 910-020, which is stamped on an upper chassis tube ahead of the right rear wheel.

As I had found driving the 906, there is not a lot of headroom, and mercifully the 910 has a removable roof panel, without which it becomes an open-top roadster with unrestricted headroom for the taller driver. Fitting the roof panel is a fiddly two-man job, one on either side of the car, though it is as light as a feather; it has two pins that tuck in the back of the rollover hoop, while the front lip tucks into the top of the windscreen header rail. The doors need to be fully open and the engine cover unclipped and canted right back so you can locate the pins in the roof panel. The 910's (partly contemporaneous) successor, the right-hand drive but aerodynamically evolved 907 coupé, features a slightly taller cabin roof, which circumvents the driver's height issue.

The 910's proportions are compact, and it is a more coherent design than the slightly lumpen 906, with much flatter curves to the wheelarches and purposeful aerodynamics. There is that characteristic 1960s Kamm-tail rear end, and at the front it is more shark-like with its twin nostrils and air vent to the oil cooler, and the light covers are neatly faired into the main panelwork of the wings.

The pedals of the 910 each have a different pattern etched into the metal, with the steering column passing between the brake and clutch.

Anatomy of a 907 racing car, revealing the raw, lightweight nature of the engine cover and inner wheelarches, transmission cooling pipes and flat-6 location. This is the Jo Siffert/Hans Herrmann #022 that started the 1968 BOAC 500 from pole position, but retired with brake problems.

Cockpit of the ex-Bill Bradley 910, with original steering wheel and gear lever, bucket seats, dashboard switchgear and gauges. A piece of corrugated tube directs cooling air at the driver.

The centre-lock 13in, five-spoke aluminium wheels are fitted with Dunlop Racing tyres, 4.75/10.00-13 on the front, 6.00/12.00-13 on the back.

The layout is not much different to that of the 906; there is a hefty fire extinguisher reservoir low down ahead of the left rear wheel, and the petrol filler is in the same place behind the passenger doors. The 910's doors themselves are a better solution than the 906's gullwings, hinged on the windscreen surround and on the trailing edge of the front wing and folding forward to rest on the right-hand oil cap and on the front left wing. There are two plastic opening vents in the door windows themselves. The two-seater cockpit is like the 906, bereft of any niceties whatsoever.

Tight squeeze

When it comes to the moment of truth, the 910 is just as much of a squeeze to get into as the 906. Wriggling my legs under the Volanti Cisa steering wheel is the trickiest bit, so I imitate a driver changeover during an endurance race and come in from the passenger side – it works. The lightweight bucket seat has a full harness, and my position is comfortably recumbent. There is a dogleg first gear, but the whole gearshift apparatus looks and performs more tidily than the 906. This sense of evolution carries through to the better-co-ordinated switchboard; the layout is much the same, with the rev counter straight ahead and the oil pressure and temperature gauges also pointing at the driver from the right of the wheel. Light switches are on the left of the steering wheel, with an ignition kill switch, ignition key, indicator switch and the pumps and a pair of ignition switches to the right. There is an ignition cut-off in the door shut on the passenger side as well as an external cut-off switch, and the spark boxes are on the rear panel where the passenger's head would go. The huge rear-view mirror is right in the passenger's line of vision, and the rear window is in the rear bulkhead – so at least you can see through the window glass, which you could not do very well on the 906.

We have taken the domed roof panel off, seeing as I am tall and it is a sunny day. It allows you to see the roll hoop, simply an extension of the chassis frame, and it is not that convincing as such, as it has got two notches in it where the roof panel slots in. It needs several turns on the starter to fire the engine up, then there is that glorious aural treat – a 2.0-litre flat-6 in full cry, slightly muted by the megaphones on the ends of the pipes but still a full-blown 'braaaaagggh, ghaaaaagh'. It is lower pitched than the 906 for some reason, but with that same dramatic gunshot gear change. Slotting into first (no problem) and with revs soaring, I ease onto the Chobham track. I build the revs to 3,500rpm, accelerate hard to keep it on the cam and aim at the apex of the corner. It's an amiable car to drive, and I have got these beautifully curvaceous front wings just below eye level through the windscreen, plus the cantilevered windscreen wiper and the streamlined mirror on the left-hand wing. With its two banked sections, long straights and curving B-roads, Chobham includes the 'snake', a glimpse of the Nordschleife winding up and down the forested Barrowhills area. Here I experience for myself that beautiful vice-free tuck-in on tighter corners.

High speed has always been a bit of a no-no at Chobham. Back when it was an MoD test track you could find yourself sharing the banking with a tank transporter, and there are advisory speed limits. But we have got no such rival hardware to clog up the place today, and I gun the 910 off the end of the main straight. Past 4,000rpm, it's a rocketship, and I bite my lip as the Dunlops grip. From an apex in the banking's inner basin, I bear right, giving it throttle to send the white missile across to the outside of the track, pushing through the

In period, 910 #020 was owned and raced by Bill Bradley for 30 years, subsequently restored by Paddy O'Grady, with co-drivers including Vic Elford, Gijs van Lennep, Tony Dean and John Fitzpatrick.

Dynamic rear three-quarter tracking shot of the 910 in action on Chobham Test Track.

The author exits Chobham Test Track's meandering, hilly Snake section in the 910.

cambered corners that course through the Surrey woods. There is no run-off area, so I am not complacent, but with every lap, the car seems to be exhorting me to go a little bit harder. This one is with you and not against you.

The nose seeks the apex on the corners in response to on-off throttle, provoking oversteer and understeer; it is a lively chassis, a wonderful car that just loves to dance, and I could so easily get addicted to it. Beautiful to look at and fabulous to drive, the 910 gets my vote as the neatest race car design of the era across all marques and possibly of Porsche's entire *oeuvre* from this period; it is not as challenging in terms of power and size as the 917 and therefore not a daunting proposition. The company's rate of progress at this point in time was so rapid, one evolution after another and running concurrently, that the 910 got rather swamped. With many fans in thrall to the 917, it deserves higher status on the Porsche pantheon.

GETTING REVVED UP

Apart from the Porsche Museum at Zuffenhausen, two museums in the USA harbour amazing collections that include significant Porsches: for example, the Petersen Museum in California and the REVs Institute housing the Collier Collection at Naples, Florida. The 910 in the Petersen Museum is that of Ben Pon, shared with Gijs van Lennep. My daughter Keri works out of West Palm Beach, Florida, as a superyacht chef, and we recently did a road trip across Florida to New Orleans in a modern Mustang. Along the way, I hooked up with Fort Miers-based Marika Haapavaara, who, with her partner, has a private collection of Porsches, and she provided a selection of photos of some of the cars from her neighbouring REVs Institute, including 904, 906, 910, 908 and 917. The 910, for instance, is 910/006.

This car won the Nürburgring 1,000-kilometre race in 1967. While not the most significant victory in Porsche's history, it was perhaps the most sentimental. After a decade of trying for an overall win in Germany's most prestigious sports car race, victory was finally achieved. The home team won before the home crowd. Joe Buzzetta and Udo Schutz formed the incongruous driver pairing for this car: the American was small, the German somewhat larger – on the face of it, an ill-conceived couple – though chosen to ensure that each Porsche contained a German driver who was capable of winning. The 910's roof was discarded to accommodate the German driver, such was the price paid for a PR victory. Right behind this Porsche were two more 910/6s. Yet, despite Porsche's best racing season in years, the factory lost the prototype championship to Ferrari by a single point. As usual, the under-2-litre trophy was Stuttgart's, but Porsche wanted more. In the quest for overall victory, Ferdinand Piëch ruthlessly pared excess weight from his cars. Only in this way could the small-displacement Porsches challenge the bigger cars outright. Piëch, the quintessential laboratory engineer, disdained racing – not for the obvious reasons, such as driver fatalities – but because of the role uncontrolled variables, including driver talent, could play. Such factors often meant that inferior solutions would win over the superior ones. To him, the optimal race would test cars on a chassis dyno over a simulated race course. Yet, since real racing was the game, Piëch played to win, with an unprecedented ferocity manifest in the wild proliferation of new racing models, and in the competition department's policy regarding them. So highly stressed were the racing cars due to the search for lightness that only the brand-new ones were used to contest important races. After a single factory outing, the works' cars were routinely reconditioned and sold off to private teams. Accordingly, it was not unusual for Porsche to produce 30 to 50 cars per year in its own race department.

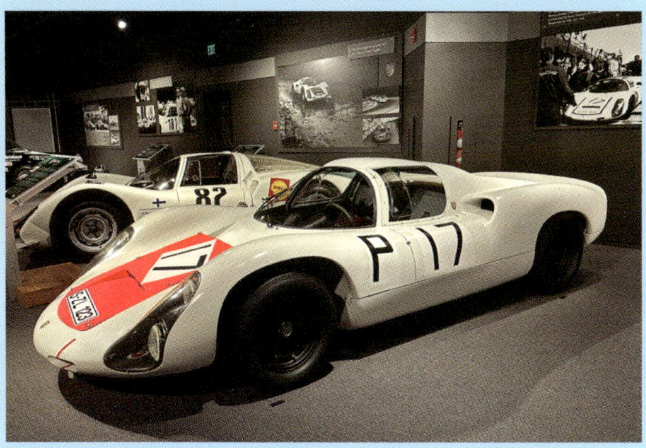

The 910 #007 that's on display at Florida's REVs Institute won the 1967 Nürburgring 1,000km in the hands of Udo Schutz and Joe Buzzetta.

THE 910 BERGSPYDER 1966–67

A single 910 Bergspyder was entered in the European Hill Climb Championship in 1966 and 1967. It was an exercise in weight-saving, differing in certain important aspects from the 910 endurance racing version, most fundamentally in that it was a spyder rather than a coupé. The use of a thin-gauge fibreglass door-less body, a very low windscreen, a small 16-litre (4.2-gallon) fuel tank, the extensive use of titanium parts and other weight-saving modifications brought the weight of the 8-cylinder 910 Bergspyder down to just over 500kg (1,102lb).

The 910 Bergspyder was built on a triangulated aluminium tube frame, fitted with the running gear of the normal 910. As the season progressed, from one hill-climb to another, further weight was saved. Beryllium brake discs were fitted, and this alone saved 31lb or 14kg. Lightweight wheels were tried, and the body was lightened even more, with

Rolf Stommelen corners the 910 #031 Bergspyder on the Schauinsland-Freiburg Hillclimb, setting 2nd fastest time of day, 13sec behind Mitter in #030.

The 1967 910 Bergspyder had adjustable rear ailerons, and weighed just 382kg (842lb).

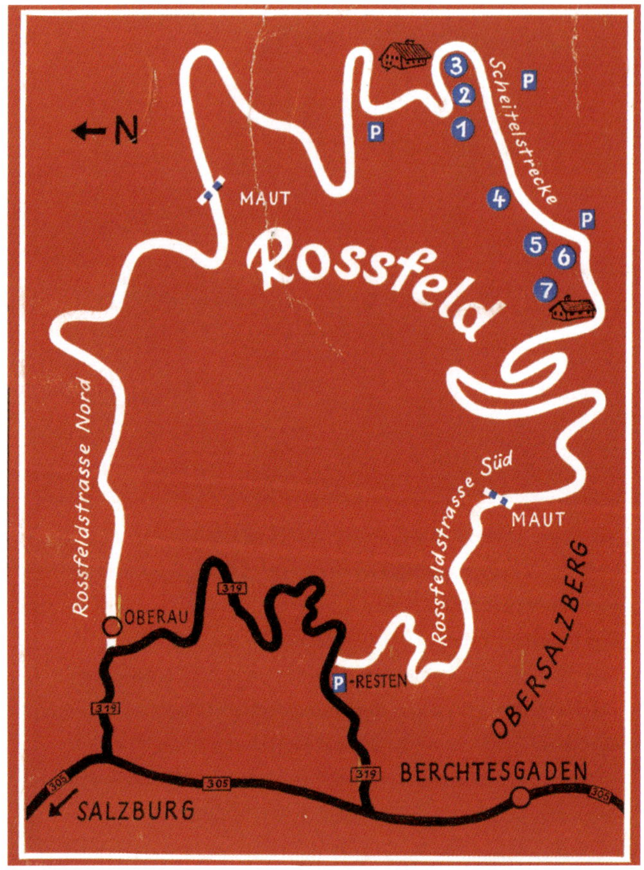

The Rossfeldstrasse is a scenic touristic route in the Bavarian Alps close to Berchtesgaden, a section of which served as the Rossfeld Hillclimb course in the heyday of the European Hillclimb Championship. The drop-offs are alarming, and there is a memorial halfway up to Lodovico Scarfiotti, killed in a 910 Bergspyder in 1968 due to a stuck-open throttle.

steel replaced by titanium, and even the 270bhp 2.0-litre Type 771 flat-8 engine was lightened by the incorporation of aluminium and magnesium until, by the end of 1967, the complete aluminium-framed car weighed only 419kg (924lb) with no fuel but with a full oil tank. The following year the generator was deleted, while the small lead battery was replaced with a lighter silver version. Even the front coil springs were eliminated and replaced by a single, much lighter cross-mounted Z-shaped torsion bar, while movable rear spoilers controlled by the rear suspension were fitted to improve tyre adhesion. Gerhard Mitter duly won his third European Hillclimb championship title.

PRIVATE LIVES

We have been concentrating largely on the factory race cars, but in many instances, the cars subsequently passed on to private owners – unlike Ferrari, who tended to destroy their cars after they became redundant or, perish the thought, obsolete.

One such Porsche was 910 #001, acquired by Bavarian privateer Walter Proebst. On a visit to Ruf Automobile at Pfaffenhausen, Bavaria, I met his daughter Verena at Alois Ruf's garage, and she provided the low-down on her father's race career.

Born in 1934, Walter Proebst was a racing enthusiast, and dropped out of college to become a lubricants engineer for a Munich-based oil company. Between the ages of 16 and 36 he raced, dirt-tracked and scrambled motorcycles

Privateer Walter Proebst took his 910 #001 hillclimbing in 1971 and 1972, as seen here at Trento-Bondone on 2 July 1972.

Many Porsche sports-prototypes had a competition life after their front-line racing heyday: this is Walter Proebst in 910 #001, which he hill-climbed in the early 1970s, as well as a 907 Spyder and Jaguar E-type.

Halfway up the Rossfeld Hillclimb is a monument to Lodovico Scarfiotti, noted Ferrari F1 and sportscar driver, who was also a major player in the Porsche works squad in 1968. He was killed when his 910 Bergspyder went off on the Rossfeld climb, presumably because the throttle. Also visible is the 991 Turbo used by the author and photographer Antony Fraser.

on a semi-professional basis, but eventually a shoulder injury led him to switch to cars. He became a hillclimb specialist, starting off in 1968 with a BMW 1800 TI and moving on to a Jaguar E-type coupé for 1970, where his first event was the 6km Rossfeld Bergrennen. I drove this magnificent route myself in a 991 Turbo, and it's an awesome, inspiring route that forges ever higher via multitudinous hairpins in an elevation gain of 548m (1,798ft). With good reason such events are called mountain climbs in Europe, rather than mere hillclimbs.

Proebst opened his account in 1971 with a couple of events in a 911 – a race meeting at the Salzburgring and Rossfeld again – before acquiring 910 #001. He did four more mountain climbs in 1971, then ten similar events in 1972, including standout climbs on the international calendar at Trento-Bondone and Freiburg-Schauinsland.

Walter Proebst's last hillclimb in the 910/001 was the Steibis Bergrennen on 15 October 1972, when he crashed. The 910 was then passed onto his sometime co-driver Hans Deffland, who swapped his March 713S with Proebst for it; Proebst subsequently drove the single-seater March in

Walter Proebst with his 910 beside the route of the Rossfeld Hillclimb. ***Verena Proebst***

German mountain climbs, initially in the F3 class and later in F2, in 1973 and 1976, and a swansong outing in 1987.

Meanwhile, Proebst acquired Porsche 907-032 and resumed his hillclimbing exploits in that, kicking off on 17 March 1974 at the Zotzenbach Bergrennen, followed by Frankenwald Bergrennen, then a race on the airfield circuit at Neubiberg, Munich, and the 1,000-km-Rennen auf dem Nürburgring 1,000km where he came 13th overall. This is followed by a host of hillclimbs with unfamiliar names – eleven in total – including Rotenburg-Fulda, Jura Bergrennen, Ruselbergrennen Deggendorf, and then the well-known Trento-Bondone, and the equally prestigious Schauinsland-Rennen Freiburg im Breisgau. He entered ten mountain climbs in 1975, including Trento-Bondone, the car now pegged as a 908, also tackling the Nürburgring 1,000kms

Trying hard on the Schauinsland-Freiberg Hillclimb, Walter Proebst takes a tight line whilst avoiding the kerbs.

again and placing 17th. After tackling three events in 1976, he effectively retired from the sport, having demonstrated admirably that racing cars such as the 910 and 907 can – and did – have a calling after their works heyday. Moreover, Walter's daughter Verena set up the Automuseum Adlkofen, east of Munich, in her father's memory, replete with 80 cars and 120 motorcycles, and she organises the annual Alex von Falkenhausen classic car rally. She would love to know where her father's cars are now so they can participate or be displayed in her museum.

TYPE 910 MAJOR SUCCESSES

1966
1st, European Hillclimb Championship, Sports class
1967
1st, 2nd, 3rd, Nürburgring 1,000Kms
3rd, BOAC 500
1st, Targa Florio
6th, Le Mans 24-Hours
1st, European Hillclimb Championship, Sport class
1968
1st, European Hillclimb Championship, Sports class
1969
6th, Le Mans 24-Hours

CHAPTER 4

THE PORSCHE 907
1967–68

The 907 #004 of Jo Siffert and Hans Herrmann came 5th overall in the 1967 Le Mans 24-Hours, having covered 3,000.62 miles (4,830.6km/h). averaging 125.06mph (201.27km/h). They also won the Index of Performance and the 2.0-litre class, and it was the first time a Porsche had exceeded a 200km/h average for the race.

In May 1967, Porsche brought a new car to the Le Mans Test Weekend. The 907 was the successor to the 910, although the long-tail configuration had been employed on the 906. Under the direction of Ferdinand Piëch and Hans Mezger, the driver's location in the 907 was installed on the right-hand side of the cockpit, bearing in mind that most racetracks ran in a clockwise direction, so the driver's weight was positioned closer to the centre of the turn. This is a short chapter, since the 907, though a significant upgrade on the 910, was joined a third of the way through the 1968 racing season by the similar-looking but bigger-engined 908.

There were few fundamental differences between the 910 and 907, which was little more than a 910 with an aerodynamically improved body, and that meant it was a slightly larger car. As it had also been recognised that right-hand steering provided an advantage in races on circuits running in a clockwise direction, the steering column was moved accordingly. The chassis remained basically the same as the 910, but the front coil springs and coaxial shock absorbers were rearranged to provide variable rate springing without resorting to variable pitch coil springs. Several coils and weight loss could be saved by this modification. On the 907, ventilated front brake discs were used from the start. Originally the 907 had the same wheels, front rims 8 inches, rear rims 9.5 inches wide as the 910, but for 1968, 12-inch-wide rear rims were used, except at Le Mans, where aerodynamic reasons dictated a return to the narrower size.

The original 907 was fitted with the 910's 2.0-litre flat-6, and its longtail bodywork was aerodynamically enhanced with movable ailerons, which we will come to in a minute. Fundamental upgrades included the driver's seating position being changed from the left to the right to optimise the car's balance for certain tracks, but the *lang-heck* bodywork rendered the car unstable at the top speed along the Mulsanne Straight.

At the end of March 1968, Porsche had four Type 907 chassis ready and brought them to Florida for the Daytona 24 Hours. Fully developed, the 907 now used a 2195cc air-cooled magnesium-alloy flat-8 with Bosch fuel injection, good for 278bhp at 8,700rpm. The 907LH (*lang heck*, or long-tail) was aerodynamically sound in principle but extremely difficult to drive fast, especially around the steeply banked section. And it is steep: I once tried to walk up the Daytona banking, but found it almost impossible (unlike Indianapolis, which is shallow by comparison). I also saw a fox run across the Daytona infield. Context, of a kind!

Porsche continued to develop the 907, refining the suspension and swapping the classic 2.0-litre flat-6 for the more sophisticated Type 771 2.2-litre air-cooled flat-8. The aerodynamics of the fibreglass body had the lowest drag coefficient of any Porsche racing car thus far produced, and the steering was shifted to the car's right-hand side to allow for the world's predominantly clockwise-oriented racetracks, giving the driver a better sense of the apexes and placing his weight on the inner side of the car on right-hand corners. It was altogether a slightly larger car than the 910 and had a rectangular front intake, rather than the 908's that had rounded-off corners. There was even a NASA-developed cool suit system to aid the drivers, who now wore dense fire-resistant Nomex race suits.

THE 907

Premiere: 9 April 1967, Le Mans test day / First win: 1968 Daytona 24h winner / Engine: 2.0-litre flat-6 or 2.2-litre flat-8 / Number Produced: ~8 units / Wheelbase: 90.6 inches / Weight: 1,320lb / Power: 256bhp @ 8,700rpm (flat-6) or 278bhp at 8,700rpm (flat-8)

FRENZIED ACTIVITY

Ferdinand Piëch's era had begun, the era when, approximately every second month, a new racing car or a significant modification was created. The new 907 was ready for the 1967 Le Mans enduro: two 907 LH (*lang heck*, long-tail) started the race, along with eight other Porsches. Running ten cars at Le Mans was a new record for Porsche, and all ten had 2.0-litre flat-6 engines. Porsche elected not to run any 8-cylinder cars because of concerns over reliability over the 24-hour race distance. So, there were two 907s, two 910s and two 906s. They came 5th, 6th, 7th and 8th after the 7.0-litre Mk II Ford GT40s and 4.0-litre Ferrari 330 P4s. The fastest Porsche was the 907 LH #41 of Jo Siffert and Hans Herrmann, and they took the 2.0-litre class victory. It was the first Porsche to cover more than 4,800km in the Le Mans 24 Hours, taking the average speed to over 200km/h. This was some achievement in 1967, with just a 2.0-litre normally-aspirated engine, considering pit stops for refuelling and driver changes. With a new

The 907 LH #007 of Hans Herrmann and Jochen Neerpasch came 4th in the 1967 BOAC 500 at Brands Hatch, the inaugural running of the annual endurance event sponsored by Great Britain's international airline.

The Herrmann/ Neerpasch 907 LH dips into Druids Hairpin during the 1967 BOAC 500 at Brands Hatch. Placed 4th overall, it was five laps behind the winning Chapparal 2F.

longtail body and suitable gearing, the 907s reached 302km/h (190mph) on the Mulsanne Straight, even though they used the reliable 220bhp 2.0-litre 6-cylinder motor rather than the more powerful 8-cylinder unit. Vented disc brakes were always fitted from this point on.

In addition to Le Mans in 1967, the long-tail 907 was used only at the Brands Hatch BOAC 500 Six-Hour race, held in April, for which it received a shortened tail – though still longer than the KH short-tail 907 that came in later.

The record-breaking performance of the 7.0-litre V8 Ford Mk IV at Le Mans had triggered rumours about an imminent rule change, and Porsche started to prepare for that in the summer of 1967. Accordingly, the 907 was equipped with the 270bhp 2.2-litre Type 771/1 8-cylinder unit, which was then modified in compliance with the rules of the new 3.0-litre prototype category that was announced in late 1967 and would come into effect in 1968. This upcoming 3.0-litre flat-8 would have to be developed first, though, to be introduced in the 908.

From 1968, the big-engined V8 and V12 prototypes of Ford and Ferrari were outlawed by the FIA rule makers, and the chances were that Porsche could secure the World

Sportscar Championship, as well as an outright win at Le Mans, since the competition from Ford, Matra and Alfa Romeo were not yet up to speed with their 3.0-litre prototypes either. Ferrari even sat out the whole of the 1968 season in protest against the rule change. Apart from the former 2000cc-class rivals, Alfa Romeo's T33/2 and the Alpine-Renault, 5.0-litre V8 sports prototypes were also permitted to enter, subject to at least 50 units having been built. This loophole was created intentionally, in order to fill the grid with cars dating mainly from 1965, like the V8-powered Ford GT40 and Lola T70.

DEAD HEAT

The 1968 endurance racing season started off in Florida with the Daytona 24-Hours. An army of five long-tailed Porsche 907 LHs lined up, supported by twenty mechanics and engineers – a large number of personnel for the time. One 907 was equipped with the 2.0-litre flat-6, and the four factory team cars with 2.2-litre flat-8s, developing 271bhp and 166lb ft of torque. The drivers wore cooling vests developed by NASA as the oil-cooler and the hot oil pipes caused excessive heat in the closed cockpit bodywork. In the race, a rival competitor dropped oil on the track, and Gerhard Mitter lost control of his 907 #53. Going sideways

The Herrmann/Neerpasch 907 LH in the paddock enclave occupied by the Porsche System works team during the 1967 BOAC 500, with a row of 907 KHs in front of it.

The winning 2.2-litre 907 LH #005 of Vic Elford and Jochen Neerpasch on the infield during its winning run in the 1967 Daytona 24-Hours. Stommelen, Siffert and Herrmann also had a go in it so they could all claim the victory. To the right is the crashed 907 of Mitter/Stommelen and the Ferrari 250LM of Piper and Gregory, which also crashed out.

The five 907 drivers credited with winning the 1968 Daytona 24 Hours have a laugh with an Alitalia hostess; left to right: Rolf Stommelen, Jochen Neerpasch, Vic Elford, Ms Alitalia, Hans Herrmann and Jo Siffert.

onto the grass infield, the car flipped. Then a Ferrari got loose on the oil and hit 907 #55 driven by Dieter Spoerry, and two 907s were out. By dawn, all the Ford GT40s had retired, and the three remaining 907s were leading. One of them, #52, experienced a throttle linkage problem, and #51 had its alternator replaced. Car #54 of Elford, Neerpasch and Stommelen – the latter having joined them after Mitter rolled their 907 – was leading.

Racing manager Huschke von Hanstein also had Herrmann and Siffert do a stint in the leading car as well – not simply the-more-the-merrier, but as a statement not only of the car's mechanical superiority, but Porsche drivers too. And then, to confirm the point, with twenty-three and a half hours gone, von Hanstein ordered the three leading Porsches to drive side-by-side. All credit to von Hanstein, it was a smart move in terms of marketing because it left an indelible impression of the marque's supremacy. Ford had done the same thing at Le Mans in 1966, but it backfired when the organisers calculated the result on McLaren and Amon's location in the starting line-up and said they had gone a little bit further in the 24 hours. The other amusing anomaly was that five drivers were credited with 1st place in one car, while Herrmann and Siffert were also credited with 2nd place in another one. Ignominiously, the three Alfa Romeo T33/2s were beaten by a Ford Mustang.

Just down the road, the 1968 Sebring 12-Hours resulted in a 1-2 finish, with the Jo Siffert/Hans Herrmann 907 winning and the Vic Elford/Jochen Neerpasch car coming 2nd. The Gerhard Mitter/Rolf Stommelen and Lodovico Scarfiotti/Joe Buzzetta cars suffered engine failures, though on the upside, consecutive victories at Daytona and Sebring marked Porsche's first back-to-back major outright wins in the WCM.

The next race was the BOAC 500 at Brands Hatch on 7 April 1968. On that fateful day, everyone's boyhood hero Jim Clark was supposed to drive one of the new Ford F3L P68 prototypes with the 3.0-litre Cosworth DFV Formula 1 engine, entered by Alan Mann Racing. For various reasons, contractual cock-up or bad communication, Jim Clark was instead driving a Formula 2 Lotus 48 at the Hockenheimring in a round of the European F2 series, partly to show off the new John Player Gold Leaf sponsorship livery, and also because the Scotsman honoured his Lotus commitment, rather than he and Lotus team-mate Graham Hill driving the Ford F3L at Brands. He was killed when a tyre came off its rim at 120mph and, despite his valiant attempts to save it, the car crashed into the trackside forest trees. No Armco

The 1968 BOAC 500 gets underway, with the Porsche 907s out in front, Mitter/Scarfiotti leading Siffert/Herrmann and Elford/Neerpasch into Bottom Bank Bend (now Surtees Bend), followed by the JW Automotive GT40 of Ickx/Redman that would ultimately go on to win, and the remarkable Howmet Turbine of Thompson/Dibley.

Jo Siffert moves the 907 KH he shared with Hans Herrmann in the 1968 BOAC 500 out of the Brands Hatch paddock assembly area to head down to the starting grid. They would end up retiring after 106 laps with brake problems.

Diving into Paddock Bend in the 907 KH during the 1968 BOAC 500, Vic Elford and Jochen Neerpasch finished in 3rd place, two laps down on the Mitter/Scarfiotti 907, which finished on the same lap and a scant 22 seconds behind the winning GT40.

barriers then, and no seatbelts, let alone a harness. A bunch of us were spectators at Brands Hatch that day, and news of Clark's demise spread like a horrible plague through the enclosures. The incredulous feeling of helpless loss was palpable – and this, at a time when driver fatalities were, sadly, only too commonplace.

Meanwhile, Jo Siffert and Hans Herrmann were fastest in practice for the BOAC race – an activity known more recently as qualifying – ahead of Bruce McLaren and Mike Spence in the new Ford F3L. However, the updated John Wyer-entered Ford GT40 of Jacky Ickx/Brian Redman won, ahead of the remaining two Porsche 907s, after being only 5th on the grid.

In races on faster tracks like the Monza 1000km, these modified Ford GT40s entered by John Wyer's JW Automotive proved to be an unexpectedly strong force. The loophole for these 5.0-litre sportscars was accessible provided at least 50 units had been built, an avenue also pursued by Lola T70 and Chevron B8 owners. For 1969 the minimum number required for homologation into group 4 was lowered to just 25 cars.

So, for the Monza 1,000kms run on 25 April, there was an entry of 75 cars, run over 100 laps of the combined flat circuit and banked track, the speeds on the concrete banking being kept down by chicanes at the start of each banking section, which brought the cars right down to first gear. The Porsche factory team was out in force with Stommelen and Neerpasch in a long-tailed 907 with the 8-cylinder 2.2-litre engine, Siffert and Herrmann, and Scarfiotti and Mitter crewing two long-tailed 908s with 8-cylinder 3.0-litre engines.

A 908 undergoing aerodynamic testing on the Weissach Test Track in 1968, with woollen threads stuck on the body to monitor the airflow over the long-tail coupé bodyshell. Porsche also conducted aerodynamic tests on the skidpan.

ENTER THE 908

We have reached a point in the chronology of this book where several models overlap: the 907 has very quickly reached its zenith, with the incoming 908 making an immediate impact, whilst the 910s are still very competitive, as well as privateer 906s. We shall follow the 908's development, evolution and race history more comprehensively in the next chapter, but as far as the timeline of the 1968 season goes, the race record in this chapter covers both 907 and 908.

Of particular interest at Monza were the two 3.0-litre Porsche 908s, making their first race appearance, although they had appeared in public at the Le Mans Test Weekend.

Claudio Roddaro enters the pit lane during Classic Le Mans 2018 in the 908 LH, capable of hitting 200mph (320 km/h) on the original Hunaudières/Mulsanne Straight. The livery is that of #004 in which Lodovico Scarfiotti and Gerhard Mitter placed 11th in the 1968 Monza 1,000Kms.

The body and chassis units were similar to the 2.2-litre long-tail 907s, based on a triangulated tubular spaceframe with the glass-fibre body bonded onto it. Designated the 908, the new cars had entirely new engines and gearboxes, the only similarity to the 2.2-litre cars being the layout of the 8-cylinders as a flat-8. The 2.2-litre 8-cylinder engine had been developed from the old Type 753 1.5-litre Grand Prix engine, with bevel gear and shaft-drive to the camshafts, and a horizontally-mounted cooling fan situated on top of the engine. The 3.0-litre 8-cylinder engines were developed from the 6-cylinder series, with chain and gear drive to the four camshafts from the front of the crankshaft, and a vertical cooling fan driven from this drivetrain.

The gearboxes were also a new design, being six-speed and having the clutch mounted on the extreme end of the gearbox, and fully exposed, a U-shaped member surrounding the clutch carrying the exposed operating arm, pulled by a Bowden cable running under the engine from the flywheel on the rear of the crankshaft. A short, splined quill shaft was connected to a long shaft that ran right through the gearbox to the rear-mounted clutch, the drive then going forwards on a concentric sleeve-drive into the gearbox and final-drive unit.

During practice for the Monza 1,000Kms, the aforementioned short quill shaft gave trouble, but during the race, the new engines and gearboxes ran well. The gearbox had

The 2.0-litre Type 771 flat-8 engine of the 909 Bergspyder produced 275bhp at 9,000rpm. However, the fuel feed system incorporated a 15-litre pressurised accumulator, which proved incapable of enabling the car to deploy full power.

full pressure lubrication delivered on a dry sump principle, with an oil tank mounted in front of the left rear wheel, while external oil pipes on the gearbox casing directed oil through jets to the gears. The oil tank for the engine's dry sump system was mounted just behind the left front wheel, and there was an oil radiator in the nose of the car, as on the 907. And, like the 907, the 908 also had a right-hand steering position in the narrow cockpit and a right-hand gear lever, with a cooling duct blowing air onto the lever. Porsche's own-make 13-inch alloy wheels were fitted – a diameter that seems tiny nowadays but was quite the thing at the time – with a single central hexagonal nut fitting, tightened by a pneumatic impact spanner or a socket spanner and lever of enormous proportions. This type of wheel and fixing was also used on the 910, which was now in limited production, with fifteen cars already sold to privateers to run in the Sports/Prototype category. In the GT category, the Porsche brigade consisted of the lighter and less lavishly trimmed 911 T/R models, with all the permitted homologated modifications to bring them up to 911 S standard, complete with alloy wheels and three triple-choke Weber carburettors. The rest were private teams, with Ben Pon and Gijs van Lennep in a new 910, replacing the one wrecked at Brands Hatch when a steering arm broke, Bill Bradley's similar car with Vic Elford as co-driver, plus Gerhard Mitter, Rudy Lins, Andre Wicky and Jean-Paul Hanrioud, and Carlo Facetti also in 910s. The Swiss Hart Ski Racing team went out when Spöerry crashed their newly acquired 907 during first practice. So, opposition came from Alfa Romeo GTZs, the Gulf GT40s and privately entered Ferraris, with the V8 Alpine-Renaults an unknown quantity. While the new 908s were experiencing transmission troubles, they were quickest, along with the Gulf GT40s. The leaders scrapped furiously, with the two pale blue and orange GT40s giving the works 908s a very hard time, with Jacky Ickx leading for many laps. At the end of a dramatic race, punctuated by numerous mechanical failures and breakdowns, the Hawkins/Hobbs GT40 was the winner, with Stommelen and Neerpasch's 2.2-litre 907 in 2nd place and the Alpine-Renault of Depailler and De Cortanze 3rd, with the Koch/Lins 910 in 4th place.

TYPE 907/8 MAJOR SUCCESSES

1967
5th, Le Mans 24-Hours
4th, BOAC 500
1968
1st, 2nd, 3rd, Daytona 24-Hours
1st, 2nd, Sebring 12-Hours
2nd, 3rd, BOAC 500
1st, 4th, Targa Florio
2nd, Le Mans 24-Hours
1971
7th, Le Mans 24-Hours

ELFORD HEROIC IN SICILY

Porsche had high hopes of success in the 52nd Targa Florio. Having withdrawn from the Monza 1,000Kms, it was clear that the Alfa Romeo works' Autodelta team was putting all its efforts into the Targa Florio, with every intention of challenging the Porsche équipe and taking on the role normally occupied by Ferrari. After practice around the 44-mile mountain circuit, the best Alfa Romeo T33 was in 3rd place behind two Porsche 908s in the 3.0-litre class, and comfortably heading the works Porsches in the 2.0-litre class. Local loyalties were divided, because Nino Vaccarella was driving for Alfa Romeo, and Lodovico Scarfiotti for Porsche. On

Vic Elford achieved a remarkable victory in the 1968 Targa Florio, driving the lion's share in the 907 KH over co-driver Umberto Maglioli, and never giving up when all looked lost due to various problems, including a puncture, loose wheel nuts and a seized stub axle.

the first lap of practice, Scarfiotti's 2.2-litre 8-cylinder 907 caught up with Vaccarella in the 2.5-litre V8 Alfa Romeo, and in the ensuing dust-up, the Porsche went off the road and was completely wrecked, luckily without injury to Scarfiotti. The Porsche team had a spare car that had been used all week as a practice car by all the drivers, so that was tidied up and fitted with a new engine and replaced the wrecked car on race day. As was traditional in the Targa Florio, the 67 entries left the grid individually at 22-second intervals, the smaller and slower cars first and the larger and faster ones last. A line of Lancia Zagato Fulvias set off at 8.00am, all driven by Italian drivers, followed by a mixed group of old and new Alfa Romeos, Porsche 356s, Sprites, MGBs, an Austin-Healey and a couple of Fiat 124 Spiders, all in the 1600 GT class. The 2.0-litre GT class consisted of six 911s, driven by a mixture of Italian, Swiss and French drivers, and then the up-to 5.0-litre Group 4 class started to leave, including Terry Drury/Terry Sanger in a GT40, and David Piper in Paul Vestey's Ferrari 250LM, and the 906 of Karl von Wendt. Vaccarella was undoubtedly the crowd favourite, storming away at 8.25am in the Alfa Romeo T33, and then Hans Herrmann was away in the first of the 907s with the 2.2-litre 8-cylinder engine and short-tailed body, its nose painted blue for recognition. Next away was Elford in a similar car, with the yellow front panel but with a hole cut in the roof to allow room for his co-driver Umberto Maglioli to sit in the cockpit without his crash helmet touching the roof. As a tall bloke, I can testify that there are few things more irritating than your head rattling against the roof when driving any kind of car with a helmet on. In the spirit of the age, when Colonel Bogey-playing air horns were all the rage, all the 907s were fitted with multiple air horns below their right front wing to warn away errant spectators and animals – and Elford's had three red ones poking out like poppies. Then Siffert was away in a green-fronted 907, and finally Scarfiotti in an orange-fronted 907, this being the rehashed practice car. The Porsche crew occupied one end of the pits, listening in on their shortwave radio to their outpost up in the mountains at Polizzi, halfway around the 72-kilometre lap. Little did they know that at very moment, Elford, the fastest runner in practice, was in trouble for, just after Cerda village, the locknut on the right rear wheel had come undone and the wheel had slipped off the driving pins. Vic stopped and tightened it up with a huge socket spanner carried in the nose of the car along with the spare wheel and carried on to Polizzi, where he stopped to have a new nut fitted. Meanwhile, Rudi Lins in the works 910 was leading the 2.0-litre class, eleven seconds ahead of Giunti in the first Alfa Romeo T33. Vaccarella was going well, with a lap of 37m 2.029s but Scarfiotti had caught up and, with a lap of 37m 0.7s was leading the favourite Alfa Romeo by 22 seconds on time, though still behind on the road. Behind them, Elford was in more trouble with the same hub nut coming loose again, this time with disastrous results, as it happened on a fast bend, and a sudden loss of drive sent the car all over the road, and it struck a rock with the right-hand front wheel and burst the tyre. A lot of people would have given up, but not Elford; he fitted the spare wheel, threw the tools in the passenger seat, and charged off again. His troubles were not over: the outer taper roller race on the right-hand front stub axle seized up and mangled itself to pieces, and he arrived in the pit with everything smoking. The mechanic set to work to change the hub assembly, fitted a new front wheel, inserted a new spare in the nose, tightened all the nuts with the compressed air spanner, topped up the fuel tank, and Elford roared away, eighteen minutes down on schedule but determined to set a new lap record, even if there was no hope of winning the race.

On a mission

On the second lap, Scarfiotti increased his lead over Vaccarella to 28 seconds. Herrmann was not feeling happy with the steering on his 907 and had dropped down to 4th place behind Linz. So, the order after two laps was 907, Alfa Romeo T33 2.5, Alfa Romeo T33, Porsche 910, and 907 – and before the start, a lot of people had expected the four 907s to cruise round in formation. On the third lap, there was a driver change as Rudi Lins handed over to Rico Steinemann, and he went away with full tanks, while Scarfiotti handed over to Mitter. But, having filled the tanks on his emergency stop, Elford went straight through on his third lap and continued, logging a shattering all-time lap record of 36m 02s, an average of 119.8km/h, taking almost a minute off the old lap record. He still could not see any hope of really featuring in the race, but pressed on anyway. And on the 4th lap, the whole situation changed. Only 14 kilometres after leaving the pits, Schutz lost control on some loose gravel, slid into a wall and wrecked the Alfa Romeo. Elford had experienced a moment on the self-same corner, the only one that had broken up badly during his lap record-breaking stint, and Vaccarella had not warned Schutz about it. Then Mitter in the leading Porsche had stopped near Caltaveturo and was seen looking into the transmission. He got going again and stopped at Polizzi to report that the right-hand driveshaft rubber doughnut had split. As he set off again, the Porsche radio alerted the main pits, who got a completely new driveshaft ready to fit. The 907 came into the pits, and work started on changing the shaft; it was still leading the race on time, but as the work proceeded and the minutes ticked away, the Alfa Romeo of Galli/Giunti was away on its 5th lap, but still five minutes behind the stationary Porsche.

Elford stopped at the end of four laps, his shattering pace having got the car up to 7th overall, and Maglioli set off with every hope now of figuring in the results, thanks to the trouble the leaders had been having. Neerpasch had taken over the badly steering Porsche from Herrmann, but they were only just holding the pace of the 910 of Steinemann/Lins. The Porsche driveshaft was changed, and Mitter was back in the race and, during the 5th lap, regained most of the lost time in the pits, so that at the end of the lap, he was just over three minutes ahead. The Alfa Romeo had actually gone into the lead during the 5th lap for a short time, only to lose it when Mitter got going again. On time, at the end of five laps, which was half distance, Scarfiotti and Mitter were leading the Galli/Giunti T33 by 3m 9s, followed by the Casoni/Bianchi T33, the Herrmann/Neerpasch 907, the Steinemann/Lins 910, slowed by an inoperative self-locking differential, the Baghetti/Biscaldi T33 and the Elford/Maglioli 907.

Although this was the situation on time, it was not the case in fact, for the leading 907 came into the pits at the end of five laps. The front brakes were sticking on, and the engine was losing power as the broken driveshaft had flattened one of the tailpipes. Some fiddling around behind the pedals cured the sticking front brakes, and the tailpipe assembly was removed, and a new one put on – though while the old one came off easily enough, the hot manifolds had expanded, and it took a long time to get the new tailpipes on. The minutes ticked away, and the slender lead was lost to the Galli/Giunti T33 and then 2nd place to the Bianchi/Casoni T33. Eventually the Porsche exhaust was fitted and Scarfiotti went back out into the race. But the flattened tailpipe had caused overheating, and soon after starting the 7th lap, the engine succumbed shortly before Cerda.

All Porsche hopes now rested on the Elford/Maglioli car, which had refuelled after seven laps, and Elford was away to drive the last three laps. Due to refuelling stops, the Casoni/Bianchi T33 led momentarily from Galli/Giunti, with Herrmann/Neerpasch 3rd and Elford 4th, now only two and a half minutes behind the leader and with three laps to go. When Bianchi took over from Casoni, the Alfa Romeo's oil pressure was sinking fast, and Giunti soon got back into the lead again. But Elford was catching up at such a rate that victory was in sight, no matter how hard the Italian tried. Elford reeled off two remarkably consistent laps, within two seconds of each other on the tortuous mountain circuit.

And before the end of lap nine, incredibly, he was in the lead. Herrmann could not keep up with the two Alfa Romeos, and the Siffert/Stommelen car was going well but was much too far back to offer a challenge. Alfa Romeo were content to be holding 2nd and 3rd, even though Bianchi was having an anxious time with the failing oil pressure. It was now all over: Elford completed his last lap without trouble and seemed almost incredulous at winning, having driven seven laps, while Maglioli had kept up the pressure on his three laps. The 910 of Steinemann Lins had started its last lap secure in 3rd place ahead of the ailing Alfa Romeo, only to have a driveshaft break. The lack of a self-locking differential was giving the driveshaft a hard time on the hairpins, provoking furious wheelspin on the inside wheel. Herrmann stopped at the pits before beginning his last lap as he was sure the steering mechanism was falling off, but nothing could be found amiss, so he carried on. During the last lap, Siffert had an electrical fault behind his instrument panel, and after stopping to tear off some hot wires, he finished the tenth lap very late in 18th place. The 906 of Karl von Wendt and Willi Kauhsen came 7th overall, with Lins/Steinmann's 910 in 9th behind Claude Haldi's 911.

Victors Elford and Maglioli covered ten laps of the Piccolo Madonie circuit, 720 kilometres, in 6hrs 28.47min, averaging 111.112km/h. In the Porsche advertising poster celebrating the win, only an exhausted yet smiling Elford was shown, glowing with sweat – and, doubtless, with fag on, rather than the cars, as was usual in their ads.

The 2.2-litre 907 #032 of Willi Kauhsen/Rudi Lins is prepped for the 1969 BOAC 500 in the Brands Hatch paddock. They started 18th but retired due to an accident on lap 44.

ON A ROLL

Next up, another victory as Vic Elford, partnered with Jo Siffert, won the Nürburgring 1,000km with the new 3.0-litre 908, then Siffert won the Zeltweg 500kms with Herrmann 2nd, both in 908s. Gerhard Mitter won the European Mountain Hillclimb title for the third consecutive year, driving the 2.0-litre 910 Bergspyder – a lightweight, topless 910 – and winning seven out of eight rounds. Rolf Stommelen was runner-up in a similar car with several 2nd and 3rd places. Herrmann and Stommelen won the Montlhéry 1,000kms from Elford and Lins, both pairings driving 908s, while an interesting partnership of Jo Bonnier and Masten Gregory came 5th in a 910. Elsewhere on the Group 4/ Group 6 calendar, Siffert won at Enna-Pergusa (Sicily) in a 910, and Herrmann won at Hockenheim in a 3.0-litre 908.

This set the stage for a showdown at La Sarthe as, due to political turmoil in France that year (the storming of the Sorbonne, etc.), the 1968 Le Mans 24-Hours was postponed from its traditional mid-June date to the end of September. This year, Le Mans was run to the new 3.0-litre formula for Group 6 cars and 5.0-litres for Group 4, and the new chicane before the pits was in use, so that cars had to brake heavily after the White House Esses and negotiate the two 45mph corners before accelerating up the gradient past the pits. In view of the long hours of darkness, the race ran from 3.00pm on the Saturday to 3.00pm on the Sunday, and apart from four hours of rain in the night, conditions were fine. The race was a straight fight between the JW Automotive Gulf GT40s running in 4.9-litre format as Group 4 cars, and the works Porsche team of 3.0-litre 908 prototypes, with the unknown quantities of Alpine-Renault V8s and a lone Matra-Simca

The 907 #028 of Gerhard Koch and Hans-Dieter Dechent came 10th in the 1969 BOAC 500, 26 laps behind the winning GT40, having started from 25th on the grid.

630 V12 running the Grand Prix engine, plus the Autodelta Alfa Romeo T33s. The Porsche team consisted of Siffert/Herrmann, Stommelen/Neerpasch, Patrick/Buzzetta, and Mitter/Elford, all in 908s. In 907s were entered Soler-Roig/Lins, Steinemann/Spöerry, Linge/Buchet, and Hanrioud/Wicky in a 910. The Gulf-Fords were driven by Rodriguez/Bianchi, Hawkins/Hobbs and Oliver/Muir. A greater part of the 1968 season had shown up Porsche's lack of reliability, with the new 908 being relatively unreliable, and Le Mans simply confirmed the fact. Anyway, as anticipated, the four 908s led the opening phase of the race and then, one by one, they fell by the wayside, so that after about four hours, the Pedro Rodriguez/Lucien Bianchi GT40 took the lead and was not seriously challenged for the rest of the 24 hours. However, the Fords were also in trouble, and with second place almost a certainty, the Matra was put up by a punctured tyre that disintegrated and damaged the bodywork and electrical system. This allowed Steinemann and Spöerry, the two Swiss drivers, into second place in the factory-loaned 2.2-litre 907 – with cracked brake disc – and only one 3.0-litre 908 lasted the distance, arriving in third place, the others going out with clutch trouble in the case of Siffert/Herrmann and alternator trouble for Mitter/Elford and Patrick/Buzzetta. So, the JW Automotive GT40 won the race and the Manufacturers' championship for Ford.

That was not close of play for the 907; during the following seasons, several 907s were entered by privateers, scoring occasional top-10 finishes with a podium at Monza in 1969 and a 7th for Wicky Racing's Brun/Mattli at the 1971 Le Mans 24-Hours and then 18th (and last) in 1972 being some of the more remarkable results. By this time, the all-conquering 917 was obsolete in the WSC, but the 907 and 908 – and 910 – were still competitive.

THE 909 BERGSPYDER

There was surely no competition for Porsche less uncompromising in appearance and specification than the Type 909 Bergspyder, created for the task of conquering the mountain climb routes of the 1968 European Hillclimb Championship. The 909's two-seat open fibreglass body was bolted to an aluminium tube space frame, while two front-hinged doors gave access to the cockpit. The front and rear structures were detachable and two movable flaps or spoilers connected to

Rudi Lins prepares to do a demo run in the 1969 Type 909 Bergspyder. The 2.0-litre flat-8 engine is comfortably surrounded by the tube-frame chassis.

The 909 Bergspyder ran in only two hillclimbs in 1968: Gaisberg and Mont Ventoux. Here is Gerhard Mitter on the run up Gaisberg; although he set the fastest time in the 910 Bergspyder, his run in the 909 was unclassified.

Driving 909 Bergspyder #002, Rolf Stommelen was 3rd quickest up the 1968 Gaisberg Hillclimb. Starting them young is Porsche designer and sometime race chief Wilhelm Hild.

the rear suspension were fitted to the rear of the car in an effort to maintain equal rear-wheel grip. The 909 was the successor to the 910 Bergspyder, whose drastic weight saving had ironically made it increasingly more of a handful for its drivers. To achieve a better weight distribution without forsaking the lightness achieved by the 910 Bergspyder the gearbox was moved ahead of the rear wheel axis, which moved the engine forward correspondingly, so the driver now sat almost on top of the front axle with his feet ahead of the front wheel axis, which itself had been moved back about 38mm (1.5 inches). The weight of the 909 was 430 kilogrammes, or 948lb.

The suspension was by transverse wishbones and radius arms, front and rear, with progressive rate coil-springs and double-acting telescopic dampers. The front springs were made of titanium, and both rear anti-roll bars were infinitely adjustable. The rack and pinion steering had a ratio of 12.2 to one. Beryllium brake discs were fitted all round, and to compensate for the reduced rear weight bias, 12-inch wide, 13-inch diameter cast light-alloy rear rims were fitted, with 8-inch rims at the front. The tyres were 4.75/10.00 x13 and. 6.0/12.00 x13 front and rear respectively. Even though, apart from testing, the 909 was only entered on a couple of hill climbs – it did Mont Ventoux and Gaisberg – and though it did not win, it was nevertheless significant as the ancestor of the very successful 3.0-litre 908/3, which appeared two years later. In its two events, the 909 was powered by the Type 771 2.0-litre 8-cylinder engine, which, in its latest form, produced 275bhp at 9,000rpm. The extra power was obtained by a slightly raised compression ratio and a higher rev limit permissible for the full-on short duration of a hill climb. As it turned out, the novel fuel feed system proved unsatisfactory, and did not allow the engine to fully develop its power. The regular five-speed gearbox was modified to adapt it to its new position ahead of the differential, but otherwise the Type 909 transmission was similar to the Type 906. All gears had Porsche split-ring synchromesh, while the shift lever actuated rod linkages. The final drive was by spiral bevel ring and pinion via a multi-plate limited slip differential and universally jointed and splined half shafts. The single disc dry plate clutch had a diaphragm spring, with increased clutch pressure, in keeping with the engine's high power output.

CHAPTER 5

THE PORSCHE 908 1968–71

The winning 908 KH #008 of the 1968 Nürburgring 1,000kms, shared by Vic Elford and Jo Siffert, averaged 99.3mph (152.9kph) over 6hr 34m on the Nordschleife.

There are several humps on the Nürburgring Nordschleife where cars get airborne momentarily, including the Flugplatz and Pflanzgarten; here, Jo Siffert gives a perfect example of getting air under the 908 he shared with Vic Elford to win the 1968 1,000Kms.

Vic Elford and Jochen Neerpasch shared 908 #010 KH in the 1968 Spa-Francorchamps 1,000Kms, starting from 4th on the grid, but retired due to an accident on lap 36.

The 908 was introduced at the Monza 1,000Km in April 1968, having run earlier at the Le Mans practice weekend. Whilst not exactly replacing the 907, with which it overlapped during the 1968 season, it was yet another demonstration of the relentless dedication within Porsche to gain the upper hand on the racetrack. It was sufficiently different mechanically from the 907 to justify apportioning different chapters to the two cars, plus the 908 had a much longer racing shelf life in its 908/2 and 908/3 Spyder configurations, as well as in private hands.

NEW RULES ON CAPACITY LIMITS

When the FIA set the engine capacity limit for prototypes at 3.0-litres and sports cars at 5.0-litres in October 1967, Porsche was well prepared, having picked up earlier on not-so-well-concealed rumours to that effect. As early as July 1967, designs were started on a completely new 3.0-litre 8-cylinder engine, to be dropped into a chassis derived from the 907, to become the 908 coupé. The first trials with the new 3.0-litre engine took place at the Le Mans test weekend in 1968, when two such engines were installed in two 907 long-tails. The first short-tail 908 to be built, 908/001, was also virtually identical to a 907, including its 13-inch diameter wheels. The first appearance of the new model in 908 KH short-tail format, with 15-inch wheels and more appropriate larger cast iron brake discs with aluminium callipers was at the Nürburgring 1,000Km race.

Later in the season, at Watkins Glen, one of the cars was built up in an aluminium tube frame chassis that weighed 20 kilogrammes, 44lb less than its steel-tube frame siblings. The lighter alloy frame was adopted for all cars built from chassis #908/012 onwards.

Before the 1969 Le Mans race, both the short- and long-tail coupés were again assessed in the wind tunnel, and consequently the long-tail cars, which had the same frontal area as the short-tail version, were fitted with a rear body section culminating in a pair of tail fins that were connected by a wing incorporating a moveable flap on either side. These flaps were connected to the rear suspension in the same way as they were fitted on the 909 Bergspyder Hillclimb cars. Racing experience and exhaustive test runs in 1968 also led to the use of reinforced front uprights, more durable wheel bearings, stronger half-shafts with larger flange bolts, and a completely new Type 916 five-speed transmission. As run at Le Mans, the long-tail cars weighed just over 700 kilogrammes or 1,543lb and reached 320km/h or 200mph

Vic Elford hugs the apex on one of the tighter corners on the Nuremburg Tribune-based street circuit in 908/2 #015, entered by Tony Dean, during the 1969 Norisring 200-mile race. Vic placed 2nd overall, having come 3rd in Heat 1 and 2nd in Heat 2.

down the Mulsanne Straight. Because the new international rules included neither a spare wheel nor a minimum weight where prototypes were concerned, no short-tail coupés were entered, with Spyder versions being run instead alongside the long-tails.

The first Spyder-bodied 908 – the 908/2 – was tested in the wind tunnel at the end of 1968. It had the advantage of being about 100 kilogrammes or 220lb lighter than the long-tail coupé, but being an open-top car, it had a higher drag coefficient. Its aluminium tube space frame was very similar to that of the coupé, but in the first version, two of the diagonal tubes that formed a pyramid brace within the chassis were eliminated from the rear part of the substructure. Exhaustive tests resulted in all Spyders being equipped with titanium front stub axles and titanium hubs all round. Another novelty was an air valve fitted to one of the aluminium spaceframe tubes, which made it possible to pressurise the frame and check it for cracks or failures by measuring the pressure drop after a given time. This practice was continued for all subsequent tubular chassis designs, including the 917.

FLAT FISH

For the 1969 Nürburgring 1,000 Kms, the new Spyder appeared, the 908/02, nicknamed the Flounder (*Flunder*) because of its flatfish-like shape, though it had a higher front end and higher waistline than its coupé predecessors. A long-tail version of this Spyder ran at Le Mans – 908/2

Pit stop for the Gerhard Mitter/Udo Schutz 908/2 #015 during the 1969 Nürburgring 1,000Kms. They started 3rd from on the grid, but finished 31st, ten laps in arrears. To the left of the car, Mitter is quenching his thirst, as Porsche R&D chief Helmuth Bott and Race Director Peter Falk oversee proceedings.

#028, entered by Hart Ski Racing and driven by Jo Siffert and Brian Redman, and it was nearly as fast in a straight line as the three long-tail coupés. To reduce its sensitivity to crosswinds, the long-tail Spyder sported twin tail fins rather than the transverse wing arrangement. From the start, Siffert was able to match the pace of the 917s and was in the lead come the first refuelling stops, only to be sidelined after six hours when an oil pipe to the gearbox broke. Meanwhile, the 917 had reached a point where Porsche could go racing with it, and so by the end of 1969, it became clear that the career of the 908 as a works car had reached its end, and they were sold off accordingly to private teams.

However, because the bigger and much more powerful 917 might not be the ideal answer to such winding venues as the Targa Florio and the Nürburgring Nordschleife, a new version of the 908 Spyder was developed with just those two tracks in mind, which was the 908/03. It was, in fact, a completely new car, somewhat reminiscent of the curtailed Type 909 Bergspyder, and only the 3.0-litre engine was carried over from the previous 908 series. The first wind tunnel tests began in the autumn of 1968, but the project was subsequently shelved in favour of the 917 and 908/02 developments. As the 908/03 was to run only on serpentine circuits, rather than the flat-out blinders, it could be very specialised, and every effort was made to keep it as small and as light as possible. Its polyurethane-foam-reinforced fibreglass body, for example, weighed only 12kg or 26.5lb. Extensive use of titanium and other lightweight materials kept its total weight down to 545kg or 1,201lb, with the full complement of oil.

Setting off on its way to winning the 1969 Targa Florio and leading a Porsche 1–2–3 is 908/2 #014 driven by Gerhard Mitter and Udo Schutz, covering 720km in 6hr 45m.03, averaging 117.46km/h.

Pedro Rodriguez and Leo Kinnunen shared the JW Automotive 908/3 #011 in the 1970 Nürburgring 1,000Kms, but failed to finish because of an off-course excursion.

The 908/2 Flounder of Robert Fink/Marco Werner is pursued by a 906 at the 2012 Le Mans Classic, eventually coming 18th in Plateau 5.

The 908/03 had 13-inch diameter wheels with 9.5-inch and 14.5-inch-wide rims front and rear, respectively. For 1971, 15-inch rear wheels were used, which required different uprights, and the rim widths were increased to 11 and 17 inches. After running the 908/03 in two races – which they won in 1970 – the cars were shelved for almost a year. Then they were ready for action again, virtually unaltered except for 17-inch rear tyres, bigger wheels and the addition of vertical tail fins. This, and some additional safety equipment, raised their weight to 565kg, or 1,246lb. At the end of the season, some of the works 908/3s were offered to select customers, and as late as 1975, three of them appeared in events counting towards the World Championship for Makes now with the turbocharged engine, like the unit that had powered the factory's 911 Carrera prototype in 1974, a 2.1-litre flat-6 developing at least 450bhp. The engines had been adapted to the old cars by the service department of the Stuttgart factory. The cars were almost unrecognisable, having been extensively re-bodied with front and rear sections from the normally aspirated 917 PA Can-Am Spyder, providing sorely needed downforce. A large air intake box, similar to those used in Formula 1 at the time, and indeed the 936, provided the intercooler with the necessary cooling air. These air scoops were later modified several times on all three cars built. The aluminium tube frame had to be locally reinforced in view of the increased performance and slightly extended rearward to carry the tail section and its large wing.

FLAT-8 DEVELOPMENT

In July 1967, the engine technicians began designing the Type 908 3.0-litre 8-cylinder engine. Just four months later, the first engine was assembled. The first time it went on the dyno it produced 320bhp, and after four months of development, it had become sufficiently reliable to try its luck in long-distance racing. At Monza, the engine's first race, the power was up to 335bhp, and in the final version, the best examples developed nearly 370bhp, still with two-valves-per-cylinder and four chain-driven camshafts. Other solutions were tried experimentally but never raced. The valves were all sodium-filled for improved cooling, and the compression ratio was 10.4 to 1. The peculiarity of the dry sump lubrication system was that the lubricant was fed axially to the front end of the drilled crankshaft to lubricate the big ends, while the main bearings were fed from the main oil gallery. The conrods and rod bolts were of titanium. Pressure of time dictated the use of the same bore and stroke dimensions as in the six-cylinder type 901 engine: 84mm x 66mm.

However, before the Le Mans race, the bore was increased by 1mm to bring the capacity closer to the 3.0-litre limit. The cylinder barrels and heads were made of aluminium, the crankcase and all covers of magnesium alloy, and the complete power unit weighed 178 kilogrammes or 392lb. The firing order originally chosen produced severe vibrations, so it was altered after the first race at Monza. Experimentally, a

Mid-race pitstop for the 908 LH #013 of Stommelen/Neerpasch, which finished the race 3rd overall. Behind the car, Rolf Stommelen reports back to Ferdinand Piëch.

crankshaft was machined with hollow crank pins, and appropriate balance weights were added. In the course of further development, the following modifications were made: a new, more heat-resistant magnesium alloy was used for the crankcase, the injection pump was altered to include a space cam, twin V-belts were used for the cooling blower drive, the alternator mounting was modified to reduce vibration, and a different starter motor and alternator were used. A new flat-plane crankshaft was finally employed to balance out the second-order forces, which still caused severe vibration. In this it was successful, though it significantly complicated the exhaust system. The engines with the flat-plane crankshaft could easily be recognised by the fuel injection lines that were crossed over the pump instead of being neatly divided left and right.

The 908/03's 3.0-litre engine remained practically unchanged. The only modification was the addition of a fluid coupling incorporated in the hub driving the cooling blower aimed at preventing V-belt breakages caused by sudden engine speed variations. A further development never left the experimental department, which was a four-valves-per-cylinder engine that had water-cooled heads in order to cool the valves adequately. Air cooling was inadequate for four-valve heads. The engine was fully developed

Hans Mezger designed the Porsche air-cooled flat-6 engine, and in 1965, he became head of race car design and was responsible for the overall construction of the 917 LH and its 12-cylinder engine. In the background, from left, are Gerhard Mitter, Udo Schutz and Peter Falk.

on the dynamometer, but it was judged that performance gains could not offset the additional weight penalty of a water radiator. In 1975, some private teams fitted their old 908/3s with a turbocharged 2142cc 911 flat-6 engine as used by the factory in the 1974 World Championship for Makes series.

The transmissions used in the 907 and earlier models were not strong enough to transmit the torque of the 3.0-litre engine. As a stopgap, the six-speed gearbox designed for the 909 Bergspyder was fitted, in combination with a small diameter triple plate clutch located at the far end of the box, driven by a solid shaft. The low inertia of the clutch enabled very quick gear changes. From the clutch, the drive to the gearbox was taken forward through a pair of quickly interchangeable gears, facilitating the alteration of the overall ratios. The twin universal half-shafts were each divided by a cushioning Guibo doughnut. However, this transmission weighed 25 kilogrammes or 55lb, which was considered excessive. Consequently, a new five-speed gearbox, the Type 916, was developed, in which the gears ran in a deep wet sump, which proved simpler and more reliable rather than being jet-lubricated by means of a small gear pump and separate pipes directing oil spray directly onto the gears.

SPA-FRANCORCHAMPS 1,000KMS

By the Spa 1,000kms, held on 26 May 1968, the 908 was obviously here to stay. Whilst Alfa Romeo did not show up, there were two Gulf GT40s pitted against the works Porsches, four cars and six drivers, who complained of the long-tailed 3.0-litre 908 coupés wandering badly under braking, although they were much quicker between the corners. Elford and Neerpasch and Herrmann and Stommelen were paired in the remaining two short-tailed 908s, with Mitter and Schlesser taking the 2.2-litre 907. They were also facing the latest Alpine-Renault and a single Alan Mann Racing Ford F3L Cosworth. There were plenty of privateer 910s, such as those of Koch/Linz and Spöerry/Steinemann, with a number of 906s in the under 2.0-litre

The 908 KH Coupé of Hans Richrath and Ingo Putz in the pit lane during 2012's Le Mans Classic, placing 19th in Plateau 5.

A moment of relaxation in the Nürburgring pits ahead of the 1968 1,000Kms race, as team personnel chat and eventual winner Jo Siffert sits in his 908's bucket seat reading a newspaper.

Group 4 category. During practice, the Porsche drivers found the long-tailed 908 much in need of development, despite its promising straight-line speed. The early leader was Jacky Ickx in the GT40, with Mitter 2nd in the 2.2-litre 907, Herrmann third in the 908, and Karl von Wendt in his Group 4 Carrera 6 leading the 2.0-litre section by a long way. Ickx had lapped the entire field by 12 laps, except for Mitter and Herrmann, and Elford was tearing back up the field after an early delay, moving from 20th to 12th and then 6th on lap 13. After one and a half hours of racing, von Wendt made his first scheduled pit stop, handing over his 906 to Willy Kauhsen. Pouring rain and spray made overtaking difficult and dangerous – though these were just the conditions in which Ickx excelled. Elford had got by Hawkins into 4th place, and handed over to Neerpasch. Stommelen took over Herrmann's car, and the last of the major contenders to stop, Mitter, brought in the 2nd place 907 for Schlesser to take over. So, the final results were Ickx and Redman 1st, Mitter and Schlesser in the 8-cylinder 907 2nd, Herrmann and Stommelen in the 3.0-litre 908 were 3rd, Koch and Lins 5th, Spöerry and Steinemann 6th, Bill Bradley and Chris Lambert 7th in the former's 910. In sodden conditions, requiring narrower tyres to be fitted, the 2.2-litre 6-cylinder 907s had shown they still had the pace to beat the 8-cylinder 908s.

TYPE 908 MAJOR SUCCESSES

1968
1st, Nürburgring 1,000Kms
2nd, 3rd, BOAC 500
3rd, Le Mans 24-Hours
1969
2nd, 3rd, 4th, Sebring 12-Hours
1st, 2nd, 3rd, BOAC 500
2nd, Le Mans 24-Hours
1st, Targa Florio
1st, Monza 1,000Kms
1st, Spa-Francorchamps 1,000Kms
1st, 2nd, 3rd, 4th, 5th, Nürburgring 1,000Kms
1st, International Championship for Makes
1970
2nd, Sebring 12-Hours
1st, Nürburgring 1,000Kms
1st, Targa Florio
3rd, Le Mans 24-Hours
1971
1st, 2nd, 3rd, Nürburgring 1,000Kms
1st, European Hillclimb Championship, GT class
1972
3rd, Le Mans 24-Hours
1973
1st, European Hillclimb Championship, Sports class
1980
1st, Nürburgring 1,000Kms

Almost a sideshow on the international stage, the RAC Tourist Trophy was nonetheless significant, historically, on the British racing calendar, with precedents on the Isle of Man, Ards, Donington Park, Dundrod, Goodwood and, subsequently, Silverstone. Between 1965 and 1969 it was held at Oulton Park, and for the 1968 event, after much rapid switching of engines ahead of the event to comply with Group 6 as opposed to Group 4 regulations, it was won by Denny Hulme in Sid Taylor's Lola T70 with David Piper's Ferrari 330 P3/4 in 2nd and Paul Hawkins' GT40 3rd, with Tony Dean's Ferrari Dino in 4th. They were chased home by a trio of 906s driven by Bill Bradley, Jeff Edmonds and Jeremy Delmar-Morgan.

Paul Hawkins, Jo Siffert, Hans Herrmann and Kurt Ahrens share a joke after the Austrian Grand Prix held at Zeltweg on 25 August 1968. Siffert came 1st in a 908 KH, Herrmann/Ahrens 2nd in a 908 KH, and Hawkins 3rd in his GT40.

The Watkins Glen Six Hours was the eighth round of the ten-race series for the International Championship for Makes, run as a six-hour endurance event on the 2.3-mile Watkins Glen circuit in upper New York State. The organisers were possibly fortunate that Le Mans was postponed till September due to that year's ongoing political crises – the harshly crushed Sorbonne student sit-in during May and further reverberations. Had it not been for this, it is doubtful that this third American race in the 1968 series would have attracted the entry that it did. With four victories and two 2nd places to their credit, Porsche went into the race with 42 points from their best five finishes, and a win at Watkins Glen would have wrapped up the title for them. Ford, on the other hand, had three victories and one 3rd place, adding up to 31 points, and they had to win to keep their championship hopes alive. Porsche's works' entries consisted of four short-tailed 3.0-litre 908s for Siffert/Elford, Herrmann/Attwood, Patrick/Ikuzawa. Buzzetta had driven for the team on several occasions, while Patrick probably had more experience with Porsches of this calibre than any other American driver.

MOVEABLE FLAPS

The only changes to the Porsches since they ran in the Spa 1,000Kms was an air scoop mounted on top of the left front wing to cool the oil tank behind the left front wheel, and two stabiliser flaps at the rear. These flaps were 1ft wide and 7in high, pivoting on rods attached to the body, above and slightly behind the rear suspension. They were connected to the lower suspension arms by means of a short horizontal arm and a long vertical rod. The flaps were raised at a 35-degree angle and setting. On the straights, they acted simply as spoilers. However, the linkage was arranged in such a way that when the car cornered, the angle of the flap on the outside loaded rear wheel was reduced, thus reducing the aerodynamic pressure on that side of the car. Conversely, the angle of the flap above the inside rear wheel, which, of course, tends to rise in a corner, is raised, and the air pressure on that flap is increased. The combined effect of the two flaps is to flatten or stabilise the car. This was a development experimented on in conjunction with Nissan. Similar flaps were tried on Porsche's hill-climbing 910 Bergspyders in 1968, but not on the endurance racing cars. They were of little or no benefit on slow corners, but Vic Elford said they probably helped on fast, sweeping bends. It was not a good race for Porsche, with two GT40s occupying the first two places and the Howmet Turbine 3rd, followed by two privately entered 906s, and in 6th place the 908 of Herrmann, Attwood and Japanese F3 star Tetsu Ikuzawa.

In 1968, there were noticeably more sportscar races on the international calendar, one such being the Solituderennen, held at Hockenheim on 21 July due to the non-closure of Solitude's country roads that made up that circuit. When Jo Bonnier's Lola T70 dropped out, Piper's Ferrari and Herrmann's 3.0-litre 908 battled for the win, the Englishman taking the win by half a second. In 910s, Vic Elford battled with Alex Soler Roig and Gerhard Koch for 5th, with Erich Bitter class winner and 8th in his 906.

As we have seen, in the previous two years, Porsche had progressed rapidly from the 2.0-litre flat-6 powered 906 and 910 through the 2.2-litre flat-8 907 to the 908, developed under hands-on Technical Director Dr Ferdinand Piëch, a grandson of founder Professor Ferdinand Porsche, and later CEO of the Volkswagen Group. The Porsche 907's 2.2-litre flat-8 generated around 270bhp, whilst the 908 model's 3.0-litre flat-8 produced 350bhp at 8,400rpm. The beautiful 908 LH 'Langheck' version was also developed for the exceptionally high speeds that

Jo Siffert in the 908 KH on his way to winning the 1968 Zeltweg 1,000Kms held on the Austrian airfield circuit, pre-Österreichring.

The 1968 Nürburgring 1,000Kms was a triumph for Porsche, placing 1st and 2nd; further down the order, the Team Caltex 906 of Jöst/Bitter came 11th, and the 910 seen here of Koch/Lins finished 20th. The 906 and 910 are split by the GT40 of Hobbs/Redman that came 6th.

The 908 LH of Jo Siffert and Hans Herrmann is wheeled out onto the grid for the 1968 Le Mans 24 Hours race, with Peter Falk helping push on the passenger door and Hans Mezger at the rear. Siffert led the first three hours, clocking 205mph (330 km/h) on the Mulsanne Straight, but retiring after four hours with transmission failure.

were achievable on the long straights of Le Mans, Spa, Monza and Daytona.

For 1969, Porsche developed an ultra-lightweight open-cockpit Spyder version – the Porsche 908/2 with a curvy 'Coke bottle' shape nicknamed the '*Flunder*' or Flounder, and, the following year, a more austere aerodynamic wedge-shape designated the 908/3.

SIX OUT OF TEN

The 1969 FIA World Championship of Makes saw Porsche 908s win six of the ten qualifying rounds, and the new 4.5-litre flat-12 Porsche 917 won a seventh race, making Porsche the World Champion marque. That year, the duo of Jo Siffert and Brian Redman dominated the Watkins Glen 6-Hour race, and the next day, Siffert drove the same car, 908/2 #016, in the Watkins Glen Can-Am Championship race.

Remarkably, the 3.0-litre Porsche punched way above its weight, finishing 6th out of 25, among 7.0-litre McLarens, Lolas and Ferrari. This car was sold eventually to French privateer Christian Poirot who raced at Le Mans into the 1970s – placing 19 overall, partnered by Jean Rondeau in 1974.

For the 1969 season, Porsche's competition programme concentrated on two major activities: long-distance sports-prototype racing and rallying. For the first time since 1963,

The 3.0-litre 908/3 prototype, pictured here at the factory, was created expressly to win on twisty circuits, specifically the Targa Florio and the Nürburgring. This JW Automotive car, #010, driven by Jo Siffert and Brian Redman, started the Nürburgring 1,000Kms from pole position but retired with low oil pressure.

Swiss driver Jo Siffert in the 3.0-litre flat-8 908/2 #011 he shared with Brian Redman to win the 1969 BOAC 500 at Brands Hatch. The pair started from pole, averaged 100.21mph (161.28km/h) over the six-hour's duration, covering 681.5 miles (968.1km), and had a two-lap winning margin.

Richard Attwood rounds Druids Hairpin at Brands Hatch in the 908/2 #010, co-driven by Vic Elford to 2nd place in the 1969 BOAC 500, followed by the 5.0-litre Lola T70-Chevrolet of Denny Hulme/ Peter Revson/Sten Axelsson and Paul Hawkins/Jonathan Williams' Lola T70-Chevrolet.

One of the most iconic yet trickier corners on the Nordschleife is the banked Karussell, being negotiated here by Richard Attwood in the Porsche Konstruktionen Salzburg 908/2 #001 he shared with Rudi Lins, placing 4th overall.

Porsche factory cars would not be taking part in the European Mountain Hillclimb series. For the long-distance races, the 3.0-litre 8-cylinder 908 models would be further developed, and at Sebring in March 1969, the new open-top Spyder version complying with the 1969 Group 6 rules was entered. Herrmann, Mitter, Elford, Siffert, and Stommelen would all be staying with the team, and they would be joined by Ahrens, Attwood, Redman and Schutz, while during the season, Kauhsen and Von Wendt, and the Austrian Lins would be offered occasional drives. It was looking as though new team manager and erstwhile driver Rico Steinemann would be playing the game of musical drivers, as von Hanstein used to do, trying to pair off ability, temperament, knowledge and speed into the most suitable car for any given circuit. For the American events at Daytona, Sebring and Watkins Glen, various American drivers such as Buzzetta and Patrick would join the team. In 1968, everyone thought that the Porsche team would sweep all before it, but they spent much of the season dealing with one technical fault after another, which was attributed in part to a reorganisation within the racing department and the arrival of new young engineers under Peter Falk and Ferdinand Piëch. Commentators felt that the knowledge gained over sixteen years of successful racing and impeccable reliability during the reign of von Hanstein was not to be lightly abandoned.

BOAC 500 MILES

If there was one race that confirmed the 908's superiority, it was the BOAC 500 at Brands Hatch in April 1969. Still sponsored by the UK's premier airline, it was the European opener of the 1969 World Sports Car Championship, held in cold, windy overcast conditions, but the six-hour event proved entertaining enough to live up to its growing reputation as a championship qualifying round. It could be argued

PORSCHE REVS UP

Amongst the cars on display in the Revs Institute at Naples, Florida, is a 1969 Porsche 908 LH with an interesting history – which, of course, they all have – and, in a way, it is representative of the strategy that Porsche adopted for 1968. Despite using engines no larger than 2.2-litres, they missed out on the World Championship of Makes by just a single point in 1967. So, the factory decided to even up the odds. The FIA's new 3.0-litre prototype – Group 6 – and 5.0-litre sports-racing – Group 4 – regulations adopted for 1968 presented the opportunity. The 2.2-litre 907 began the 1968 season spectacularly, with wins at Daytona, Sebring and the Targa Florio. The 908 brought into play shortly afterwards was beset by frustrating mechanical failures, and lost the 1968 championship to JW Automotive's Ford GT40s. Meanwhile, the 4.5-litre 917, built hard on the heels of the 908, was ready for homologation in 1969 but, typically, was too untried to spearhead Porsche's assault on the World Championship. That chore fell to the troubled 908, which, by now, had undergone such major changes as an aluminium spaceframe, a newly designed crankshaft, 15-inch wheels and a new five-speed transaxle. In 1969, this car won on the ultra-fast Spa-Francorchamps long circuit in the hands of Jo Siffert and Brian Redman. But, despite its superbly efficient appearance, the long-tailed 908 LH was not an easy car to drive quickly. Beautiful but imperfect aerodynamics caused the race cars to weave from side to side as speeds approached 200mph, a tendency as daunting to the drivers as to any competitor who might be in a position to overtake. Alarmed or not, Brian Redman set the fastest lap at 145.28mph – a new course record – on his way to victory. The most successful long-tailed 908 campaigned by Porsche, this one also came second to a sister 908 LH at Monza's 1,000Kms, and retired with a broken countershaft gear at the Daytona 24-Hours. That its Spa victory and a 2nd place were sufficient for it to earn top honours is explained by simple mathematics: to win the world championship in 1969, Porsche built a total of 52 brand-new racing cars. By contrast, John Wyer's JW Automotive won the title the year before, using just three Gulf-sponsored GT40s. But numbers were irrelevant to Ferdinand Piëch. Just consider how many new racing Porsches appeared during his era. Granted, each was a logical extension of the other, but the proliferation simply overwhelmed the opposition and was unmatched by any race car builder anywhere.

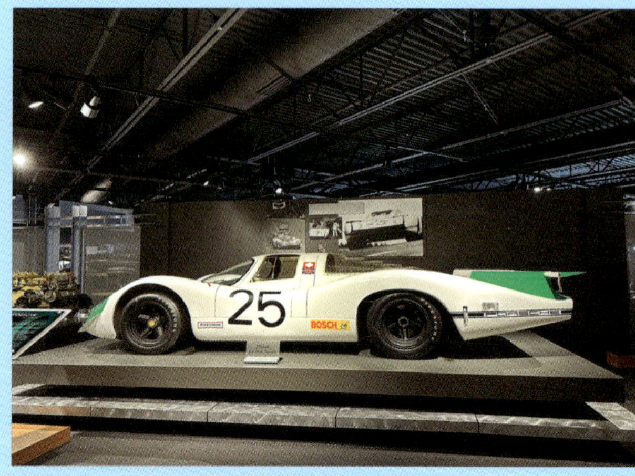

The 3.0-litre flat-8 powered 908 LH on display at the REVS Institute, Naples, Florida is #025, raced in period by Hans Herrmann, Jo Siffert and Brian Redman, with the latter pair wining the 1969 Spa-Francorchamps 1,000Kms.

that six hours is too long to let the teams fight it out at full stretch. On the other hand, it is too short for the repair of any serious damage that might arise during the course of the event. Nevertheless, six hours of racing was thoroughly entertaining for those of us present as spectators. Without a win since the Austrian Grand Prix in August 1968, the Porsche team came in force with four of its open-bodied 908 Spyders for Siffert/Redman, Elford/Atwood, Mitter/Schutz and Herrmann/Stommelen.

Opposing them in the Group 6 prototype class was one lone 3.0-litre works Ferrari 312 P for Amon and Rodriguez. The other car with any hope of winning was the new and unraced 3.0-litre Mirage-BRM, entered by JW Automotive for Ickx and Oliver. The Group 4 challenge for outright victory came in the form of eight Lola T70-Chevrolets. The dark horses were the two Alan Mann-entered Ford prototypes; however, the P-69 was now an 'illegal' open-bodied car with a hole in the roof for the driver's head.

Porsche mechanics carefully unload the Herrmann/ Stommelen 908/2 #007 in the Brands Hatch paddock before the 1969 BOAC 500.

Photographer Roger Dixon was on hand to capture the image of Porsche mechanics manoeuvring the Herrmann/ Stommelen 908/2 Flounder in the Brands Hatch paddock before the 1969 BOAC 500 race.

Jo Siffert plunges the 908/2 KH #011 into the steep, off-camber Paddock Bend during the BOAC 500 at Brands Hatch, 1969, which he and co-driver Brian Redman won.

Practice was a straight fight between the Siffert/Redman Porsche and the lone Ferrari. It also saw the tyre war heat up when Siffert elected to run on Firestone tyres for the race instead of the more customary Dunlops. Team manager Rico Steinemann had no objections as they had brought Siffert the fastest lap at 1m 28.8s. This made everybody sit up and take notice, because it was faster than his F1 lap record of 1m 29.7s set at the previous year's British Grand Prix.

On race day, the circuit was dry, so everybody kept to their usual dry tyres. Drama struck the Siffert/Redman car with only twenty minutes to go before the start when the transistor ignition system started playing up. By staying on the grid until the last minute, the Porsche mechanics managed to get one ignition circuit working, but not two, so Siffert started the race 600rpm down and with 20bhp less. But this handicap did not affect proceedings, because by the end of the first hour, Siffert and Redman had thwarted the Ferrari's early challenge, and they were almost 80 seconds clear of Elford and Attwood, followed by Mitter and Schutz, with the Ferrari next up.

The Herrmann/Stommelen 908 came next, still on 39 laps, as well as the leading Group 4 car, the Hawkins/ Williams Lola-Chevrolet T70. By the second hour, the leading Porsche had extended its lead to a lap, with Elford still 2nd, but now it began to drizzle, making the track slippery, but the Siffert/Redman Porsche continued unabated. At 3.00pm, Attwood came in to start Porsche's second string of lightning stops, while Stommelen spun on the slippery surface at the same time.

Starting from 5th on the grid, Udo Schutz and Gerhard Mitter finished 3rd in the 1969 BOAC 500 at Brands Hatch in 908/2 #008.

At the halfway stage, Porsches lay 1st, 2nd, 3rd and 5th, with the Ferrari wedged in between them. From now on, the race became processional, with the Siffert/Redman car pulling away from Elford/Attwood – Elford spinning his 908 coming out of Clearways, rejoining in a tail-happy fashion just ahead of the approaching Ferrari, which swept into what was at that point, 2nd place. However, it was short-lived, soon letting Quick Vic back into 2nd place. At 4.30pm, and with only one-and-a-half hours to go, Elford brought his 908 into the pits to begin the last series of stops, and by 4.41pm, all four cars had been refilled, and the works Porsches carried on unchallenged and unflustered, ultimately filling the first three places.

TARGA TALES

For the 1969 Targa Florio, held on 4 May, Porsche entered one of the largest factory teams ever seen on the Piccolo Madonie, with six 908/2 Spyders running 3.0-litre flat-8s. As well as all the official factory drivers, with the exception of Siffert, who was in Barcelona driving in the Spanish Grand Prix, they co-opted numerous Porsche drivers from amongst their racing customers. Factory drivers were Mitter, Schutz, Redman, Attwood, Herrmann, Stommelen and last year's winners, Elford and Maglioli. The two German drivers, von Wendt and Kauhsen, were given the fifth 908, and the sixth was driven by Gérard Larrousse and Rudi Lins,

Starting from pole position, Jo Siffert and Brian Redman won the 1969 Nürburgring 1,000Kms in the Porsche Salzburg 908/2 #006.

the Austrian privateer. In addition, the factory was also running a 911 R for Spöerry and Toivonen. The only opposition to Porsche for an outright victory was the lone 2.5-litre Alfa Romeo Tipo 33 from Autodelta, driven by Vaccarella and de Adamich. Backing up the Porsche squad were two private 2.2-litre 907 coupés: the Manfredini/Silva car and the other for Koch/Dechent. In the final outcome, Porsches filled the first four places, with Mitter/Schutz 1st, Elford/Maglioli 2nd, Herrmann/Stommelen 3rd, and von Wendt/Kauhsen 4th. The Manfredini/Silva 907 came seventh, and Larrousse/Lins were twert-first. Elford set the fastest lap, a new record at 35m 0.82s, and the winners' average pace was also a new record, knocking over 21 minutes off the previous year's race time.

The circus moved on to Spa-Francorchamps for the 1,000 kilometres on 11 May, and it was another Porsche win for Siffert/Redman in their 908, with Rodriguez and Piper second in a Ferrari 312P, and Elford and Ahrens 3rd, followed by Stommelen and Herrmann. In 5th were Bonnier and Muller in the Swede's yellow Lola T70, followed by Pilette and Slotemakker in the Alfa Romeo T33, which paints a picture of Porsche's overwhelming domination at this point.

THE BRIAN REDMAN INTERVIEW

Brian Redman makes a point during an interview at the Goodwood Festival of Speed, 2009.

Endurance racing expert Brian Redman recalls his Porsche years as if they were yesterday. He gave me a vivid, sometimes downright alarming description of life behind the wheel of 908s and 917s – a wry smile and twinkling eye never far away.

Fifty years ago, things were rosy for Brian Redman. The 32-year-old Lancastrian had made a name for himself on the club racing scene with Red Rose Racing's lightweight E-type Jaguars and, as a member of the Gulf JW Automotive team in GT40 and Mirage. In 1969, he was on Porsche's talent roster, partnering Jo 'Seppi' Siffert to victory in the BOAC 500 at Brands Hatch, Monza, Spa and Nürburgring 1,000kms, plus the Watkins Glen 6-Hours in the new 908 Spyder and Coupé. That year the pair gave Porsche the World Sportscar Championship victory it had so long craved. Some partnership: the British erstwhile mop salesman and the Swiss knife-sharp garage proprietor were maestros of the flat-8 908 in its Coupé, 'Coke-Bottle' and 'Flounder' Spyder configurations. But the brand-new 917 was something else, an unknown quantity that they were not too keen to try, as Brian explains.

The first time the 917s appeared in a race was Spa Francorchamps '69. They had all the usual long-tail 908s there, plus two 917s, and anybody who wanted to drive the 917 could do so. Jo and I agreed that we had a better chance in the 908 long-tail. He was out in our 908, it was raining, and I was sitting in the pit, and Dr Bott, Head of Engineering, said to me, 'Brian, will you drive the 917?' The last thing I wanted was to drive a 917 in the rain, because about a month before, they had rung me from Stuttgart and asked me to come and test it. I thought to myself, this is very suspicious. They've got six German drivers living close to Stuttgart, and they've got Siffert in Switzerland; why do they want me, living in England? So, I said I had some urgent business, and I would call them back in one hour. 'Please be certain to call, Herr Redman,' they said. So, I called Siffert in Switzerland and said, 'Jo, have you tested the new 917 yet?' There was a long silence, and then he said, 'no, we let the others find out what breaks first'. So, I didn't go. Kurt Ahrens went testing, the car aquaplaned off the track and under the Armco barrier, and broke in half across the cockpit. He went on down the track stuck in the back half, leaving his shoes in the front.

The 917's origins are well known.

Ferdinand Piëch was the driving force behind the whole 917 programme, and in fact the biggest risk he ever took in his professional career was ordering the construction of 25 of them. Porsche had to make that many for homologation so the FIA could come and inspect them. Of course they couldn't sell them, nobody wanted to pay whatever the modest price was, something like 140,000 DM ($30,000 in period). Porsche was incredibly busy at that time. They had seventeen, possibly eighteen, 908s in longtail coupé and short-tail Spyder form, and they had five cars entered in every race, and ten drivers for the five racecars. That's before you get to customer cars. For the first time ever, they were making a real attack on the World Manufacturers' Championship, which at that point they had never won. Of course, in the past they had won individual races by virtue of great reliability and handling, some big races, but not the World Championship. Now, because of the change of rules mandating 3.0-litres for Group 6 Prototypes and 5.0-litres for Group 4 Production cars, they thought that Aston Martin and Lamborghini and Maserati and Jaguar who all had 5.0-litre engines would come into racing. But in order to have a 5.0-litre you had to have 50 cars made like that. Well, nobody took the bait, and so in early '69 or maybe late '68 they changed the rules and made it 25 cars, not 50. I think Porsche knew about this beforehand and were already working on the cars. The 917s were really just big 908s, and *the first one had a 4.5-litre 12-cylinder engine while the 908 was 3.0-litres and 8 cylinders. The pistons and valves were the same in the 917. It wasn't until early 1970 that the 917 went up to 5.0-litres. So, in '69 the car was built, and it was shown to the FIA in April 1969. At the same time Porsche was busy with the 908s and, incidentally, it had also started to design and build a new 908, the 908/3 designed only for the Nürburgring and the Targa Florio.*

I'd driven with Vic Elford at Daytona, and Rico Steinemann asked me whether I wanted to stay with Vic, or go as number two to Jo Siffert, or as number one in my own car. I thought that the best chance of winning races was with Jo, who was tremendous, so I said I would go with him. Number Two means you don't get the limelight to the same extent, and you don't get much practice, just the minimum three laps. And you've no say in the set-up of the car. But it worked out fantastically, and Jo and I won five out of the ten World Championship races that year to clinch the title for Porsche for the first time ever.

Their success provoked some inter-team rivalry.

The German drivers constantly complained that Siffert and I got better cars, but they went quiet at the Nürburgring, because we had two new cars, Flounders, and Jo crashed one of them and Vic crashed the other, and we had to take Porsche Austria's spare car, another 908/2. And we won the race in that, and again at Brands Hatch. The cars had dual ignition, and at the starting line the technicians switched off one set of ignitions, so the car should keep running on the other set. At Brands Hatch, they switched one set off, and the engine stopped. So that meant we had one faulty ignition circuit, so we were about 30 horsepower down. But we still won the race.

I ask Brian to tell me more about his teammates: what sort of men were they?

Well, Jo Siffert was very mercurial. There was always something going on behind the scenes, wheeling and dealing. He drove most of the cars for the film Le Mans, *and he always had some business transaction on the go. After he died (at the Brands Hatch Victory Race in a BRM, 1971), Rico Steinemann (Porsche works team manager) said, 'What a pity, he was the only one out of the whole ten of you with any business sense.' That wasn't strictly true because Kurt Ahrens went on to run a successful business and so did Rudi Lins – they were Volkswagen and Porsche dealers in Austria. Udo Schutz was highly successful and became a big businessman too.*

Maybe the meagre wages drivers earned in 1970 provided a spur.

In 1970, driving 917s for the best team in the world, John Wyer's JW Automotive, we were paid £300 downtime and £750 a race, except for Le Mans, Daytona and Sebring where we got £1,000. So, ten races a year made around £7,000, about the same as people could earn doing normal jobs. We raced all the time just to try and earn a living, and in other things as well; I was driving for Chevron in the 2.0-litre B16.

Back to the ambivalence that greeted the 917. With uncertain aerodynamics, narrow rear tyres and a tendency to wander at high speed, the 917 was more of a prototype than the 908. But during practice at Spa Brian gave it a go.

I got into this 917 for the first time ever on the fastest, most dangerous racetrack in the world, 8 miles around, with no Armco to speak of. In the 908 we would be doing 180mph, and in the 917 a year later in 1970, you came into the kink in the Masta Straight – which wasn't flat out – at 215mph. The 917s were ten seconds a lap faster than Formula 1 Grand Prix cars. So, there I am, I switch to the 917 from the 908. It's the first time I've sat in it. My knees are up against the back of the steering wheel, my head is on the roof, and I am really uncomfortable. I start it up and turn on the gigantic windshield wiper, which is parked on the left side of the screen – they say it came from a Boeing 707. It took one mighty swipe to the right and flew off into the pits. So, I turn the engine off, get out and Dr (Helmuth) Bott says, 'Brian, what are you doing?' 'The windscreen wiper has broken,' I say. 'Ah,' he says, 'that's ok, just drive slowly.' Well, I did a couple of slow laps in the rain, and Seppi and I decided to use the 908 long-tail, in which we won the race and I set fastest lap (3m 37.1s, 233.8km/h). Gerhard Mitter and Udo Schutz (that year's Targa Florio winners in a 908) chose to drive the 917 and they blew it up on the first lap.

It is often suggested they purposely contrived that, though Brian is doubtful.

Former Porsche racing mechanic and manager of the Mobile Museum, Klaus Bischoff, steers the 908/2 Flounder along the Solituderennen pit lane – also occupied by one of the Carrera Panamericana 550 Spyders – ahead of the Solitude Revival in 2008.

I don't think so, but no doubt they were sorely tempted! In those days the 917 had a five-speed gearbox, 5th gear out of the gate alongside 3rd and I think Mitter went from 4th to 3rd instead of 4th to 5th After that, I did the Le Mans test in the 917, running 225mph on the Mulsanne Straight, and it was weaving all over the road because there was so little downforce. Then came the Nürburgring 1,000kms, for which the 908 was perfect. None of the factory drivers wanted to drive the 917, so Porsche brought in David Piper and Frank Gardner. But the 917 was about 45 seconds a lap slower than the 908, and that was good enough justification not to want to drive it. In August there was the Austrian 1,000kms at the Österreichring. Porsche had officially withdrawn from racing after Le Mans and the cars were ostensibly run by independent teams, though unofficially Zuffenhausen personnel were swarming all over the place. The course was very fast, I'd never raced the 917 and in fact I'd never even been there before. I got just the three laps of practice, and I had a fit of temperament. I went to Rico Steinemann and said, 'thank you Rico, I am going home. I can't start the race with Jo Siffert in a factory 917 when I don't know the track and I don't know the car, it's an absolute recipe for disaster.' And he said, 'go slowly.' I said, 'how can I?' So, in the end he put me with Richard Attwood in David Piper's 917, and we finished third. Kurt Ahrens took my place with Jo Siffert, and they won, and Jo Bonnier was second in a Lola.

The official works cars would be run by JW Automotive Engineering in Gulf livery in 1970 and John Wyer was already making plans. Brian takes up the story:

About six weeks after Austria I got a call from John Wyer asking if I'd test the 917 at the Österreichring. He said, 'Porsche are doing a test, we're taking over the official factory team next year, and we will be there with our mechanics and engineers. Kurt Ahrens is coming for Porsche, you will represent us, and we are going to try Piers Courage in the car and Leo Kinnunen – the Finnish driver who has been doing well in Group 7 Interserie races.' It was an official Porsche factory test, with the Porsche engineers [running under the Porsche Konstruktionen Salzburg banner] and John Wyer's people, so it was a bit of a fraught atmosphere. I drove the car, and so did Kurt Ahrens, and it was just like it had been six weeks before in the race. After I came in, John Wyer's chief engineer John Horsman called me over. As a test he'd put some oil on the rear deck before I went out, just behind the cockpit, and he said, 'look at this!' The oil – which should have flowed along the body – didn't go on the body at all, it just went onto the very tip of the back of the bodywork. I think the contour of this rear bodywork is what's causing the problem. He got some aluminium from Porsche, some Duct tape and some plywood and they flattened the rear deck so, instead of dipping behind the rear wheelarches, it went straight. We instantly gained three seconds a lap. The next day we tried

Firestone tyres, and we got another second. So, in the end we were four seconds a lap faster. That's how the short tail came about for 1970. John Wyer was extremely upset at Daytona on the first race because Porsche Salzburg turned up with Ferdinand Piëch. They had experimental stuff and a full-scale factory-backed team, and John had been told that he would be the only factory team.

John Wyer's team was nevertheless magnificent that year, as Brian points out:

If you look at the results from 1970, you will find that almost every time Porsche Salzburg won, the JW Wyer team had dropped out. At the Nürburgring, we had a slow pit stop in the new 908/3 (010) due to a dickey starter motor; when I joined in about 4th place, the car was very good, and I closed up. I passed Kurt Ahrens who eventually won with Vic Elford. I came up behind my teammate Leo Kinnunen on the 13km jump – where you come off the ground in top gear at about 130mph. He made a mistake and hit the banking as he took off and flew in the air. I went underneath him. I was only about 6 feet behind him when it happened. So he was out of the race, and now we were leading, and everything was good. Towards the end of my session, the oil pressure warning light flashed a couple of times, and when Jo took over, the engine was a long time starting [three batteries were applied to deliver 36 volts to the starter motor]. And when it did get going, it soon broke, as it had run out of oil. About ten years ago I was testing cars that were coming from Monterey, including a 908/3, and I saw Klaus Bischoff, the head of the Zuffenhausen museum, who in 1970 was a Porsche Salzburg mechanic. I said, 'you remember the Nürburgring in 1970 when we should've won in Wyer's car, but we ran short of oil?' 'Ja, Brian,' he said, 'At Porsche Salzburg, we knew all about this problem. So, we had bigger oil tanks!'

The 917 was radically transformed for 1970 and JW Automotive made steady improvements, so it was a very successful year with Porsche's Le Mans win and another Championship victory. Brian thought it prudent to call time, and as it turned out his assessment of the risks to come proved to be correct.

I decided to retire at the end of 1970 because I thought I was going to be killed. All my friends were perishing, and I thought I could be next. I came back in March '71 and did a one-off in the Targa Florio because Derek Bell, who took my place in the JW squad, had never done it. Jo crashed the car the night before the race and Wyer said, 'I would like you to start the race.' I said, 'what for?' because I'd never started it before. He said, 'I don't want Siffert and Rodriguez knocking each other off the track.' So, I started and immediately the handling was poor. I got 20 miles round the 44-mile track and the steering broke, I hit a concrete post on the right, in the fuel tank. This was in spite of what

The 917 #005 of Nicolas D'Ieteren and Joe Twyman comes into the pit lane at Le Mans Classic, 2018. This is the resurrected and correctly liveried car in which John Woolfe lost his life in the 1969 24-Hours race.

> *the engineers had told me before the race; they said, 'Herr Redman, if you must have the accident, do not crash on the right side.' The car exploded and I was covered in burning fuel from head to foot. I was very lucky to escape, and it took me several weeks to recover, so that was that.*

Talk of the accident that singed his eyebrows sparks memories of others.

> *It was never widely reported that at least five 917s that I knew about broke in half across the cockpit in accidents, though they very rarely broke anything in a race. John Woolfe was the first private owner to buy a 917, and Digby Martland, his co-driver, who'd raced Chevrons successfully, lost it when he went over the hump at the end of the Mulsanne Straight (at Le Mans) and then spun for about 3- or 400 yards. He didn't hit anything, but he drove it back to the pits, got out, went up to John Woolfe, said, 'thank you very much, John, I have now retired from motor racing,' and though he did race subsequently they got Herbert Linge in as co-driver. John Woolfe insisted on taking the start, but he lost it at White House on the first lap and was killed. He was the only driver to be killed in a 917 though.*

> *At the Brands Hatch 1,000kms race in 1970 Pedro put on that fantastic wet weather drive, while Seppi and I were in 2nd place, and late on I got knocked off by Chris Amon in the Ferrari who was four laps in arrears. I was probably holding him up, but I'm going into Westfield corner and the rain is pouring down, and boom! I had a pretty good accident and hit everything in sight. So, I walk back to the pits and Dr Bott comes up and says to me, 'Brian, are you ok?' I say, 'yes thank you, Dr Bott.' He says, 'now you see Brian, the 917 is a very good car to have a crash in.' I just said, 'why can't you build a proper car like Lola and McLaren?' That was my grumble with the 917.*

Brian Redman prepares to take the 917 PA Can-Am car up the Hill at the Goodwood Festival of Speed, 2009.

So that's how it stands today. The 908/3 is the Porsche that earns his top marks.

> *It was designed at a time when Porsche were under enormous pressure to build and start to race the 917s, with the 25 of them sitting there. And at the same time, they were racing 908s in both long-tail and short-tail forms, and simultaneously they were developing and building a car just for two particular races, the Nürburgring and the Targa Florio. Pretty amazing. The 908/2 in both its long- and short-tail forms was extremely nice; they were all comfortable. Interestingly, in setting the fastest lap at Spa in 1969, the 908 long-tail had just under 400 horsepower and did about 180mph. A year later, the 1.8-litre Chevron B16 Spyder was three seconds a lap quicker than a 908 long-tail with just 250bhp and a top speed of 160mph, but through the corners, the 908 Spyder would have been faster than the long-tail because the long-tail was like the 917 with the attendant cornering problems.*

The fire still burns bright in that Lancastrian heart. At Goodwood, he has driven the Can-Am 917 PA from the new Porsche Museum up the Hill, as well as at Monterey. 'I love to drive the 917 nowadays because it's a fantastic car from a fantastic era.' At Laguna Seca he was back in a Gulf 908/3, trouncing its sister 917s. Brian has lived in Florida for a while, and in late January 2024 he staged the Homestead Targa, an exclusively Porsche meeting at the southern Florida circuit. Pride of place was the 908/2 from the Revs collection. No wonder it's his favourite Porsche.

LE MANS 24-HOURS, 1969: ALMOST THERE

It does not really matter what the situation is regarding the annual Sportscar Manufacturers, Championship – all the teams simply want to win the prestigious Le Mans 24-Hours. Before the event had even begun, Porsche had won the 1969 Championship with outright victories at Brands Hatch, Monza, the Targa Florio, Spa-Francorchamps and the Nürburgring – where they had filled the first five places. And if the Championship had been their only interest, they could have justifiably stayed away from Le Mans. But unlike the F1 Drivers' Championship, whose participants are only interested in winning points, the Porsche Racing department was out to win the 24-Hour race, regardless of any Championship, and so they arrived in France with an enormous quantity of men and materials, with three long-tailed 908 coupés, powered by the 3.0-litre flat-8s, one new Spyder 908/2 with a long-tail body, and four 917 coupés with 4.5-litre flat-12 engines. One of the 917s was destined for their first customer, the Woolfe Racing team, for John Woolfe and Digby Martland to drive. But the latter, a very competent Chevron B8 racer, had tried it in practice and decided it was more than he could cope with, and, in consequence, the works driver Herbert Linge was loaned to the Woolfe team to co-drive with the owner. The Porsche works team members shuffled randomly amongst the various cars during practice, and Siffert/Redman settled on the 908/2 Spyder, while Mitter/Schutz, Herrmann/Larrousse and Kauhsen/Lins all settled on the long-tail 908 coupés, and Stommelen/Ahrens and Elford/Attwood took the 917 coupés, the factory spare not being used.

The expected Porsche domination in the opening laps went according to plan, Stommelen and Elford in their 917s setting the pace. What was not expected was a fatal accident to the third 917, which John Woolfe elected to start the race in, despite his minimal experience with such a powerful and potentially wayward car. On the opening lap, he crashed at the exit of Maison Blanche, the car broke in two and caught fire, and he was killed, gaining the bizarre distinction of being the only driver to die in a 917. Although the 917s were immensely fast, they were consuming fuel from their regulation-size tanks very rapidly, and they ran for only a few minutes over an hour before having to refill – whereas the 908s ran for more than 1hr 15mins. The Ford GT40s could last 1hr 30mins, which, in a 24-hour race, is a very significant sort of difference.

The last of the works' Porsche 908s was gaining slowly on the Ford GT40, but not quickly enough to be a certain winner, and was on the same lap at midday with two hours to run. Hans Herrmann and Gérard Larrousse had to beat Jacky Ickx and Jackie Oliver. The JWR-Gulf Team wisely kept Ickx in the GT40 for more than two hours and he drove it as if it were a sprint race. At 12.30pm, he made his last pit stop for petrol, and the Gulf mechanics rapidly got the car serviced, but not before Larrousse had gone by into the lead. Then, at 12.42pm, the Porsche had to stop for petrol and a driver change, and the Porsche mechanics worked equally fast, as suddenly, the whole outcome of the 1969 Le Mans race was equally in their hands. Herrmann set off in the 908, and as he accelerated up the pit lane, Ickx went by in the GT40. There were one and a quarter hours left to run, and it seemed that Porsche could possibly win. But Ickx was driving brilliantly, and the GT40 was equally healthy. Relentlessly, the Porsche wore down the gap, and soon after 1.30pm, with less than 30 minutes to go, Herrmann took the lead. But the next time around, Ickx was back in front.

The last few minutes of the race, Ickx was making up on corners and in braking what the Ford lacked in speed, and the two cars passed and repassed each other in the sort of wheel-to-wheel racing beloved of Hollywood. Using the slipstream of the Porsche down the long 3.7 miles (6km) Hunaudières straight – at probably over 190mph (306km/h) – Ickx kept up with and then out-cornered the Porsche on the right-hand Mulsanne corner. As the clock ticked towards 2.00pm, it was still either driver's race, and both cars were flat out. A few seconds before 2.00pm, the two cars started their final lap. They repeatedly passed and repassed each other, four or five times during that final lap, and Ickx extended the lead around Mulsanne corner again. This time he made it stick, and the Ford led the Porsche across the line by about 100 yards, and the ending of the race went to pieces. Crowds invaded the track, in spite of hundreds of gendarmes, and the traditional parade of cars, drivers and pit crews did not take place. It was a long time before Ickx and Oliver could be got together to receive the acclamation on the podium. The traditional end-of-race ceremonies went by the board, and the 1969 Le Mans 24-hours ended in chaos and confusion.

The 908 LH of Claudio Roddaro in profile on the start/finish straight during the Le Mans Classic 2018.

MASS TURNOUT AT THE ÖSTERREICHRING

Anything left on the race calendar was kind of incidental, seeing as Porsche had already buttoned up the Championship. But there was one milestone still to be achieved; victory for the 917, which came about in the Austrian 1,000kms, held on the brand new Österreichring, a fantastic new circuit with plenty of gradient changes and taxing corners. Here, on 10 August, Jo Siffert and Kurt Ahrens took the honours in one of the two 917s present. Porsche having 'retired' for the remainder of the season, the firm's Austrian subsidiary was allocated three 908 Spyders with short-tail bodywork, plus a pair of short-tail 917s and almost the entire roster of work's drivers to man them. There were three privately owned 908 Spyders crewed by top-flight drivers, including Masten Gregory, plus an inordinate number of 910s on the entry list as well. The opposition consisted of three Alfa T33s, one Matra V12 and a single Gulf Mirage, and it was the latter, driven by Jacky Ickx, that gave Siffert the most trouble, the Porsche superior on the straight, the Cosworth-powered Mirage having the better time in the turns. For 25 laps, Siffert and Ickx ran more or less nose-to-tail, in and out of the slower cars, often passing one on each side of someone who was not looking in their mirror, or going between two cars that were busily having a private race of their own. Siffert lapped the other 917, which must have surprised Attwood in the second 917 and Bonnier in his 3rd-placed Lola T70. Refuelling demands in the final laps allowed the more frugal Lola-Chevrolet to take the lead, but Ahrens focused, and caught and passed the T70 to take the chequered flag by a minute. No fewer than eighteen Porsches filled the top 21 places, crewed by well-known names in the sport, including one Niki Lauda (with Otto Stuppacher), 21st in a 910.

PORSCHE 908/03

The intensity with which Porsche pursued the World Championship for Makes in 1970 and 1971 is indicated by the 908/3. It was produced in order for them to win just two races: the Targa Florio and Nürburgring 1,000Kms, both twisty, difficult tracks, where the 917's size and power were something of a handicap. Previous 908s had been built as Coupés or Spyders – viz 908/1 and 908/2, the former virtually the same shape as the 907, and the latter characterised by a smooth, flattish shape that earned it the fishy nickname 'Flounder'. The 908/3 was produced only as an open-top Spyder. Only the engine remained the same, giving away at least 65hp to the rival 3.0-litre 312PB Ferrari. Relying on their mastery of featherweight design, Piëch's engineers produced a car virtually supernatural in its weight saving coming to the grid at a mere 540kg. Though the 908/2 had been easily the lightest car in its class, the 908/3 was lighter yet by a full 100lb through the extensive use of titanium. Its spaceframe chassis weighed but 48lb, its plastic and foam body another 26.5lb. Thirteen 908/3s were produced: eleven in 1969–70 and two in 1971. Because of their extraordinary lightness, racing pundits predicted widespread structural failures. The pundits were wrong, however. A 1–2 finish in both the Targa Florio and Nürburgring in 1970 saw to that, although the 1971 Targa was a driver error-fraught crash-out. A three-car sweep of the 'Ring put the final event back on track. The only 908/3 breakages occurred in the two cars built in 1971, and only because they had not been built to specification. Still at the 1971 Nürburgring, Pedro Rodriguez and Jackie Oliver joined in the three-car Porsche sweep, nursing their car across the finish line to 2nd place, despite a broken chassis. The 908/3's win rate was an astounding 75 per cent. Even more astounding is how long the car's basic design remained competitive. With the 908/3, Piëch and company moved far ahead from the 910 design-of-the month days. Like the 1927 Delage Grand Prix car, this Porsche was so brilliantly effective that it remained competitive for more than a decade. A 1971 configuration 908/3 won its last World Championship race at Silverstone in 1980.

The 908/3 KH of Jerome Miloe and Jean-Louis Miloe on the grid for a sportscar race during the 2007 Nürburgring Old Timer meeting.

THE GÉRARD LARROUSSE INTERVIEW

Gérard Larrousse's retirement present to himself was a Porsche 993, a car he surely earned, as one of France's most successful motor sporting personalities. Winning Le Mans, the Nürburgring 1,000kms, the Targa Florio and the Corsican Rally makes you a pretty special driver.

Born in 1940, Gérard began rallying in 1961. 'I was 21, which is kind of old today,' he frowns. 'But I was still a student studying business management in Paris. I come from Lyon, near the Alps, and people there are very keen on rallying. Friends said to me, "Come on, you are a good driver so why not try it?" I really started from zero because I never went to a racing school like Winfield, or even kart racing.'

Between 1964 and 1965 Gérard did national service while building a reputation in French club racing, and at the end of 1968 he had a proposition from Porsche to drive four or five rallies. Accepting Porsche's offer meant *au revoir* to Alpine, for whom he had just won the French rally championship, but the clincher was the prospect of circuit racing. Gérard had the taste for it having done Le Mans twice for Alpine with Patrick Depailler and Henri Grandsire, and he was also racing Formula France single-seaters. 'So, I said, "OK, Porsche is proposing some rallying, but I know that they have a lot of racing cars so maybe I will have a chance to do circuit racing," and that's exactly what happened.'

Gérard was immediately dispatched in a 911 with navigator Jean-Claude Perramond on the 1969 Monte Carlo Rally, finishing 2nd to Bjorn Waldegård: 'Bjorn was going much faster than me on snow; he was really brilliant.' But things quickly got even better, as he describes:

> *When I came to Porsche, I immediately got on with competitions manager Rico Steinemann. He said, 'Gérard, if you want to drive in France and you have sponsors, we can prepare a car for you in the factory. We give you the car and a couple of mechanics and then you devise your own programme.' They gave me the 911R, which I drove on the Lyon-Charbonnières and Neige-et-Glace. That was a very light car, 850kg with double camshaft 6-cylinder engine, revving to 9,000rpm. I won the Tour-de-France and Tour of Corsica, against all the Alpines.*

Cutting a dash, Gérard Larrousse drove for Porsche from 1969 to 1971, logging numerous successes including 2nd places at Le Mans in 1969 and 1970.

He smiles at the irony. 'It was a private team with a factory car.' Promotion came rapidly:

> *One day, Steinemann called and said, 'Ah, Gérard, you are a rally driver so you can drive the Targa Florio for us with the 908.' I replied: 'You think I can drive a 908?' and he said, 'Of course.' We had a test drive in Sicily to learn the Targa Florio course – this was the first time I'd driven a proper racing car for them. My wife Michelle and I stayed for one month in Céfalu, and it was fantastic driving a 908-2 Spyder on the open road.*

JT interviews Gérard Larrousse at Classic Le Mans 2018.

Canine collision

He coped with the inevitable potholes, sheep, goats and donkeys, but a large dog was one hazard too many:

I braked but the 908 passed under the dog and caught his legs. He went up in the air and landed inside the cockpit, falling on my left arm. So, I pushed him into the footwell, stopped the car, undid my safety belts and got out to look at the damage. But I could not get back in again as he was still alive, trying to bite me. I saw some people coming; you think you are alone, but you never are in places like Sicily, however remote. I was a little bit afraid as I thought they wouldn't be happy because I'd hit someone's dog. But they said, 'No problem,' they got their pitchforks and forced the dog out of the car. I drove back to the café where we were based and there was plenty of blood in the car, on my overalls. It was terrible!

Come the race, Gérard and Rudi Lins finished 21st, a couple of laps down on the winning 908. He placed 3rd in a Porsche 910 at Montlhéry's Coupe de Vitesse, and then came Le Mans 1969, a nerve-jangling race if ever there was one. Partnered with veteran Hans Herrmann in a 908 long-tail coupé, he finished 2nd after a titanic struggle with Jacky Ickx in the Ford GT40. But that's just the bare bones of the story.

I was a very young driver and Herrmann was an old driver, so Rico put us together just for fun. After twenty hours we were the only works car still going and it began to look like we could win. Everything changed, people's attention and attitude was completely different. They could see Mr Bott and Dr Porsche looking at the car, and we were like children. They said: 'Drive as fast as you can now!' It was very hard going because it was drizzling and there was a bit of fog. I had a fight with another Porsche driver, Udo Schutz, driving the same type of car as me, a 908 longtail. After I passed him he was pushing very hard to get back at me, and he made a mistake and finished in the guardrail at Hunaudiéres, and the car burned. It was a dreadful sight, though he was alright.

It was Gérard's first big-time experience with Porsche, and he liked the 908.

I preferred the Spyder because I drove many races in it. We had just started the Martini Racing Team and in 1970 I drove a lot of races with Hans-Dieter Dechent who brought in Martini as sponsor, and he took Gijs van Lennep, Helmut Marco and me, and we were driving everywhere with the 908.

That year Gérard drove the maximum number of races, 42 in total, so he was well able to discriminate between the 908/2 Spyder and the 908 coupé, which he found more difficult because it was actually lighter. As he tells it:

When they came to Le Mans the first time, they were fitted with aerodynamic devices on the back that were meant to adjust the stability at high speed. The Le Mans technical people said, 'No, you can't start the race with those movable wings on the rear,' so we had to fix them so they wouldn't move. It was fickle, yet it was very fast, lapping at 330km/h. There wasn't so much power, but a very good top speed.

Hans Herrmann and Gérard Larrousse brought their 908 LH to within 100m – two seconds – of victory in the 1969 Le Mans 24-Hours. Troubled by a cracked axle bearing and worn brakes, the Porsche handled less well than the marginally slower GT40 of winners Ickx and Oliver, and the result could have gone either way.

By comparison, during practice Stommelen's long-tail 917 hit 360km/h – 224mph – on the Mulsanne Straight.

> *But when Herrmann had his fight with Jacky Ickx in the GT40 we couldn't win because our brakes were not good enough. The car was fast, but not as powerful as the GT40. So, Jacky had a great opportunity to catch Hans in a straight line, and then pass him on the brakes. After that it was impossible to pass again, so we finished about 100 metres behind.*

Gérard came 13th in the Targa Florio in 1970, sharing the 3.0-litre 908/2 with Rudi Lins again. He and Koch brought their 908/2 to 7th in the BOAC 1,000kms at Brands Hatch, and Gérard came 2nd at Le Mans once more, this time with Willy Kauhsen in the fabulous psychedelic-liveried 917. Although entered by Martini Racing Team, this was really a works car like the Porsche Konstruktionen long-tail of Elford/Ahrens, but ignition problems due to rain meant it was slower than Herrmann/Attwood's winning 917, though it had been ten seconds quicker in practice. Later in the season Gérard won the Coupe du Salon at Montlhéry with its formidable banking in a 908/2, and a week later at the same Paris track, he and Claude Ballot-Lena placed 3rd in the 1,000kms driving the 908/2.

Is Vic there?

For 1971, Gérard was paired with Vic Elford in the Martini Racing Team's 917.

> *The season started at Daytona, but there were some problems with the car, and I did not drive there. But then, with Vic, we won Sebring 12-Hours. That's a big memory for me. And after that, we drove together all year.*

The duo scored another victory at the Nürburgring 1,000kms in the agile 908/3, while at Le Mans they retired the long-tail 917 from 32nd spot in hour seven, though they had been running 2nd early on. A potential win at the Österreichring with Helmut Marko in a short-tail 917 ended when a tyre blow-out spun him into the Armco.

According to Gérard, the 917 was very expensive to maintain and results suffered accordingly. 'The team hadn't enough money to keep it in good shape over the whole season,' he says ruefully. 'In fact, it was delivering less and less performance as the year rolled on, and races at the end of the year were very difficult.'

Gérard claims that the problem wasn't just the flat-12 engine – the chassis was also fragile and troublesome.

> *Some 917 tube-frames were aluminium, some magnesium, and if you had cracks in the chassis the car wouldn't handle, it was moving around the whole time. So, they put air inside the chassis tubes and if the pressure was falling it meant there was a crack somewhere. The chassis had a valve like a tyre inner tube, and they were putting a lot of pressure in to see if it was OK or not.*

Though Porsche won the 1971 World Championship for Makes there was intense rivalry between drivers in the two squads – the independent Gulf-JW Automotive and the works Martini Racing Team. 'There were a lot of fights within the JW team between Siffert and Rodriguez, and with Vic in the Martini car,' says Gérard.

Vic Elford and Gérard Larrousse drove Martini Racing Team's 908/3 #008 on the 1971 Targa Florio, but went out on the seventh of eleven laps in an accident, enough, though, to be classified 39th.

Gérard Larrousse does a demonstration lap at Classic Le Mans 2010 in the Martini Racing Team 917 LH he drove with Vic Elford in the 1971 Le Mans 24-Hours.

The John Wyer team was separate from Porsche, and they were modifying their cars, and the engineers from Porsche were not too happy about that. There was a fight between them and John Horsman, who was engineering the JW cars. At Le Mans especially there was a big fight between the Gulf cars and the factory Martini cars.

Gérard drove the 1972 Monte Carlo Rally with Jean-Claude Perramond in the Écurie Shell 911S, finishing 2nd after a ferocious battle with Sandro Munari's Lancia Fulvia.

The team was Bjorn (Waldegård) and me but with a private service crew, and the sponsor was SEB, a cooking pot manufacturer. I missed a tyre change in the Ardèche and took a minute extra on the road because I could not drive hard anymore, there were no spikes left. Otherwise, I would have won.

At the end of 1971, the 917 programme finished, and Gérard's works Porsche contract was not renewed. Driving the 3.0-litre Matra-Simca MS670B, and teamed with Henri Pescarolo, Gérard won Le Mans in 1973 and 1974. Then, as head of Renault's racing organisation, he took the French automotive giant into F1 in 1976. In 1986, in collaboration with French lawyer Didier Calmels, he established his own F1 operation under the name Team Larrousse Calmels, involving various drivers such as Philippe Alliot, Yannick Dalmas, Bertrand Gachot and Eric Bernard, plus designers Eric Broadley, Ralph Bellamy, Gérard Ducarouge and Robin Herd. The Larrousse Team's labyrinthine story – Hollywood could not make it up – concluded in 1995.

PORSCHE 908/2 #005

Chassis No. 908/02.005
Engine No. 42
Gearbox No. 916/016

Visionary Public Relations Director of Martini and Rossi International in the 1960s was Paul Goppert, an early advocate of motorsport sponsorship in the days when commercial endorsement – cigarettes, drinks, household brands – was brand new in motorsport outside the USA. By the late 1960s, he had begun sponsoring Porsche racing privateers, including that of Hans-Dieter Dechent, who, at the time, was racing a 910. Dechent's small single-car operation, German B.G. (*Blau und Gelb* = blue and yellow) Racing Team, grew quickly with Goppert's help, adding a 907 in 1969.

So, 908/02 #005 began life as a works team car, raced sparingly in 1969, first at the Sebring 12-Hours, in the hands of Vic Elford and Richard Attwood. Starting from the back in a crowded field of 70, the seasoned duo came 8th overall. A month later, #005 was used as a T-car (training car) for the Targa Florio, from which the Porsche team once again emerged victorious, their 4th Targa victory in a row. Towards the end of the 1969 racing season, Dechent's team, now known as the Martini International Racing Team and the beneficiary of Porsche's development largesse, acquired 908/02 #005, though the season's finale, the Zeltweg 1,000Km at the newly opened Österreichring, ended with a DNF for Dechent and Gerhard Koch.

During the winter of 1969–70, #005's body was reconfigured by Porsche with a longer tail – engine cover – surmounted by a pair of fins, interchangeable with the KH short-tail. Koch and Gérard Larrousse drove it in the Sebring 12-Hours, Richard Attwood joining them 30 laps in, his own 908/02 disqualified for having received a push-start, and they were rewarded with 7th overall. At the BOAC 1,000Kms at Brands Hatch, Larrousse and Koch came 6th overall behind three 917s and a Ferrari 512 S.

On show at Classics at the Castle, Sible Hedingham, in 2013, 908/2 #005 shares space with another Martini Racing Porsche, the 935 driven at Le Mans in 1977 by Rolf Stommelen and Manfred Schurti.

Gérard Larrousse and Rudi Lins shared the cockpit over the next three races, Monza, the Targa Florio and Spa-Francorchamps, taking the class victory in Belgium. At the Nürburgring 1,000Kms, the pair of Martini International Racing 908/02 Spyders finished 5th and 6th overall, behind the works' new 908/3 Spyders and a couple of Ferrari 512 Ss. With all eyes on Le Mans, Martini Racing equipped 908/2 #005 with the new long-tail LH bodywork, which enabled the incorporation of a transmission oil cooler, a factory modification unique to the 908/02 series.

The 908/02 #005 LH was driven by Rudi Lins and Helmut Marko, while its sister car, #009 (subsequently #019), remained in short-tail KH configuration, with nominated drivers Hans-Dieter Dechent and André de Cortanze. However, it was involved in an accident during practice and did not make the start. Intermittent rain storms throughout the race caused several retirements, but by midnight, #005 was lying 6th, leading the 3.0-litre sports prototype class, and had moved into 2nd place overall by 10.00am the next morning. However, during two pit stops for tyre changes, seized rear wheel nuts caused delays, and some twelve minutes were lost. They dropped just one place, crossing the line 3rd behind winners Attwood and Herrmann in the red Salzburg Konstruktionen 917 and the psychedelic Hippie 917 in 2nd place, taking the 3.0-litre prototype class victory, the Index of Performance, and 3rd in the Index of Thermal Efficiency. Chassis #005's season ended on a high note – now returned to KH short tail configuration – with a class win at the Watkins Glen 6-Hours and 3rd overall at the Österreichring in the Austrian 1,000 Kms, once again the season's finale. The car was then acquired by Jo Siffert and passed into the hands of other collectors after he died in 1971.

The Martini Racing 908/2 #005 of Miguel Amaral, Manuel and Pedro Mello-Breyner in action at Classic Le Mans 2010.

CHAPTER 6

THE PORSCHE 917 1969–71

To comply with the FIA's homologation requirements for Group 4 Sportscars, in early 1969, Porsche constructed 25 examples of the 917 and presented them in echelon for inspection by officials.

In October 1967, the FIA elected to limit the engine capacity of Prototypes running in the World Championship for Makes to 3.0-litres, effective from 1 January 1968. A minimum production volume of 25 units was allowed for sportscars, with a capacity limit of 5.0-litres. While Porsche anticipated the 3.0-litre limit, for which the 908 engine had been designed, the 5.0-litre limit for sports cars was a surprise, since it was generally assumed that the 5.0-litre cars would have a serious advantage. However, Porsche thought that very light 3.0-litre cars might still be competitive, until they learned that Ferrari was preparing to build a batch of twenty-five 5.0-litre sports cars – the 512 S. This sparked Porsche's decision to build a car that would be eligible for that class too, which was the Type 917.

The creation of the 917 began in July 1968, and because time was of the essence, the designers of the 12-cylinder engine adopted the materials, cylinder-barrel dimensions, pistons, conrod length, valve dimensions and timing of the 908 engine. However, this spec fell short of the 5.0-litre displacement limit, resulting in a capacity of 4.5-litres. The chassis was a very close relative of the 908/02, and the time saved by using so many existing components made it possible to have the first car ready in time for

Racing from Indianapolis Corner into Arnage, the Le Mans-winning 917 of Hans Herrmann and Richard Attwood was given the least chance of success pre-race, having a 4.5-litre engine against the other 917s (bar one) with 5.0-litres.

the Geneva Motor Show on 13 March 1969, where it was available to private race teams for the price of 140,000 Deutschmarks. At the end of April, the 25 cars required for homologation in the sports car group by the CSI were lined up for inspection in the factory forecourt. In May 1969, Gerhard Mitter drove a short-tail version in its maiden race, the Spa 1000 kilometres, but a broken valve caused its retirement after the first lap. Two weeks later, Frank Gardner and David Piper were invited to drive the same car in the Nürburgring 1,000-kilometre race, with orders to finish at all costs, which they did, in 8th place. At Le Mans, only three months after the 917's first outing, a long-tail version created excitement when it led the race for more than twenty hours before retiring. That was the Elford–Atwood car. After the first half of the 1969 season, however, an important conclusion was drawn. The effort put into racing the 908 and 917 models was more than the factory's technical staff could cope with, especially as the development of both racing and production cars was carried out by the same department at the time. A partner had to be found to run the still underdeveloped 917 in the World Championship for Makes the following two years, and the choice fell on JW Automotive Engineering, led by John Wyer.

Already something of a veteran, Wyer managed Aston Martin's Le Mans victory in 1959 with Roy Salvadori and Carroll Shelby in the DBR1. The 'W' in the JW Automotive name represented racing specialist John Willment, who went into partnership with Wyer, while John Horsman became chief engineer in 1962, a position he retained during the Porsche phase. Based in Slough, and supported by the Gulf Oil Company, the collaboration was initiated in 1970, when the factory was also able to link up with another private organisation, Porsche Salzburg, headed by Dr Porsche's sister, Louise Piëch. The following year, the Austrian team changed sponsors and became the Martini Racing Team. There was an important difference, however, between Wyer's link with the factory and that of the other teams running the 917. JW Automotive was served directly by the experimental department, while the other teams, including Porsche Salzburg, were dealt with by the Sport Service Department.

The 917 scored its first victory in the last race of the 1969 season, the Austrian 1,000 kilometres at Zeltweg, when Jo Siffert and Kurt Ahrens beat all comers in a short-tail car entered by Karl von Wendt. In the first race of 1970, the John Wyer team triumphantly inaugurated its collaboration with Porsche by taking the first two places in the Daytona 24-Hours with drivers Pedro Rodriguez/Leo Kinnunen and Jo Siffert/Brian Redman. It prefaced an astonishing track record of success: from 1969 to the end of 1971, in the 24 World Championship races for which the 917 was entered, as well as the 908, Porsche was beaten on only five occasions. Wyer's Gulf JW-Automotive team won eleven races with its blue and orange cars. The factory won one race in 1969, Porsche Salzburg won one race in 1970, which was Le Mans, and the Martini team succeeded in winning one. Up to the close of the 917 project at the end of 1971, the tally of cars built included 36 short-tail, two Spyders and five long-tail cars.

PRICE INDEX

Porsche's 917 programme cost an estimated 15,000,000 Deutschmarks (£6.5m), which breaks down to 350,000 Deutschmarks (£153K) per car. It is not surprising therefore, that from the initial 140,000 Deutschmarks, the price of a race-ready 917 short-tail had risen to 280,000 Deutschmarks, which was about $77,000 in 1971. After Porsche's two decades of uninterrupted participation at Le Mans, in 1970, Hans Herrmann and Richard Attwood drove their Porsche-Salzburg entered short-tail 917 to victory, presenting the firm with endurance racing's most coveted prize, marked by a triumphant drive from the Zuffenhausen factory through Stuttgart to the City Hall. After three consecutive victories in the World Championship for Makes in 1969, 1970 and 1971, Porsche decided pragmatically to retire from the series. From 1972, the engine capacity for World Championship racing prototypes was again limited to 3.0-litres, which would not in itself have deterred Porsche from entering, had not a minimum weight of 650 kilogrammes (1,433lb) been imposed. Without this limit, the power handicap inherent in an air-cooled engine could have been acceptable, and offset by lightweight design, an accomplishment in which the factory excelled. But 650 kilogrammes was a good 100 kilogrammes (220lb) higher than what could be easily achieved, as proven by the 800kg 908/03, which won at the Nürburgring and Targa Florio in 1970 and 1971. So, Porsche opted out.

Vic Elford on his way to 2nd place in the 1969 BOAC 500 at Brands Hatch in the 908/2 #010 shared with Richard Attwood.

VIC ELFORD'S VIEW

'Quick Vic' came into endurance racing via rallying, a discipline he excelled at, putting the 911 on the map by winning the televised Lydden Hill Autocross in 1967, then winning the 1968 Monte Carlo Rally with David Stone.

Over the years, I enjoyed several meetings with Vic. I had witnessed him in action numerous times, even during the 1968 season when he won Class C of the British Saloon Car Championship in the semi-works AFN 911. Memorably, Antony Fraser and I lunched with him and his wife Anita Fol during the Targa Florio centenary when he was in charge of the 987 Cayman course car. And on the 2008 Rallye Monte-Carlo Historique, when Vic and his veteran co-driver David Stone were reprising their Monte victory of 1968 in a 911, Mrs T and I were tasked with ferrying their partners, Anita and Bébé, the length and breadth of France each day for evening rendezvous with Vic and David wherever the rally fetched up – Reims, Valence, Éze, Monaco – at the behest of Porsche GB, who had kindly furnished us with a palatial Cayenne Turbo V8 for the event. Predictably, we both got booked for speeding, despite our celebrity bi-lingual passengers' intercessions with the apprehending gendarmes.

Competition manager Huschke von Hanstein gave Vic the opportunity to run a 911 in the 1966 Tour de Corse, with David Stone as navigator: they finished 3rd, and the die was cast. 'In 1967, I should have won the Monte-Carlo, but we slipped up on the tyres,' commented Vic. Nevertheless, 3rd place was a decent result. But Vic's top-line career was well and truly underway: winner of the 1968 Monte-Carlo Rally with David Stone, he also shared the winning 907 LH prototype with Jochen Neerpasch in Porsche's 1-2-3 finish at the Daytona 24 Hours – the first time that Porsche had taken victory in a big-time WSC event. Although the finish was staged so that the 907s crossed the line three abreast, Vic, at the wheel of the winning car, was actually five laps ahead of his teammates.

A couple of months later came the tortuous Targa Florio, the toughest round of the World Sports Car Championship. On the first lap of the Piccolo Madonie, up in the Sicilian hills, Vic's 907 had a loose wheel and then a puncture, and had to return to the pits on the space-saver spare. All this lost some sixteen minutes, and for Vic the race seemed over. He started the second lap of the rustic 44-mile circuit eighteen minutes behind. As he recalls, 'I thought, "that's it, there's no possibility I can win, but I'm going to make damn sure that every lap is a record!"' Staying in the cockpit for more than five of the six-and-a-half hours (to the exclusion of co-driver Umberto Maglioli), he pounded the mountainous course, shattering the lap record, and taking the victory by almost three minutes.

F1 taster

Meanwhile, Vic was co-opted into the Cooper Formula 1 team, and came 4th in the uncompetitive Cooper-Maserati T86B at Rouen in his first Grand Prix. It was a result he never bettered in F1, and it's his career in sports-prototypes that he is best known for. His rocket-like trajectory into the upper echelons of sports-prototypes began in 2.0-litre 910s – principally the well-known Bill Bradley car, 910-020 – that he helmed in 1968. This was the car that I drove at Chobham test track. Vic's first outing in 910-020 was the Monza 1,000Kms in April 1968, and he ensured it was quickest of the five 910s present. 'In 1968, Porsche had too many works drivers,' he commented, 'so we each missed one race. Monza was my turn to drop out, and so I drove with Bill.'

At the start, Vic was well up with the works GT40s and factory 907s and 908s, but a wheel came off during Bradley's stint, and thus, a secure 4th place receded to 9th overall. Vic drove this 910 several times that year, retiring at Mugello, 'because it broke', and crashed out at Nuremburg's Norisring in June after a collision with Frank Gardner's Lola T70. He fared better at the Solituderennen, staged at Hockenheim in July. Vic remembered that:

> *I had a great race. I missed some of the practice because it was wet, so I started way down at the back and had to work like a dog, without slipstreaming, to catch up to the pack. Which I did, and I passed them all to win the 2.0-litre category.*

After a huge scrap with Alex Soler-Roig in another 910, Vic placed 4th overall behind the big bangers and ahead of a load of other 910s and 906s.

> *We had different cars for every race: the 907 long-tail coupé for Daytona, the short-tail for the Nürburgring and Targa Florio, and for hillclimbs we had the Bergspyder 909 and 910 Spyders. Then came the 908 coupés, and at some races we had both the 907s and the 908s in long-tail and short-tail bodies. We won Daytona, the Targa Florio and Nürburgring 1,000kms with the 907, and by the end of the year they'd started making the 908/2 and the 917.*

For 1969, Vic was behind the wheel of the 908/2 Spyder. 'We were using tube-frame chassis,' he points out, 'although the Spyders had different chassis from the coupés, and at Sebring the uneven surface broke them, although that was the last race we had such problems.' After that, Vic and Kurt Ahrens, Jo Siffert and Brian Redman won just about everything. But not Le Mans: Hans Herrmann and Gérard Larrousse with the 908 long-tail came 2nd by not much more than 100 metres.

Huschke von Hanstein was effectively replaced by Ferry Porsche's nephew, Ferdinand Piëch, aided and abetted by Peter Falk.

Vic Elford takes the restored 1969 Targa Florio-winning 908/2 Flounder around Glemseck Corner in a demonstration run during the 2008 Solitude Revival.

Kurt Ahrens and Vic Elford on the podium after winning the 1970 Nürburgring 1,000Kms in Porsche Konstruktionen Salzburg's 908/3 #008.

Until then, Porsche had been happy to win its class all over the world, but Piëch wasn't content with that. He wanted outright domination and he set about getting it: hence the 907 then the 908 and ultimately the 917. It was very different from the fatherly relationship I'd had with Huschke. Piëch was two years younger than me, and he wasn't an easy man. But he and I wanted the same results, and we had the same philosophy about how to get there – hard work. Before the Targa, Piëch would take over the car park under the Hotel Santa Maria in Cefalù and establish a practice schedule starting at 6.00am each day. If you were five minutes late you had to buy a crate of beer for the mechanics. If they had to get up at 5.00am, so did we. I liked that.

Over lunch in a Termini Imerese restaurant, Vic Elford recounts some of his Porsche exploits in the Targa Florio.

To take advantage of the 5.0-litre Group 5 rules, Piëch sanctioned development of the flat-12 917. The FIA deemed a minimum of 25 should be produced to qualify for Group 5 and so Porsche threw together 25 917s and lined them up in front of the factory for the FIA delegate Dean Delamont (from the RAC) to inspect. We called them the 'secretary cars' because everybody in the place who could hold a spanner, even down to the secretaries, was press-ganged into helping to build them. When Delamont arrived, he was told, 'Choose any car, and you can drive it.' Fortunately, he declined!

The early 917 was pretty horrible, but I wasn't afraid of it, even in the wet. I suppose my rallying background meant that I'd come into racing with some extra disciplines. Rallying the 911, there wasn't much grip on asphalt, and on snow and ice, virtually none. I was used to an unstable car, which I then stabilised in my own fashion. That's why I loved the rain. Spa in the wet and Rouen with those downhill sweeps: lovely. But at Le Mans, my philosophy was always, 'I don't want to race, I just want to have the fastest car'. With the 917, I had it. None of us had ever done much more than 190mph before and here we were doing 225mph-plus. I loved the 917 for that. That first 917 year, 1969, with the long-tail, Richard Attwood and I had a 50-mile lead with three hours to go, when the clutch packed up. The 1970 short-tail car was more stable: you could move it around a bit. But for Le Mans, we had a new long-tail. With that you had to be very precise to get it right first time. Once you'd committed to a corner you had to stay committed. And that year it rained. But I found that I could go through the Mulsanne kink flat at night in the rain at 240mph. Took a while to work myself up to it, though. In practice I'd ease off a little, but once I kept it absolutely flat through there, the car loved it. My pole position average was just over 150mph, and I set fastest lap in the race.

Porsche had now split its race management responsibilities between John Wyer's JW Automotive and Porsche Salzburg Konstruktionen, effectively run by Ferdinand Piëch. 'There was lots of rivalry between the two teams, between the personalities of Wyer and Piëch. I led the Salzburg team, fighting Wyer's cars as much as the Ferraris.' In 1971 the Martini Racing Team replaced Porsche Salzburg. Vic won at Sebring with Gérard Larrousse and scored his third Nürburgring 1,000Km win.

However, the demise of Group 5 ended his long relationship with Zuffenhausen.

Vic Elford in discussion with Gérard Larrousse in the 908/3 #008 they shared to win the 1971 Nürburgring 1000Kms. Their winning margin over the similar JW Gulf 908/3 of Siffert/Rodriguez was 1m 44s. Behind Vic is Hans-Dieter Dechent, boss of the Martini Team (in hat), and Hans Herrmann, with Peter Falk (head of Porsche pre-series and racing department) behind the car talking to mechanic Fritz Spengler.

> *I lived through an entire racing era at Porsche, and I loved every Porsche I drove. I liked all the people – Norbert Singer, Peter Falk, Helmuth Bott, Hans Mezger, as well as Piëch and Huschke. This was when Piëch packed his bags and went off to Audi. He didn't just want to be the rich nephew taking over the family business. He went on to great things at Audi of course and then Volkswagen. I think that after his grandfather, he is arguably the greatest automotive engineer of the twentieth century.*

Despite all this, in nine attempts, Vic never won the Le Mans 24 Hours, the last go being 1984 with Anny-Charlotte Verney in a Rondeau M379C, though there were two class wins, in 1969 with Ben Pon in a 906 and 1972 with Claude Ballot-Léna in a Ferrari Daytona, plus of course several outright victories in WSCC endurance races. He was also game for anything, trying his hand at NASCAR, Trans-Am, and Can-Am with the Chaparral 2J 'sucker' car – reunited with Vic at the Goodwood Festival of Speed a few years ago. He also guested in recent years at Classic Le Mans and Laguna Seca and, back in the day, he was awarded the *Chevalier de Ordre National du Mérite* for bravery at Le Mans in 1972, stopping his Alfa Romeo T33 mid-race and trying to rescue the driver of a Ferrari Daytona in the incident that killed his friend Jo Bonnier. It was this accident, as much as anything else, that prompted him to declare his retirement from racing – conscious of the risk of life-changing injuries as much as fatality – though he was tempted back occasionally: witness his drive in the 2008 Historic Monte. You might say he was old school: Vic was kind, thoughtful, considerate, supremely brave, and especially gifted behind the wheel of a competition car.

SPECIFICATION OF THE 917

Overseen by Hans Mezger, the 917 body was developed in the Porsche design department. A 1:5-scale plasticine model was made, followed by a 1:1 model that was used for wind tunnel testing at the Research Institute of Automotive Engineering and Vehicle Engines at the University of Stuttgart (*Forschungsinstitutes für Kraftfahrwesen und Fahrzeugmotoren an der Universität Stuttgart* – FKFS). Further aerodynamic development was carried out by Charles Deutsch at his Paris-based SERA research institute (*Société d'études et de réalisations automobiles*). The final body design included two adjustable side-mounted air flaps in the front and rear, which feature on both the short-tail and long-tail versions. Like its predecessors, the 917's body was made of fibreglass, and the central cabin section was bonded to the aluminium tubular spaceframe chassis in a similar fashion to its immediate ancestors, while the front and rear lids were detachable. The tube-frame chassis weighed only 45 kilogrammes, but it still begs the question why, when F1 cars had been constructed around aluminium monocoque chassis since the Lotus 25 of 1962, did Porsche persevere with the – admittedly tried-and-tested – multi-tubular spaceframe? The 936 that persisted until 1981 was still constructed on a tube-frame chassis, and not until the 956 of 1982 did Porsche embrace an aluminium monocoque. Fair enough, the contemporary Ford GT40 was based on a triangulated tubular frame, as were the more complex Ferrari 330 P3 and 512 S.

Weight shift

Back to the 917: shifting the cockpit and driver's seat further forward from the precedent set by the 908 meant that the wheelbase could be kept at 2,300mm despite the considerably longer 12-cylinder engine. The outer skin was 1.2 millimetres thick, but opening parts, such as the doors and the engine cover, were reinforced with aluminium tubes or polyurethane foam. The windscreen was 4.2mm laminated glass, while the door windows were Plexiglas. The body panel extending over the engine was made of transparent Plexiglass to provide rearward visibility and was louvred to admit air into the engine compartment. The complete body, including all covers, seats, closing aerodynamic devices, wiring, the harnesses and, in the case of the long-tail car, it weighed only 95 kilogrammes or 209lb. The rack and pinion housing was magnesium. The rack itself was made of Aluknet, a wrought aluminium alloy. The steering ratio was 11.4 to 1. So,

The 917 LH's fibreglass body was bonded to the aluminium tubular spaceframe chassis, which weighed only 45 kilogrammes. Shifting the cockpit and driver's seat further forward than the 908 meant that the wheelbase could be kept at 2,300 mm despite the longer 12-cylinder engine.

conceptually, it was not so different from its predecessors, the 906, 910, 907 and 908. Research into the effect of aerodynamic forces on the racecar's behaviour led to the adoption of movable flaps, which, after some experimentation, were only used at the rear. They were controlled by the rear suspension in such a way that they increased the downforce when rear wheel travel was extended and decreased it when the suspension was compressed. The flaps were actuated by links to the suspension. The CSI banned such movable devices from June 1969, although the 917s were allowed to use them at Le Mans by special permission, and they then had to be abandoned. The driver's seat consisted of two parts. The shell had a removable seat pan, individually shaped for each driver and could be changed when one driver took over from the other in long-distance races. The seat was adjustable for reach, and the steering column was both for reach and height. Flexible tubes carried fresh air into the cockpit, while the drivers were further insulated from the prodigious heat within the cockpit by means of cooling tubes plugged into their race suits. In addition to the tachometer, oil pressure and temperature gauges, the instrument panel carried warning lights for fuel level, generator charge, oil pressure, and brake pad wear. The fuel tanks, with a capacity of 140 litres (37 gallons), were made of sheet aluminium and carried as panniers on either side of the cockpit, where they helped lower the car's centre of gravity. They were connected by a thick tube, so the car could be filled up from either side or simultaneously from both sides. For homologation, 25 examples – long-tail cars – were built as required by the racing rules at the time – but a short KH tail sold with it could quickly be substituted. Two long-tail cars were entered by the factory in 1969, one of which led the 24-Hours of Le Mans for twenty hours. That was the Vic Elford/Richard Attwood car, which I describe in detail later on. Neither shape was very satisfactory, but the factory cars remained unchanged throughout the 1969 season. Only David Piper's

The lull before the storm: the 917 KH #044 of Rodriguez/Kinnunen in front of the JW Automotive pits, with John Horsman in hat in the pit and Ferdinand Piëch in overalls to the rear of the car. The headlights have a protective film to be removed later in the race.

privately-owned 917 KH short-tail appeared at the end of the season at Kyalami with modified rear spoilers.

Crucially, JW Automotive's John Horsman was present at a test with the 917 at the Österreichring in the autumn of 1969, and he is generally credited with making a crucial observation in understanding the inherent instability of the 917. Dead flies were splattered all over the car's nose and windscreen, but there were relatively few on the twin rear spoilers. That suggested that the aerodynamic appendages above each wheel were somehow out of the airstream. With Porsche's permission, Horsman and his crew then made modifications to the 917's bodywork, raising the rear deck and creating the distinctive KH or short-tail shape for what then became known as the 917K. The front end was little changed, but from the central part of the cockpit back, the waistline was raised in a nearly continuous line over and behind the rear wheels. The previous Plexiglass engine cover was banished, leaving the horizontal cooling blower and the air intake pipes in the open air. The first car to appear with this configuration was again David Piper's in the Buenos Aires 1,000-kilometre race. Two weeks later, the works cars first appeared at Daytona in JW Automotive's Gulf livery.

For the Le Mans 24-Hours, the Gulf-JW Automotive cars sported a small spoiler across the car's tail. As this proved to be more stable and not very much slower in a straight line than the long-tail version, JWA used this type of tail for most of the races in 1970. The following year, so-called shark fins were added to its somewhat lowered tail, reducing the drag coefficient by 15 per cent, although the finned tail was only occasionally used by JWA. A pair of fibreglass air boxes were also tried over the air intakes, but these brought no improvement, and were never used in races – and again, we will look at that point later on.

Readily identifiable by the cuts of meat delineated on its bodywork, the 'Pink Pig' 917/20 #001 rests beside the pits during the 1971 Le Mans. To the right is the 917 of van Lennep and Marko and, far right, the 908/2 #026 of Ballot-Léna and Chasseuil.

THE PINK PIG

An interesting crossover between the short- and long-tail versions was the Porsche 917/20, of which only one example was built, and went on to become something of a legend, despite unconvincing results. The design of this car attempted to achieve the low drag factor of the long-tail version without exceeding the length of the short-tail car. Its shape was a joint effort by Porsche and the French company, SERA. The large lateral overhang and the rounded edges of the wheel openings were noteworthy. Liveried in pink, delineated by various cuts of meat as found in a butcher's, the Pink Pig appeared in the Le Mans test weekend in April 1971, brand new and completely untried and, driven by Willi Kauhsen, it won the three-hour race that concluded the three days of practice. In the actual 24-Hour race, it proved to be faster than the wind tunnel tests had suggested, but Kauhsen's co-driver Reinhold Jöst crashed at Arnage in the night while running 5th.

A meaty prospect: the 917/20 'Pink Pig' was a guest of honour at Classic Le Mans, 2018.

Before that, Porsche had already collaborated with SERA on the development of the two long-tail cars that were entered for Le Mans in 1970 by Porsche Salzburg and the Martini Racing team. The latter car had been lent to that organisation, which did not yet represent Porsche officially, because JW Automotive, the Porsche factory's official racing stable, did not trust the long-tails and did not regard them as fully developed. This particular car finished 2nd in the hands of Gérard Larrousse and Willi Kauhsen. However, Porsche felt that the car still needed further development, and for the 1971 Le Mans race, new bodies fabricated in very light polyurethane foam reinforced sandwich were fitted. The front end was modified by the addition of an air-dam, brake cooling ducts, and oil cooler air intakes were modified, as were the front wheel openings and housings. The cockpit ventilation was improved, the Coke-bottle humps over the rear wheels were lowered, and the rear fins were also modified. The handling was so much improved that even John Wyer and team manager John Horsman were persuaded to enter two cars in this configuration. Jackie Oliver lapped the circuit in practice with one of them at 155.66mph (250.457km/h) and was timed on the Mulsanne Straight at an eye-watering 240mph (386km/h). In 1970, a new rule required reducing the tank capacity to 120 litres (31.7 gallons), which could be contained in a single safety tank on the right-hand side of the car. As a general rule, the type of suspension and its geometry directly depend on the tyres' characteristics and dimensions and properties, as was typical racing practice to keep deflections and suspension pick-up points as small as possible. Conventional rubber bushings, as found in road cars, could not be used. As in all Porsche racing cars beginning with the 906, all suspension parts of the 917 were pivoted on Teflon-lined solid spherical bushings and adjustable ball joints. The suspension itself was by transverse wishbones, front and rear, combining light weight with great flexibility in the choice of geometries. Anti-roll bars were used front and rear to control body roll and consequent undesirable wheel camber changes. The 15-inch diameter wheels were magnesium castings carried by titanium hubs. The coil springs were also in titanium, mounted coaxially with the gas-filled shock absorbers. A four-piston brake caliper was developed especially for the 917; the bridges between the two caliper halves were aluminium, but the caliper halves themselves were of a forged titanium alloy. The pads were 18mm thick and the radially vented discs were 28mm front and rear, operated by dual circuits, each with its own master cylinder. The more highly stressed front brakes were additionally cooled by air ducted from the front of the body, with provision to extract hot air from the brakes. No important suspension changes were made for 1970, except for detailed modifications dictated by the development of even wider tyres and by the efforts to improve the straight-line stability. Wheel rim width varied according to the particular race circuit, normal combinations being 10.5 inches at the front and 15 inches rear, or 12 inches front and 17 inches rear. Configuration of the 917 braking system was meticulous. JW Automotive fitted Girling brakes with four-piston calipers to its cars in 1970, and Martini followed suit in 1971. Larger piston calipers were fitted to the Porsche Salzburg cars, which retained ATE brakes, which also had twin titanium calipers, later in aluminium, to which the piston carriers were bolted. Further development led to the use of discs made of copper-chrome alloy. They were lighter than the cast-iron discs but were heat-sensitive so that they could only be used for the less highly stressed rear brakes. They were employed successfully at Daytona in 1970, but a more reliable and cheaper means of increasing the braking efficiency and reducing the weight was to drill the ventilated cast-iron discs in a specific pattern, right through the cooling ducts and vanes. These drilled discs were used throughout the 1971 season, except at Le Mans. The Martini-Porsche 917 #030, built in January 1971, was involved in Teldix electronic anti-lock brake tests, and was entered for the last race of the season, the Austrian 1,000 kilometres at Zeltweg, driven by Helmut Marko and Gérard Larrousse. In practice, the system worked all right, but the drivers found it difficult to adapt their technique to the anti-lock brakes and take advantage of the possibilities they offered to brake much later and enter corners with the brakes still firmly applied. Unfortunately, a tyre failure caused the car's retirement in the race itself. The car was then used for another year for anti-lock brake tests, and in 1975 it was bought by Count Gregorio Rossi, part owner of the Martini-Rossi concern, who had it adapted for road use, driving the car between Paris and his various country estates. Images of it are still regarded with incredulity on social media.

Some of the complexities of the 917s tubular chassis frame are evident with the engine cover removed, as well as the flat-12 engine with horizontal cooling fan and transmission cooling funnels.

FIA regulations for endurance racing required Group 4 Sportscars to carry spare wheels, located above the transmission and exhaust pipes.

FLAT-12

The 4.5-litre flat-12 Type 912 was an air-cooled 4-stroke engine, with twin overhead camshafts per bank of cylinders, fed by fuel injection. The cylinders had the same dimensions as the type 908's 3.0-litre engine, 85mm x 66mm. In view of the crankshaft's torsional vibration, the power take-off was in the middle of the crankshaft where a 32-tooth straight-cut spur gear mashed with a 31-tooth gear driving the power take-off shaft. The diameter of the power output shaft, which resembled a torsion bar, was kept as small as possible. The long crankshaft, which could be the source of considerable torsional vibrations if power was taken off at one end, as is normal practice, was thus turned into two shorter crankshafts with a much higher fundamental vibration period, putting resonance periods outside the speeds reached by the engine.

There were two spark plugs per cylinder, each plug having twin platinum electrodes. The individual cylinder heads were permanent mould castings made of a temperature-resistant aluminium alloy. The four camshafts were spur gear-driven from the central crankshaft gear, the five straight-cut intermediate gears on either side running in needle bearings. The valves were actuated by bucket tappets, and the one-piece camshaft ran in nine 2mm steel-backed bearings. An axial blower made of fibreglass reinforced plastic provided the engine cooling air. Its outside diameter was 330mm (13 inches) and it had 658mm (2.3 inch) blades.

Accessibility to the internals of the 917 KH #008 is good, as demonstrated here with the engine lid up and the windscreen-hinged doors open.

At the Italian World Championship 1,000Km race run at Monza in April 1970, the 917 appeared for the first time with a bigger engine. Its bore had been increased by 1mm to 86mm while the stroke had gone up from 66mm to 70.4mm, giving a total capacity of 4907cc instead of 4494cc. There were no other modifications, but the power went up from 580bhp to 600bhp. None of the other engine specifications was changed. For 1970, a new exhaust system was also developed in which all exhaust pipes from one bank of cylinders merged into a single megaphone tailpipe, in which all individual pipes had exactly the same length, measured from the exhaust valve to the merging point, a set-up that involved a lot of clever plumbing. The cooling blower was driven by bevel gears from the lay shaft running parallel to the crankshaft. At 8,400rpm engine speed, corresponding to peak power, it delivered 2,400 litres (85 cubic feet) of air per second, absorbing 17 horsepower. The engine's maximum power being 580bhp, this represented only 3 per cent of the total power. The engine had twin ignition, the two distributors being located at the front end and at the rear end of the right-hand crankcase half. The dry sump lubrication system comprised seven pumps: one pressure and six scavenger pumps.

The 917's front lid is removed to access the pedal box and clutch and brake fluid reservoirs.

Despite knowing that the era was drawing to a close, at the end of the 1970 season, Ferrari came out with the Type 512M, intending to give the Porsche 917 a run for its money – and with which Jacky Ickx actually beat Jo Siffert's works 917 in a non-championship race. Porsche responded with a slightly larger capacity engine. The bore was increased from 86mm to 86.8mm to raise the capacity to 4998cc, within just 2cc of the allowed limit. The new engine first appeared in April 1971 at the Brands Hatch BOAC 1,000-kilometre race. In addition to the increased bore, there was another important change. The Chromal cylinders were replaced with Nikasil aluminium alloy cylinders, their bores coated with nickel-silicon carbide. Thanks to the reduced friction provided by the new material, the engine produced an extra 30bhp.

Driver's footwell with pedal cluster and fuse board, shot from the passenger seat in the 917 cabin.

In some races, five-speed transmissions were used, in others, four-speeds, and if the box contained five gear sets, there was a lockout in the selector mechanism to prevent the driver inadvertently selecting the wrong gear. All forward gears were Porsche synchronised. The triple plate dry clutch was bolted to the engine power output shaft and the ring gear for the starter was mounted on the clutch housing. A multiplate limited slip differential was used. Its locking factor could be altered, but for most races was set to 75 per cent. The engine and transmission unit was attached to the multi-plate limited-slip by three rubber supports and welded-on gearbox supports. The half-shaft featured two universal joints, one damping doughnut and 100mm long ball splines. Initially, the five-speed gearbox was used in conjunction with a Fichtel and Sachs triple-plate clutch, but in the course of the 1969 season the clutch was changed for a Borg and Beck of a similar type, which was more reliable. The initial weakness of the gearbox housing, which tended to crack, was solved by increasing the number of stiffening webs in the matrix.

Engine cover raised to reveal the 917's flat-12 engine and transmission, triangulated chassis tubing and cool air ducting.

JW AUTOMOTIVE

JW stands for John Wyer and sleeping partner John Willment. The JW Automotive team was headed by Wyer, with John Horsman as Chief Engineer, David Yorke as Team Manager, and Arnold Stafford (former 500cc racer) as supply source manager.

The ink on the contract making John Wyer manager of Porsche racing for 1970 was barely dry when Wyer was stunned to find out his most significant opponent,

Driver change, as Derek Bell prepares to take over from Jo Siffert in the JW Gulf 917 LH during the 1971 Le Mans 24-Hours. Race director John Horsman looks on as mechanics tape the race numbers securely, but the car retired in the 18th hour whilst lying 6th due to a gearbox oil leak.

in addition to the usual Italian rivals, would be Porsche itself. Austrian Porsche Konstruktionen, known familiarly as Porsche Salzburg, was the team of Louise Piëch, whose son Ferdinand (his grandfather's namesake, and Ferry Porsche's nephew) headed the factory racing programme. Despite Porsche Salzburg's status as an independent team, familial ties ensured that Frau Piëch would receive new development updates as soon as, and sometimes before, Wyer's official factory team. For most of 1970, this did not particularly matter. Porsche Salzburg won Le Mans, but Wyer's Gulf Porsches dominated the season. The 917 won every major race entered save one: the Sebring 12-Hours, during which a new and hastily developed larger front hub bearing failed on all cars entered. A Ferrari 512S aimed at challenging Porsche in the 5.0-litre class emerged victorious in southern Florida. In 1971, 917 #019 was entered by the Martini Racing Team, the new name Louise Piëch gave her organisation in line with sponsorship from Martini & Rossi. Again, the Piëch team took Le Mans, the winning car driven by Helmut Marko and Gijs van Lennep, and sporting numerous experimental features, including a magnesium tube frame. And again, Wyer's Gulf-JWA Porsche team dominated elsewhere and won the championship for the second consecutive year. Marko and van Lennep raced 917 #019 three times in 1971, although the results were not as fortuitous as they enjoyed at Le Mans. At the Daytona 24 Hours, with Rudi Lins as third driver, a crash put the car out on the 462nd of 688 laps, while at the Monza 1,000Kms a throttle linkage was the culprit mid-race. Engine failure put 917 #019 out at Spa, its last race.

THE GIJS VAN LENNEP INTERVIEW

Two-times Le Mans winner for Porsche, Gijs van Lennep's glittering career as a sports car driver also included a spell in F1. But it is mainly as a Porsche racer that he is best known and, indeed, he is a Brand Ambassador, representing the company at events like Rennsport Reunion.

I have sampled his prowess at the Abbeville circuit – from the passenger seat – on several occasions, handling exotic 911 RSs belonging to Belgian Porsche collector Johan Dirickx. Harnessed and helmeted, I have been dazzled by Gijs's prowess behind the wheel. Power on, the wide-arched 3.0 RSR hangs mid-corner in suspended animation, its broad slicks cleaving the asphalt. Then it flicks straight and hurtles off along the straight, crisp shifts modulating the ear-splitting barp. It is poetry in the hands of the Targa Florio and double Le Mans winner, and clearly, the fire still burns. Over lunch in the circuit's pavilion, Gijs (pronounced Ghys) recalls the highs and lows of his fifteen-year career that took him from karts to Formula 1, and a handful of Le Mans podiums for Porsche.

Gijs van Lennep spent most of his racing career driving a variety of Porsches, culminating in victories at Le Mans in 1971 and 1976, and the final Targa Florio in 1973.

A spry figure, still sporting his distinctive orange crash helmet, Gijs has worn well: born a Netherlands nobleman in 1942, he was taken to the seaside aged six – not to the beach but to Zandvoort's inaugural F1 Grand Prix in 1948. 'My father was a sportsman who loved shooting, rowing, a bit of boxing and tennis, and he took me to the first Dutch Grand Prix. I saw all of them bar two, when I was racing somewhere else.' Gijs got started early: 'When I was four, I had a pedal car but pedalling didn't make it go fast enough so I pushed it with my feet to go quicker.' Self-propulsion gave way to mechanical power when the Van Lennep brothers got hold of their mother's Fiat 500. 'My brother was five years older than me, and when I was nine, he taught me to use the clutch and gearshift.' Gijs was naturally adept mechanically. 'From the age of twelve I had mopeds and took them apart and put them together again to make them quicker, up to 40km/h, though I was not allowed to ride them in public at that age.'

The writing was on the wall; clearly a career in motoring competition beckoned, and Gijs built his first kart aged fifteen.

> *The local bicycle shop sold go-karts imported from America, though I built karts to my own design. I had my first race in 1957 on a cinder track with a 100cc motorbike engine, and I was quickest because I had bigger wheels than the ones from America. The engine seized just before the start, and I was presented with a miner's lamp as a consolation prize because I was the unluckiest guy that day, and that was my first trophy.*

A couple of years later, Gijs tackled a sprint at Zandvoort in his mother's Fiat 600 and rolled it in the slalom. 'My father was in the stands with his friends, and he remarked dryly, "The roof of my wife's car is a little lower than it was before." Naturally enough, my mother wasn't very impressed.' Next came a Beetle, and soon enough, its 1200cc flat-4 was replaced by a 75bhp 356 motor courtesy of friends from the local car mechanics college. At about the same time, he began attending Rob Slotemaker's skid school at Zandvoort.

'I think one of the reasons I'm still alive today is because of the car control I learned at Slotemaker's,' speculates Gijs. 'As a sixteen-year-old, I always won the slalom in every car I drove. If you go sideways, it's a nice sensation to control the

Gijs van Lennep on the Nürburgring during the 1966 1,000Kms, in the Racing Team Holland 906, finishing 7th overall.

car, but it's nothing to do with racing. But if you come upon oil on the track, you have to react and stay on the road.' Gijs knows only too well the implications; ironically, Slotemaker was killed in 1979 when his Camaro spun on oil and crashed into the car of a doctor attending another accident. In the mid-1960s, when Slotemaker was a successful race and rally driver, his school cars were BMWs.

> *We would drive the circuit in the wet, right on the limit, with full opposite lock at 130km/h, holding the slide on the throttle. If it is more slippery you dump the clutch, but then the slide drops and you have to turn in very quickly otherwise you lose it. It's really difficult, and if you are over the limit you are gone.*

His first World Championship race was with his brother at the Nürburgring 1,000kms in 1966, of which Gijs drove five of six hours.

> *There were thirteen Carrera 6s, and I finished 1st in class and 7th overall. It started raining one lap before the end when I was running 3rd in class, and I used my experience at the skid school to climb a couple of places higher.*

In the ditch

In 1967, Gijs mostly drove a 911R, but suffered a bad crash at Spa in a 906.

> *It was just pre-safety belts, and I pitted to have the rollbar adjusted. Then I went out again, but they hadn't fastened the engine cover properly and one of the catches broke as I went left up to Malmedy. I just changed to 5th gear and the hood came off and it was like an aircraft taking off. I spun, but there was no guardrail or anything, and the track was about a metre higher than the surrounding land and the car carried on going for about 200m. I dropped out and fell into a ditch and at first, they couldn't find me. I broke only one little bone on my first finger, and I had a lot of sand in my eyes underneath my helmet. My boots were gone, my trousers were gone, but I was bloody lucky as I should have been dead. A lot of my racing friends killed themselves at that time; between 1966 and '76, I lost a lot of mates. That's the other side of racing.*

The Porsche connection began in earnest in 1968 when Huschke von Hanstein hired him as a works driver for the season-opening Daytona and Sebring races, partnering Udo Schutz.

> *He hit a rabbit at Sebring, and it broke the suspension. He was a big guy, quick, but his hands were too strong, and after 90 minutes, there was no gearshift left. The gearbox of a Porsche is fantastic, provided you don't jerk it, and it lasts forever. But in this case, there was nothing left!*

Gijs drove AAW's Porsche 917 at Le Mans in 1970, sharing with David Piper. They had run as high as 3rd for a few hours, but first Piper crashed, and Gijs went off with a high-speed blow-out at Hunaudiéres in the repaired car. It was another memorable moment:

In '70, when Richard Attwood and Hans Herrmann won, we were already six minutes in front of them at 11.00 o'clock at night, but then it started raining, and David spun it, and he was in the pits for three-quarters of an hour for repairs. I took over, and on the straight in 5th gear at 320km/h, bang, a tyre exploded. I held tight, keeping it in a straight line – but then you don't know how fast is fast. From 340–350km/h on the straight, it seems like an hour before you stop. Eventually, I pulled it onto the grass.

The following year Gijs drove the Martini-liveried 4.9-litre 917s in the World Championship for Makes, partnered by Dr Helmut Marko, and they took a memorable victory at Le Mans. It was the last year of the traditional Le Mans start, where drivers sprinted across the track to their cars, and the speed record down the Mulsanne Straight was broken – 236mph (380km/h). A record 33 Porsches were entered, and the Van Lennep/Marko car not only won outright, it won its class and the Index of Performance, and they set a distance record that stands to this day: 3,315.20 miles (4,769.923km) at 138.13mph. Gijs said:

It was beautiful to drive, though I wouldn't have said that in '69 when the 917 was very scary. Porsche was very clever with aerodynamics and tried all sorts of configurations. We were in one of the Martini cars [Jöst/Kauhsen drove the Pink Pig, and Elford/Larrousse crewed the other Martini-entered 917] against John Wyer's Gulf cars. There were three KH short-tails – we had one of them – and three LH long-tails. We were the lightest car, but the long-tails did 370km/h on the straight, and we did 350. Every pit stop, they put new bulbs in, and we won, though as a Martini car, the JW Automotive squad didn't like that very much. That was my first great victory.

Added drama from the Martini Racing pit crew as the van Lennep/Marko 917 KH heads out during its victorious run in the 1971 Le Mans 24-Hours. Porsche Technical Development Director Helmuth Bott (in blazer) points the way, and in the background are Peter Falk and Hans-Dieter Dechent.

The champagne corks are about to pop for 1971 Le Mans winners Gijs van Lennep and Helmut Marko, with Martini Racing Team director Hans-Dieter Dechent on the left about to do the honours. They set a new distance record, covering 5,335km (3,315 miles), which lasted until 2010. Dr Marko has, in recent years, been an advisor to the Red Bull F1 Team.

Gijs mimes the posture required to hold a 917 on the banking at Daytona:

> *It was scary, and the steering was so heavy you couldn't sit in a normal position. The car was always wanting to go up the banking, so I had my right arm braced against the seat with my left elbow jammed between my knees, holding the bottom of the steering wheel. You didn't do anything but just hold onto the car, though you were aching quite a bit. It was flat out, of course, and the car had very good balance, but the thing you were afraid of, what happened to Vic Elford, was a flat tyre, and then you were gone, there was so much G-force. Vic got a flat tyre and went up to the top of the banking from the grass and back again.*

Incoming rule changes for 1972 excluded big bangers like the 5.0-litre 917s and Ferrari 512s, forcing Porsche to focus its energies on the Martini-liveried 911 Carrera RSR. Gijs brought one of these swollen-arched beasts to 4th at Le Mans in 1973, partnered by Herbert Müller, following home two Matras and a Ferrari prototype and heading a trio of 908s.

> *The big boss said: 'You go as quick as you can, all the way, just look after the gearbox nicely and everything else will take care of itself. The rest you go like hell.' We were confident it wouldn't break so we pushed it all the way, and I've never been so tired in my life!*

That year, Gijs and Herbie Müller also won the Targa Florio in the final running of the Sicilian classic as a Championship race. Gijs had become a Targa talent, having driven the event from 1970 to 1973. Gijs recalls:

> *The first year, I drove the 908 for the Finnish team with Hans Laine. That was before he killed himself – and we finished 4th overall behind the factory 908s but ahead of the Alfa. Not long before the finish, I came into the pits for a tyre change, and Laine went out, and about 15km before the finish, he lost his left front wheel. If you go faster, it goes*

The Le Mans 1974-winning Martini Racing crew of Herbert Müller, Norbert Singer and Gijs van Lennep share a joke in the pits.

> *up onto three wheels, and he was doing 250km/h on the straight and driving on the disc on the corners! He made it back to the pits like that, and they sent him out again with another wheel – and we still finished 4th!*

In 1976 Gijs teamed up with Jacky Ickx to drive one of the two new mid-engined spaceframe 936 Spyders to victory.

> *We had the 2.1-litre turbo engine, the same as in the 911 RSR turbo, and we were fastest in practice. If you drive behind a 936, you notice that everything glows red-hot in the back because the turbo is spinning at 80,000rpm, and it's red-hot all the time. The 936 was more subtle to drive than a 917, a little easier and a lighter car. But in fact, the 917 was fantastic and drove like a go-kart, which you wouldn't believe for such a big car.*

Historically, Gijs is one of fourteen Dutch Grand Prix drivers – he had eight F1 races – and since then has been scheduled to drive a Porsche 550 Spyder in certain historic events, including the Mille Miglia and Classic Le Mans, with Dutch F1 star Jan Lammers who also won for Jaguar at La Sarthe in 1988. 'The 550 Spyder is a nice car,' comments Gijs, 'but it is dangerous even though it is only 130bhp, and not so quick at 180km/h. There is nothing to it, it is small and light and not very structurally rigid. It's easy through the corners, though, and nice to drive.'

Nevertheless, Gijs is careful about what events he agrees to do, critical of barging tactics that cause accidents and destroy valuable classics.

> *I pick and choose what I do. You don't go 100 per cent, you drive 90 per cent. I have very good eyes still. My eyes are fantastic, and I can see really sharply and also in the dark. I shoot, and I like to play golf a lot to keep fit, although I still smoke a bit.*

Today, he is a freelance instructor, working for old comrade Ben Pon's business – the Dutch Porsche importer – teaching the Porsche and Audi Quattro driving experiences at Zandvoort. It is no surprise to find him sideways in a 911 today. 'You go mad as you get older. Cornering is okay, but late braking goes off a bit. I like to drive in the snow. Again, that's down to car control, so I am still quite quick, – as he amply demonstrated on Abbeville's tight turns. 'I was very lucky to drive a lot of Porsches. In fact, I still do, and that is very nice.'

THE 1970 RACE SEASON

Maintaining tradition, the season began in Florida with the Daytona 24-Hours and the Sebring 12-Hours. Both events should have been a 917 walkover, but although Siffert/Redman and Rodriguez/Kinnunen scored a one-two at Daytona, Ferrari had in the meantime sorted the 512S suspension, and Andretti/Merzario got pole at Sebring. The Autodelta squad looked like it meant business too. However, the leading Siffert/Redman 917 was delayed by an electrical problem, the Herrmann/Lins car suffered an over-revved engine, and Vic Elford was sidelined when a Fiat pulled up right in front of him whilst waiting for a spinner to rejoin the race, and the 917 was badly damaged. Thus, the Ferrari 512 of Giunti/Vaccarella/Andretti came 1st, followed just 22 seconds later by the Solar Productions 908 driven by Steve McQueen and Peter Revson. The actor was a dab hand at racing, hence going on to make the acclaimed movie *Le Mans*.

Brands Hatchings

Back at Brands Hatch for a very wet BOAC 1,000km race, the entry was headed by cars from Porsche, Ferrari and Matra, backed up by some good Group 6 3.0-litre cars as well. In recognition of the fact that the cars covered way more than 500 miles during the six-hour race, it was renamed the 1,000kms, falling in line with the majority of races in the Championship too. There were a few non-starters, including Piper's 917, whose engine had swallowed a stone, with dire results, and the Martini 908, which Tony Dean crashed heavily in practice. The race was scheduled to start at midday, and half-an-hour beforehand, the cars were allowed three exploratory laps. When the flag dropped, it was Elford away first, pushing the white Austrian 917 into the lead ahead of Ickx' Ferrari 512 S, Siffert and Brabham in the Matra-Simca V12. The torrential rain was really going to play havoc with ignition systems, and one of the first to suffer was the 908 of Van Lennep, which

Photographer Roger Dixon captured the spectacularly tail-sliding Gulf 917 #016 of Pedro Rodriguez coming out of Druids Hairpin on his way to winning the rain-drenched 1970 BOAC 1,000Kms with Leo Kinnunen co-driving.

stopped at the end of the first lap to be dried out. It ran perfectly from then on, eventually climbing up to 5th place overall.

On lap 2, Ickx took the Ferrari past Elford into the lead, and then Pedro Rodriguez' JW 917 was seen to overtake several cars under the yellow flag and was black-flagged for a warning, which he ignored for a couple of laps. Eventually signalled in by his own pit crew, he was duly reprimanded by the clerk of the course and set out from the pits very sideways with the bit now firmly between his teeth.

Siffert had probably also been affected by an accident, as his 917 picked up a flat tyre and pitted for a quick pit stop just before Rodriguez came in, but it dropped him down the field. The leading Ferrari was not going well because Ickx was having trouble seeing out due to a defective windscreen wiper, and he made a couple of stops for new blades before finally stopping for a new wiper motor. So, it was Elford out in the lead once more, with Amon challenging him and all the while Rodriguez was making excellent progress, fully justifying his reputation as one of the best wet weather drivers. By lap 15, he was up into 3rd place. And meanwhile, Amon was all the time trying to get ahead of Elford's 917.

He finally succeeded on lap 16 and, two laps later, Elford was relegated to 3rd place by the presence of Rodriguez. On lap 20, the Mexican took the lead by diving on the inside at Paddock. Immediately he started to pull out a lead by lapping five seconds faster than anyone else. By lap 30, Rodriguez was over half a lap ahead of Elford, and Brabham was up to 3rd with the Matra, leading the Group 6 category ahead of Siffert, and Merzario, who had taken over early from Amon, Pescarolo and Bonnier.

Braving incessant rain during the 1970 BOAC 1,000Kms, the Porsche Salzburg Konstruktionen 917 KH #023 of Vic Elford and Denny Hulme overtakes the Ferrari 512S of Chris Amon and Arturo Merzario coming out of Druids Hairpin. This 917 finished 2nd, the Ferrari came 5th.

By lap 50 of this 235-lap, 1,000km race, the leading order was Rodriguez, Elford, Siffert, Brabham, Attwood, Amon, Servoz-Gavin, Bonnier, Larrousse and Van Lennep. By 100 laps, the rain seemed to be abating, and Rodriguez had moved two laps ahead of his team-mates Siffert and Redman, with Elford and Hulme 3rd, although the New Zealander did not have a very high opinion of a Porsche 917 in the wet. Ferrari were now out of the hunt with the Amon/Merzario car 4th, but six laps down. In 5th was the steadily-driven Attwood/Herrmann car, with van Lennep/Laine moving the AAW 908 up to 6th place to head to the Group 6 class, with Beltoise/Brabham in pursuit. The field was thinning, with Blatzheim rolling his 907 spectacularly at South Bank Bend.

The first 100 laps had taken almost three hours, which was expected to be half distance, but speeds were still down although the track was starting to dry. At 3.24pm, Rodriguez came in after his marathon stint and handed over to Leo Kinnunen, who now had a big responsibility on his hands. During the next period, Siffert closed to within 30 seconds of Kinnunen, while the Elford/Hulme car held station in 3rd place. The race had speeded up. Merzario, who had been going well in the wet, was having to fight for his 4th place and was overtaken by Attwood and then Van Lennep. He was summoned in, and Amon then took over, soon moving the car back to 5th place. He then caught Redman on the road, though he was actually four laps ahead, and the pair engaged in a spirited battle. This ended suddenly when Redman lost control of the 917 at Westfield, left the track, clouted the bank, and was out of the race. At the 200-lap mark, it was still a Porsche 917 trio at the front, but with the Rodriguez/Kinnunen car five laps ahead of Hulme/Elford,

The winning JW Automotive Gulf 4.5-litre 917 KH of Pedro Rodriguez and Leo Kinnunen passes inside the Martini Racing 3.0-litre 908/2 of Gérard Larrousse and Gerhard Koch, which came 6th in the rain-sodden BOAC 1,000Kms at Brands Hatch, 1970.

with Attwood/Herrmann a further three laps down. The van Lennep/Laine car was now up to 4th ahead of Amon/Merzario, and the Koch/Larrousse 908 was just ahead of the Bonnier Lola T70. Chris Craft had handed his Porsche 910 back to Alain de Cadenet, who promptly spun and then retired with a broken gearbox. The closing minutes were kept alive by Amon stopping for fuel and dropping back to 5th. At the end of six-and-three-quarter hours of gruelling racing, Rodriguez crossed the line to take the chequered flag, no fewer than five laps ahead of the two Salzburg 917s. The Van Lennep/Laine 908 took a fine 4th place, just ahead of the Amon/Merzario Ferrari. And then came Koch/Larrousse, Bonnier/Wisell, while another Porsche 910, driven by Beuttler and Gold was 11th, ahead of the Brabham/Beltoise Matra. The BOAC 1000 was a sweeping success for Porsche, and the Gulf-JW Automotive cars were more than admirably backed up by the Porsche Salzburg team.

TYPE 917 MAJOR SUCCESSES

1969
1st, 3rd, Zeltweg 1,000Kms
1st, Kyalami 9-Hours
1970
1st, Daytona 24-Hours
1st, BOAC 1,000Kms
1st, Monza 1,000Kms
1st, Swedish Grand Prix
1st, 5th, Spa-Francorchamps 1,000Kms
1st, 2nd, Le Mans 24-Hours
1st, Zeltweg 1,000Kms
1st, Watkins Glen 6-Hours
1st, International Championship for Makes
1971
1st, Buenos Aires 1,000Kms
1st, Daytona 24-Hours
1st, Sebring 12-Hours
1st, 2nd, Monza 1,000Kms
1st, 4th, Spa-Francorchamps 1,000Kms
1st, 2nd, Le Mans 24-Hours
5th, Nürburgring 1,000Kms
1st, Austrian Grand Prix, Zeltweg (Österreichring)
1st, Paris 1,000Kms (Montlhéry)
1st, International Championship for Makes

In the Ardennes

The Monza 1,000kms staged on 25 April was won by Pedro Rodriguez/Leo Kinnunen in a 4.5-litre Gulf 917. But 5.0-litre Ferrari 512s filled the next three places, followed by two Matras and an Alfa T33. It was a close-fought race, and clearly the Porsches were not going to have the clean-up that may have been envisaged at the start of the season. The circus moved north to the Ardennes.

Most of the familiar names were on the entry list for the Spa-Francorchamps 1,000kms, headed by the JW Automotive 917s of Siffert/Redman and Rodriguez/Kinnunen and the Porsche Salzburg 917s of Elford/Ahrens and Attwood/Herrmann. There were two privately-entered 917s in the hands of Juergen Neuhaus/Helmut Kelleners representing the Gesipa Race Team, and a yellow car for Hans Laine/Gijs van Lennep from the Finnish AAW team. There were two Martini 908s for Larrousse/Lins and Dechent/Marko, and a 2.0-litre 907 for Blatzheim/Kraus. Post-Monza and the Targa Florio, it seemed that Ferrari had gained fresh impetus, and Jacky Ickx was paired with John Surtees (who then currently held the Spa F1 lap record with a V12 Honda) to drive the 512S. Peter Schetty and Arturo Merzario were in another 512, Ignazio Giunti and Nino Vaccarella in the third one, and Ecurie Francorchamps brought along a customer 512 S for Derek Bell and Hugues de Fierlant. There were also several Lola T70s and Chevron B8s and B16s amongst the entry, plus seven 911s, no less.

Tyre creep

The JW Automotive Team were having trouble with their tyres creeping sideways on the rims and letting the air out. Siffert had two go down and Redman one, so Rodriguez was told to take it easy, which he did – at 3 minutes 27 seconds, which was inside the existing lap record. The Ferraris were using narrower rims, and their Firestones were behaving. Both the JW Gulf 917s were using 5.0-litre engines, and the team had the Daytona-winning car with a 4.5-litre engine present as a training car. The bigger engines, with their vastly superior mid-range power and torque were really coming into their own on the brutally fast circuit, but the Porsche-Salzburg team were not so happy. The Elford/Ahrens 917 did the first practice session with a 4.5-litre engine installed, but it would not handle properly. On the Saturday afternoon, ahead of the race, the JW Gulf mechanics had got over their 917s' tyre problems by metal-spraying the wheel-rim shoulders. Rodriguez really

Jo Siffert and Derek Bell came 2nd in the 1971 Spa-Francorchamps 1,000Kms, a scant 0.4 seconds behind winners Rodriguez/Oliver. Behind them is the Müller/Herzog Ferrari 512M and the yellow and green 908/2 KH 326 of Claude Ballot-Léna and Guy Chasseuil, which came 5th.

began to demonstrate the pace and power potential of the 5.0-litre engine, lapping in the 3m 24s bracket. Though Surtees did most of the driving of the leading Ferrari, even when it got going properly, he was not in the same class as Rodriguez and the 5.0-litre Porsche. A more aerodynamic tail was fitted to the Rodriguez car, with the valley behind the engine filled in and a very low angle spoiler installed, and he went out and did 3m 21.2 seconds, and then 3m 19.8 seconds. Ickx, in the leading Ferrari, could only log 3m 24.4s, which gave him third fastest, because Siffert had got down to 3m 23.9 seconds: all these quick times on the 'old' 14.120km (8.77 miles) circuit were making the two-year-old lap record look very slow. Relatively. Even the private 917 of Kelleners/Neuhaus got below the record with 3m 29.7s. The pace of these 5.0-litre 917s was shattering. Meanwhile, the Elford/Ahrens Salzburg 917 had been fitted with a 5.0-litre engine during the morning, but it still would not handle correctly, and a broken chassis frame tube was suspected, most of practice being spent pumping 80lb per square inch of air pressure into the frame and looking for leaks. The break turned out to be at the front of the chassis frame, and it was repaired ahead of the race.

The two blue-and-orange Gulf 917s took off together and circulated in close company – so close that Siffert and Rodriguez touched door handles going through Eau Rouge, possibly the most daunting corner on the circuit. It looked as though they had already got the race sewn up. But Ickx got the Ferrari in between them after Rodriguez had taken the lead. The rest were left behind, as these three erstwhile Grand Prix drivers demonstrated their superiority. Both 917s had headlights blazing, clearing a path through the back-markers they were lapping, and the slower cars certainly knew when they had gone past, being knocked sideways by the draught as the three leaders went by at close on 200mph (320km/h) along the 3-mile-long Masta straight (given the notorious Masta kink in the middle) down to Stavelot. The old Grand Prix record went by the board, even while the circuit was drying out, and the pace got faster and faster. By rights, Elford should have been up there with them, but having done very little practice – and that with a car that did not handle properly – he now had to settle himself into the high-speed circuit.

After fourteen laps, Siffert called into the pits, less than an hour into the race. The JW Gulf pit's gravity feed system did not work too well, and it was a slow stop. The following lap, Rodriguez and Ickx came in together, and the refuelling system for the Gulf car worked better; it was away before the Ferrari, which was being refuelled from old-fashioned churns because somebody misinterpreted the regulations and thought pressure or gravity refuelling was not allowed. The race panned out with all the stars leading at some point, mostly gaining and losing the lead during fuel stops. After 4hrs 09m, the Siffert/Redman 917 was the clear victor, by

2m 30s, from the Ickx/Surtees Ferrari 512 S, and Elford/Ahrens a lap down in 3rd. The Giunti/Vaccarella Ferrari was 4th, followed by the Laine/van Lennep 917 and Attwood/Herrmann 917. The 3.0-litre 908s of Larrousse/Lins and Dechent/Marko were ninth and 11th, the 910 of L' Aimie/Nelson 12th and the 2.0-litre 907 of Blatzheim/Kraus 13th, with Brits Paul Vestey and Peter Sadler 14th in their 910. Amazingly, just a handful of seconds separated the latter quintet after 1,000 kilometres' racing on one of the most demanding circuits in the world.

Spa-Ring Partners

In the wake of the better races in the Championship – the Monza 1,000 kilometres, the Targa Florio and the Spa 1,000 kilometres – the long-distance racing scene looked set for another good race at the Nürburgring. Although Porsche had won the previous three races, there were all the signs that Ferrari was becoming a serious threat with its 512 S Spyders, and the battles between these 5.0-litre sports-prototypes were hotting up. All the indications were that Ferrari had Porsche on the run, lacking little in performance and proving remarkably reliable, and with Ickx and Surtees the recognised *Ringmeisters*, the ADAC 1000-kilometre race held great promise. In addition, Alfa Romeo was taking the races seriously, as they had done in the Targa Florio with their T-33 3.0-litre V8 prototypes and, like the two 5.0-litre sports car teams, they did a lot of pre-race testing. With the weather bright and sunny, by the time the competitors gathered for the opening practice on Friday before race day, the anticipated battle was fading fast. Porsche made the sort of technical manoeuvre that Mercedes-Benz was wont to do, which completely demoralised the opposition. They had had a private test day and run the 5.0-litre 917s back-to-back with the 3.0-litre 908/3 Spyders, and were soon satisfied that the Targa Florio cars were the best bet. While a 917 could be driven adequately fast around the Nürburgring, it required a lot of physical effort, whereas the 908/3 Spyders could be driven hard indefinitely. In addition, there was the bonus of better fuel consumption from the 3.0-litre engine, which would cut out one pit stop compared with the 917. Ahead of practice, they made it known that the improved fuel consumption was going to be a vital factor, apart from

Crowds of Sicilian enthusiasts cram the roadside as Brian Redman rushes by, keeping a clean line in the distinctively liveried JW-Gulf 908/3 #010 on its way to victory in the 1970 Targa Florio.

The Porsche Salzburg Konstruktionen 908/3 #008 of Vic Elford and Kurt Ahrens won the 1970 Nürburgring 1,000Kms, 5min 13.6sec ahead of JW-Gulf's Rodriguez/Kinnunen 908/3 #011.

the lower fatigue factor for the drivers. They allocated two of the Targa Florio 908s to the JW Gulf team and two to the Salzburg Porsche squad. The drivers were Elford/Ahrens, Siffert/Redman, Rodriguez/Kinnunen and Attwood/Herrmann.

The 908/3 had the smooth-fronted but slab-sided open-top Spyder bodies, all to the same specification, a stockier look compared with the 908/2 Flounder, with the 3.0-litre flat-8 air-cooled engine mounted well forward in the chassis and the gearbox between the engine and the final drive unit. The markings on the Gulf blue cars were the same as in Sicily, with two orange arrows on the Siffert/Redman car and just one arrow on the left-hand side of the Rodriguez/Kinnunen car. The Porsche Salzburg team had simpler hues, white for the Elford/Ahrens car and yellow for the Attwood/Herrmann car. The Gulf JW cars ran Firestone tyres, but the Salzburg Porsches were on Goodyears. So much for the pre-race strategy.

The result was a victory for Vic Elford and Kurt Ahrens, followed by Hans Herrmann and Richard Attwood, both crews in Salzburg Konstruktionen cars. Ferraris were 3rd and 4th, with Larrousse and Marko 5th in a Martini team 908, Lins/Kauhsen 6th in another Martini 908, Koch/von Wendt in a 908, Greger/Leuse in a 908, and in 9th, Wicky/Cabral in a 907. Formidable stuff.

Le Mans: achieving the pinnacle

The pundits tend to be scathing about the 1970 Le Mans race; the traditional start where the drivers sprinted across the track at flag-fall, leapt into their cars that were all lined up in echelon, rather than grid-fashion, and sped away, was now banned. From a perfectly sensible safety point of view, the driver was obliged to be strapped into his race seat and go on the green light. The idea of the second driver performing the cross-track sprint and switching on the car's external ignition key was abandoned, though there was still a flag to signal the start, waved on this occasion by Dr Ferry Porsche, with a relay of flag marshals opposite the lined-up cars to convey the start signal.

The first thirteen cars in the line-up were big Group 5 sports cars, most of them 5.0-litres, the first 3.0-litre prototype being the Matra 650 Spyder of Brabham and Cevert. The 5.0-litre 917 coupés were driven by Elford/Ahrens, Siffert/Redman, Rodriguez/Kinnunen, and the 4.5-litre 917 coupés were driven by Hobbs/Hailwood, van Lennep/Piper, Attwood/Herrmann, Larrousse/Kauhsen. The opposition consisted of no fewer than eleven Ferrari 512 S, including four Factory cars for Ickx/Schetty, Vaccarella/Giunti, Bell/ Peterson, Merzario/Regazzoni, Scuderia Fillipinetti 512s for Müller/Parkes, Bonnier Wisell and Manfredini/Moretti.

At the start, Elford and Siffert ran away from everyone, and none of the Ferraris ever looked like being a challenge. The event's title, the Grand Prix of Endurance, looked most apt. On the third lap, the leaders started lapping the slower 911s while the complete absence of Renault-Alpines was also noticeable. The race had barely been going for 30 minutes when the rain began, and what had started as a not-very-exciting race now became positively dreary. The big cars were running for less than one hour before having to stop for fuel, and Elford was timed at 206mph (331km/h) along the Mulsanne Straight. It looked as if it was going to be a 5.0-litre Porsche walkover, but that was not the case. Rodriguez had his 917 engine blow up, Siffert retired in the biggest cloud of smoke imaginable, and Elford's 917 broke its engine disastrously. It was raining extremely hard, and cars were spinning off in all directions. Hailwood crashed the 4.5-litre

Driver swap for Vic Elford and Kurt Ahrens in their Porsche Salzburg Konstruktionen 917 LH #042. Having set fastest time in practice, they retired in the 17th hour while lying 4th. Dr Bott stands arm outstretched at the front of the car, while Ferdinand Piëch observes the action, standing at second right.

Gulf 917, while the Larrousse/Kauhsen 917 was leaking oil, and during the heavy rain in the early hours, the leading 917 of Attwood/Herrmann was misfiring very badly with water getting into the air intakes. Of the 51 starters, only 19 were running at midday on Sunday, and many of those were very sick.

But the red short-tail 917 (917-#023) of Attwood and Herrmann was running well, while the long-tailed 917 Hippie car (917-#043) of Larrousse and Kauhsen was 2nd and the 908 Spyder (908-#050) of Lins/Marko was 3rd. Due to the appalling conditions during the night, the average speed was low, and many cars were behind the minimum distance schedule. And when a major cloudburst flooded the pit area, the cars were reduced to 50mph or less, such was the lack of visibility and risk of aquaplaning. The privately entered 908 3.0-litre Spyder of Lins/Marko was in command of the Index of Performance, and even the Sonauto 914/6 of Guy Chasseuil and Claud Ballot-Lena lay 6th. The Solar Productions film company of Steve McQueen had entered his 908 as a serious entry driven by Linge and Williams, and they had unobtrusively been filming the action as they raced, with cameras mounted fore and aft, built into the car. A long delay earlier in the race, when the starter motor failed, put them out of the running, and stops for camera loading put them too far back to be classified, but nevertheless they were still running at the end of the 24 hours. Some of the footage found its way into McQueen's epic take on the race in 1971. As Sunday afternoon turned out bright and sunny, a vast crowd stood patiently drying in the sun, waiting for the finish, which was as traditional as the start, back in the day. The race over, as each survivor of the gruelling 24 hours crossed the finishing line, the co-driver normally clambered onto the car, together with mechanics and pit staff, and the cars stopped at the top of the pit straight where they were turned around and sent back in front of the 20,000 or so spectators opposite the pits.

From the first to the last car, the crowd applauded, and all those involved soaked up the joy, regardless of what position the cars finished in. The gendarmes tried in vain to control the crowds that surged onto the track, to acclaim the winners, who were up on a platform with flowers and champagne. Entralled fans milled around the surviving cars, which they had watched from afar for 24 hours. It was chaotic, but it was joyous, an appropriate ending to the Le Mans 24- Hours. In consequence of the chaos from the previous year, when Ickx beat Herrmann by 100 yards and the crowd got out of control, such was the excitement and enthusiasm, a new post-race ending was planned for 1970, about which the public were not informed until the last minute. As the cars finished their last lap, they were impounded in a guarded enclosure and the winning drivers put in the back of a lorry and sent off for a lap of honour. It was actually a lap of dishonour, because the lorry looked like a dust cart setting out to pick up the rubbish. There was no public presentation and no sign of the cars, so a very disillusioned public just went home, feeling thoroughly cheated, having been deceived at the start and robbed of all the excitement at

Conditions were far from ideal during the running of the 1970 Le Mans 24-Hours, with visibility down to virtually zero due to spray, as experienced by Attwood and Herrmann in the winning 917 KH #023.

The 917 LH #042 of Vic Elford and Kurt Ahrens takes the Ford Chicane during the 1970 Le Mans 24-Hours; having started from pole, it retired in the 17th hour while running 4th due to engine failure.

the finish. It was said that the traditional start and finish of the Le Mans race gave a human dimension to a purely mechanical affair, and the spectators felt they had been misled. And whilst it was the first outright Le Mans victory for Porsche, it was at some expense, and it was not a very joyous one, because the whole race had been like the weather: cold, wet and miserable. Porsche won by sheer weight of numbers, and they also won the Index of Performance, the Sports Car category, the Prototype category and the GT category. In fact, they won everything that it was possible to win. However, it could have been observed better.

HEADING STATESIDE

Next up, the endurance racing entourage shipped over to the United States for the Watkins Glen Six Hours on 11 July. Heading to Upper New York State for the endurance race held on the short but fast Watkins Glen circuit, the entry comprised Group 6 Sports-Prototypes, Group 5 Sports cars and Group 4 GT cars. It was significant in that it witnessed the final demise of the 3.0-litre Group 6 cars, which the FIA had been pushing to exclude and, since Porsche and Ferrari had each built 25 cars to comply with the FIA regulations for Group 5 sports cars, the days of the 3.0-litre Sports-Prototypes were numbered – apart from an occasional race such as the Targa Florio and the Nürburgring, where their alacrity and nimbleness was very effective. In spite of having to carry road-going equipment such as a spare wheel and use a full-sized windscreen, the 5.0-litre Group 5 Sports Cars were too fast and too powerful for the 3.0-litre prototypes to match.

The 1970 Le Mans-winning 917 KH of Hans Herrmann and Richard Attwood on a demonstration lap at the 2016 Zandvoort Historic Grand Prix meeting.

Le Mans was the ultimate showdown, when the fastest 3.0-litre car could only manage 14th place in the starting line-up. So, when the entry for Watkins Glen was drawn up, all factory 3.0-litre entries had been withdrawn, with Matra and Alfa Romeo giving the race a miss. The odds were on the side of Porsche, as they gave factory support to two teams – Gulf-JW Automotive, and Porsche Konstruktionen of Salzburg, the latter having much stronger support from Stuttgart in the shape of mechanics and engineers, the Gulf team being much more self-sufficient. JW Automotive fielded two blue and orange 5.0-litre 917s, driven by Siffert/Redman and Rodriguez/Kinnunen. Meanwhile, the two 5.0-litre Salzburg 917s were entered by the Porsche-Audi Division USA, and, in deference, were painted blue with white stripes and driven by Elford/Hulme and Attwood/Ahrens. The New Zealander was joining the team as a replacement for Hans Herrmann, who had retired from racing after winning Le Mans, having been on the scene since 1952. In a supporting cast, the German International Martini Racing Team was running a 4.5-litre 917 liveried in the Hippie colour scheme for Larrousse/van Lennep, plus a 908 driven by Lins/Marko, with another 908 in the hands of Tony Dean and Peter Revson. At the end of six hours' racing, the winning car was Rodriguez/Kinnunen, followed by Siffert/Redman, with the Ferrari of Andretti/Giunti in 3rd, and in 4th were Vic Elford and Denny Hulme, with the Ickx/Schetty Ferrari 5th, and Attwood/Ahrens coming in 6th. If you were to propose a pecking order in the succession of talent, this result might provide a useful indicator, though, of course, it does not allow for mechanical tribulations.

The 1970 season-closer was the Austrian 1,000Kms, staged on the fabulous new Österreichring. Porsche was represented by the two regular teams: Gulf-JW Automotive, with two 917s driven by Siffert/Redman and Rodriguez/Kinnunen, and Porsche Konstruktionen Salzburg entering two 917s for Elford/Attwood and Ahrens/Marko. The rival Alfa Romeo Tipo 33-3 with 3.0-litre V8 engines somewhat resembled the Targa Florio Porsche 908/3. Once again, the winning car was a JW Automotive 917 driven by Siffert and Redman, with an Alfa Romeo 2nd, Larrousse/Lins 3rd in a 908, and Elford/Attwood 4th with a 917. The highest-placed Ferrari was 7th.

DOWN IN HOLLYWOOD

Meanwhile, actor Steve McQueen, famous for his cool-guy performances in *The Great Escape*, *The Thomas Crown Affair* and *Bullitt*, was, with his Solar Productions crew, hard at work at Le Mans between June and November 1970, producing the *Le Mans* blockbuster movie that came out in 1971. Whilst McQueen had fully intended to drive the actual 24-Hours race himself, his backers refused to support him making the movie if he did. Nevertheless, he assembled a throng of genuine Le Mans cars, including 917s, 908s, Ferrari 512 Ss and Lola T70s. Forty-one professional drivers were hired to do the driving during the making of the film, including six previous and future winners of the 24-Hours – Jacky Ickx, Richard Attwood, Gérard Larrousse, Jürgen Barth, Masten Gregory and Derek Bell – plus Brian Redman, Mike Parkes, Jo Siffert and David Piper. McQueen would of course star in the film as 917 driver Michael Delaney, with arch-rival Siegfried Rauch as Erich Stahler in a Ferrari. Most aspects were genuinely authentic and reflected a certain reality, given the story's odd fatality, retirement and romance. The unfortunate David Piper really did lose part of a leg in an accident during filming. A Ferrari that was demolished in an accident was actually a Lola T70 disguised to look like a Ferrari, and in order to capture footage for the race scenes, McQueen entered a 908 driven by Herbert Linge and Jonathan Williams in the race as a camera car. Additionally, McQueen sent out a Ford GT40 camera car driven by Johnny Servos-Gavin ahead of the race start, so that the camera mounted on the car's nose filmed the circuit completely devoid of other racing cars, but with all the special effects such as marshalls, fire crews, ambulance men, police and the crowds, all at the ready. Only one man ever sees a racing circuit in that situation, and that is the driver who leads away from the start. As McQueen said, 'When you're racing, it's life. Anything that happens before or after is just waiting.' The result? A Porsche 1–2, with McQueen/Delaney finishing 2nd.

During the making of the movie *Le Mans* in 1970, actor Steve McQueen's Solar Productions engaged around 40 racing drivers to perform or act as extras in the film. Some of the senior drivers on set included (from left) Mike Parkes, Dieter Spöerry, Jean-Pierre Jabouille, Gérard Larrousse, David Piper, Jonathan Williams, Steve McQueen, Derek Bell, Masten Gregory, Hughes de Fierlant, Herbert Linge and director Lee Katzin.

THE RICHARD ATTWOOD INTERVIEW

On the pantheon of Porsche protagonists, Richard Attwood ranks alongside the likes of Siffert and Rodriguez, having notched up Porsche's maiden Le Mans victory; what's more, he is still racing in a 928, sponsored by Porsche GB and run by its northern UK dealerships.

In 1968 Richard was called back to BRM to drive the P126 V12, opening his account with a fine second place at Monaco. There was a fourth at Monte Carlo the following year with Team Lotus, deputising for the injured Rindt, but that was effectively the end of Attwood's Formula 1 career.

Having enjoyed a lifelong career in top-line motorsport, ranging from F1 to endurance racing – which included chalking up Porsche's first Le Mans win – Richard Attwood continues to support the brand as a marque ambassador and was still racing a 928 in 2016.

His debut with a racing Porsche was in privateer Bill Bradley's Carrera 6 at Zeltweg in 1965, but the first factory outing was not until 1968. 'Huschke von Hanstein suggested they give me a try, so I was invited to drive the Watkins Glen 6-Hours with (F3 star) Tetsu Ikusawa in a 908 with a 3.0-litre flat-eight engine.' They came 6th in a race dominated by the Gulf GT40s, with much driver swapping and mechanical failure in the Porsche camp. It was seen as a trial run for the following year, the trio of 908s being fitted with pivoting stabiliser flaps on the end of the rear bodywork, which acted in consort with the rear suspension, and which would reappear on the early 917.

Under Ferdinand Piëch, Porsche was already committed to winning the World Sportscar Championship with the 907 and 908, and the experienced Attwood was one of its leading drivers, along with Elford, Siffert, Redman, Herrmann and Stommelen. But it was not a certainty. In 1969, Attwood's choice of team rested on the flip of a coin; he could sign for John Wyer's JW Automotive to drive GT40s, or for Porsche. 'I thought Porsche had the more modern cars – and I could see the effort going on there. The GT40 was obsolete, even though it won Le Mans again that year. Wyer wanted Ickx and Oliver, and me with Hailwood.' But Porsche it was.

The first round of the 1969 championship was the Daytona 24-Hours. It should have been a Porsche steamroller, since they were more numerous (five works 908 coupés) and quicker than the Lola T70S and Gulf GT40s.

> *All the 908 long-tails had engine problems, because the fibre gear between the crankshaft and the camshaft failed (subsequently, it was aluminium), but anyway it was too weak and they all broke.*

Attwood, paired with Joe Buzzetta, was leading at six hours when his engine failed.

> *My car broke fairly early on, and they said, 'Have you finished?' I said I'd like to carry on because the cars were new to me. They were quite shocked to find a driver who actually wanted to go out again! I drove three cars until they all broke, and I was in the last one which broke. It was miserable for Porsche, and they were really upset about that.*

Next, he shared a 908 Spyder with Vic Elford at the Brands Hatch BOAC 500. 'We had a good result there, finishing 2nd.' It was a factory hat-trick, with a trio of 908s taking the first three places on the swooping Kentish circuit.

Porsche was running a computerised programme which timed every factory car in the race, and they were assessing the drivers' pace and consistency. They checked lap times and aggregate times, and found that Siffert was fastest and the second guy was me! And we all thought Elford was quick!

Unstable aero

By late April 1969, the 917 was up and running.

The first 917 I drove was at Le Mans in '69, and it was dreadful, in that it was aerodynamically very unstable because of the shape of the body. If you look at the 917 and the 908 long-tail they look much the same, but the 917 was that much faster. The 908 long-tail was very unstable at the bow, but it would only do about 195mph – that was its terminal speed. Then it would literally be off the ground. The 917 had a bit more weight, so it was off the ground at about 210mph, but thereafter it really was horrendous.

Attwood was co-driver to Vic Elford:

I didn't know until three years ago that the reason I drove the 917 at Le Mans that year was because Vic had nominated me to drive with him. I didn't want to drive it, at all; I wanted the 908/1, and I could have killed him – because I'm not a brave bloke, you know! I knew of the 917's reputation because they had run the first one at Spa with Mitter and Schutz. It was dry in practice, but then the race came and it was raining, and they knew it was going to be hell. So they did half a lap and I'm sure one of them just dipped the clutch and gave the engine a good rev – and then all of a sudden the engine went bang which, of course, it would do. They weren't about to drive it in the rain at Spa, and I don't blame them either, it was that bad.

Richard is underplaying his talents, since he and Elford established a comfortable lead in the befinned 917 *langheck*, out in front from the fourth to the 21st hour.

We were on 9-inch wheels at the front and 12-inch at the back, and the tyres were chunking so we had to slow

Leaping on the Nordschleife, the Porsche Salzburg Konstruktionen 908/2 #001 of Richard Attwood and Rudi Lins came 4th in the 1969 1,000 Kms.

down a bit. Dunlop made us cut the speed from 235mph to about 215mph, which made it just about bearable for us to run the race.

When Attwood pitted with a slipping clutch he had a four-lap lead over the Ickx/Oliver Ford GT40, but the makeshift repair failed with three hours to go, and the car retired – to an ovation from the grandstands. Attwood remains unmoved:

I hated the car, and I was happy to get out of it. It had four exhausts, two out of the back and one underneath each door. The noise from the one underneath the driver's door was just so horrendous that I got a headache after the first session – and I had that headache thereafter.

For 1970, the factory split the race teams three ways between Porsche-Austria (Porsche Salzburg Konstruktionen) with the cars painted red or blue with white stripes, JW-Gulf in blue and orange, and Martini Racing in the drinks company's livery, silver with red and blue stripes.

We were all officially signed up by the factory, but split between notionally different teams. Porsche-Austria was the same deal, with Strasse as the team manager but really run by the factory. If ever the factory wanted to do anything they just changed everybody around, and whoever they wanted was given the job. Elford and I were allocated to Porsche-Austria, which pissed Wyer off.

His Gulf cars were driven by Siffert and Redman, Kinnunen and Rodriguez, while Elford had Ahrens as co-driver and Attwood had Herrmann.

For Le Mans, Elford and Ahrens had a special 917 long-tail, which really got up Wyer's nose because he thought he was officially the works Porsche squad. So there was a lot of foul-mouthing and bad language going on. It wasn't as civilised as it might have seemed.

That spring, Porsche asked Attwood what configuration 917 he would like to drive at Le Mans.

I was asked in the February before Le Mans which car I wanted to drive. I don't know why; maybe they had seen the disappointment from the year before. So, I chose the car and the driver for reliability reasons, and because I wanted to do better than I did the year before. I wanted a straightforward short-tail

Richard Attwood gets his 908/2 sliding out of Druids Hairpin at Brands Hatch during the 1969 BOAC 500 race. The Lola T70 Chevrolet in pursuit is the Sidney Taylor-entered car of Denny Hulme, Peter Revson and Sten Axelsson.

car, sorted and aerodynamically stable, with the smaller 4.5-litre engine because I didn't want any transmission problems.

They also asked who he wanted to drive with:

I reasoned that Elford was very fast and always started on pole or got the fastest lap, but he'd never finished Le Mans. At Le Mans you needed a consistent, non-heroic driver and Hans Herrmann fitted the bill. So I asked for him and they said OK.

Although their 4.5-litre car went well in qualifying, it proved the slowest 917 – three others had the 4.5-litre engine and three had the 5.0-litre version. Two of the seven 917s had five-speed 'boxes, the rest had four-speeders. Elford's pole time in the 5-litre long-tail Salzburg car was 3m 19.8s, while Attwood/Herrmann managed 3m 32.6s.

Hans Herrmann didn't speak a word of English and I couldn't speak German, so we never had a conversation, just sign language. He was very ambitious to win Le Mans, having been pipped at the post in 1969. The highest I'd ever got was seventh, with David Piper in the Ferrari 275LM in '68. I'd done it six or seven times without finishing, and that was normal – most people didn't finish. To actually finish was an achievement, let alone win it.

The plan was for Attwood to do the start and Herrmann to take the finish. Ninth in the first hour, the Anglo–German pair moved into the lead with eleven hours gone as car after car retired. Attwood recalls:

We weren't allowed to use first gear so, to conserve the gearbox, we had three gears to go from 30mph to 220mph. We lost about six seconds a lap coming out of Mulsanne and Arnage corners, which are right-angles, just waiting for the power to build up. So, at first, we weren't getting anywhere. But that year there was a huge attrition rate, and it was one of the wettest Le Mans anyone could remember. Three Ferraris went off in one accident, and Hailwood famously went off under the Dunlop Bridge in Wyer's car and Wyer wouldn't have him back. Apart from Larrousse and Kauhsen (placed second in the psychedelic Martini car), all the other 917s retired with mechanical problems.

Attwood did not intend to win from the front.

Richard Attwood hands over the 917 LH #008 to Vic Elford at the Le Mans 24-Hours, 1969. To the left (in Porsche T-shirt) is Ferdinand Piëch.

I didn't want to be in the lead, because it means you've got to defend it for the next fourteen hours. All that time you're listening for things that might be going wrong. Anyway, all the fuel stops went perfectly and it was one of the most undramatic races I've ever been in. I had one big slide and that was it. The biggest problem was trying to keep the engine free of misfires because of water getting into the electrics, and trying to keep it artificially as warm as we could because it was running very cold, anyway. So we were revving it higher in the gears and even blipping it coming into corners. In the end we won easily. Porsche was always going to win it that year, and team orders said whoever happens to be in front, he wins it.

Just seven cars were classified finishers in 1970, and five of them were Porsches – two 917s, a 908, a 914/6 and a 911. And the post-race party?

Not for me. And there was no podium that year; we were put on a truck and taken around a third of the track, away from the crowd, so that was a great disappointment, so there was no elation after the race. I couldn't really care, cos I was not really feeling too well. The relevance of the win didn't come to me until later. Le Mans is a big race, but to me it was just another race in the championship at the time and, yes, it was nice to have a win, but it didn't seem very special to me. For the Porsche family, it was a great relief. We should have won it the year before; indeed, we could have won it the year before, and I don't think they thought the 917 would last as long as it did. It was an experiment, and it was relatively tentative. The problems that we had at high speed were really bad, and when I dropped out of that '69 race I was very happy to still be alive, and I couldn't have cared less that I hadn't won Le Mans. People probably don't believe that, but it's absolutely true: I was so uncomfortable, I had a blinding headache, and I had neck ache 'cos of the power; I had never experienced power like that before, and I was in such discomfort that I couldn't have cared less when the car broke.

At Classic Le Mans, Richard and Vern are in a 1971 car. So, the 917s that he has driven subsequently, I ask, presumably there has been no mechanical evolution, the tyres are the same. Is it a similar experience doing this demo?

Le Mans winners in 1970, Hans Herrmann and Richard Attwood greet each other warmly at the Classic Le Mans reunion in 2012.

It's the same as it was in '71. It's just as dangerous, and the tyres aren't much different. They're slicks, and they're quite grippy, but they were in their day anyway. From '67 to '69, there was a big development in tyres; in '69, we were still on the old Dunlop treaded tyres, and then in '69–'71 we went from 12-inch rear wheels to 19 inches, so there was a massive enlargement of rear wheels in a very short space of time.

Fun car

Richard's favourite Porsche is not the most obvious one.

We all thought the most fun car, the most reliable and the easiest to drive, was the 908/3 Spyder. The long-tail was not so good, although it was much quicker at high speed as it was built purely as a projectile. You could thrash it, and it was pretty much unburstable. It was really well put together, and there was just enough power to be interesting. It was a balanced car, and the aerodynamics didn't have problems; you could almost drive it on autopilot.

So, not the Le Mans-winning 917, then?

We all knew the 917 was going to be a problem, a bit of a wild card. We didn't really want it at the time, and none of us wanted to test it. Brian (Redman) had been asked to drive it, and he rang Jo Siffert to ask his opinion, and Seppi said: 'Brian, we let one of the others try it first, because the 908 is a good car and we just wait to see what the result will be.' Fortunately, I didn't drive it in its earlier days. At Spa, Mitter and Schutz drove it, but one of them took it out, deliberately, I think. In its early days it wasn't a difficult engine to blow. We used to race them to 8,000rpm; they were safe to 8,400rpm, but at 8,600rpm they burst.

Richard could not resist owning one, though. When Brian Redman wanted to buy a house in 1978, Attwood helped him out by buying his 917. At first they thought it might be the re-bodied wide-track 'Pink Pig' (917/30) used by Jöst and Kauhsen in 1971, which would have been exalted provenance enough, but it turned out to be none other than McQueen's Solar Productions car that Attwood drove during the making of the movie. Identification proved straightforward.

There were some switches on the dashboard for the cameras, and under the front cover were a few aluminium tubes with a mounting for the camera.

Strapped for cash in 2000, Richard sold it at auction in the United States.

I drove it onto the rostrum, gave it a big rev and everyone cheered. But there were no bidders beyond $1m, and the auctioneers eventually sold it privately to collector Jerry Seinfeld.

In 1971, Attwood only drove a couple of races for Porsche, coming second at Le Mans with Herbie Muller in a short-tail JW Automotive car and winning the Osterreichring 1,000kms with Pedro Rodriguez.

I spent a lot of time working on Steve McQueen's Le Mans film, so I wasn't desperate. I made very good money out of that, better than if I'd been racing. I drove the Solar Productions 917 camera car, which they'd bought from Stuttgart. It was car number 20, Steve McQueen's race car in the film. We had cameras at the front and back, and sound recording equipment on board.

After that, Attwood's professional racing career drew to a close. He had married two years earlier and regarded marriage and motor racing as incompatible. The prospects for top-line sports car racing did not look too promising, either. 'The 5.0-litre formula was coming to an end, and 3.0-litres wasn't going to be as interesting. So, at the end of '71, I joined the family business.'

Attwood has a keen sense of his place in motor racing history. Maybe he lacked the killer instinct, ultimately putting marriage and family before the sport. A good call, given that the attrition rate amongst his peers was still dreadfully high. Nevertheless, he is one of the nice guys, personable, unfailingly charming and pragmatic about career opportunities that did not quite pan out. What is impressive is that he can still do the business in top-flight classic meetings. Racing runs deep through his veins – this is a guy who was in F1 from 1964 to 1969, remember – and he was courted back to Le Mans in 1984 to drive a Nimrod Aston Martin. He has also starred at a number of events, including the Goodwood Revival – winning the TT race with Mark Hales – and the Spa Six Hours, where he placed third in a lightweight E-type in 2006. More recently, in 2017 Antony Fraser and I watched him in action in a 928 in an HSCC Historic Road Sports race at Croft. And he is still a consultant at the Porsche Driving Experience at Millbrook and Silverstone.

The JW Automotive 908/3 #011 of Richard Attwood and Bjorn Waldegård follows the Alfa Romeo T33/3 3.0-litre V8 of Andrea de Adamich and Piers Courage on the 1970 Targa Florio. The 908 came 5th, 9min 31sec behind the winners Siffert/Redman; the Alfa was classified 41st, having crashed out.

CAN-AM CHALLENGE

The 917 Can-Am cars are not covered in this book, partly because Pete Lyons' book *Can-Am History* covers it fully, and, more specifically, because Can-Am is outside Porsche's involvement in the World Sportscar Championship. Obviously, it should not pass without a mention, though.

From 1966 to 1987, Can-Am racing was extremely popular in North America, dominated in the late 1960s by Bruce McLaren's works team – with Denny Hulme helping him clean up as his regular second driver – and the Lola T70s (John Surtees was the inaugural Champion), both marques mostly employing 7.0-litre Chevrolet power. Other marques to feature as open-top big-bangers were

Dario Franchitti motors the 917 PA out of the assembly area at the 2014 Goodwood Festival of Speed for a run up The Hill.

Karlsruhe-based vintage Porsche specialist Manfred Freisinger drives 917/10 #006 at Hockenheim in 2012. The car was formerly entered by Californian Porsche distributor and race team owner Vasek Polak for Milt Minter in Can-Am events in 1972.

Chaparral, Shadow and March. Run by the SCCA to the FIA's *Formule Libre* Group 7 regulations, there were two races in Canada and four in the USA. Since North America was Porsche's best export market, a Porsche Can-Am car followed naturally. Group 7 – a class constrained by almost no rules, neither a maximum engine capacity nor a minimum car weight being specified – was a playground at the time for the two mega-horsepower ultra-light Chevy-powered Team McLarens. Porsche's first venture into this new arena would be in something of an underdog role. The decision to enter the highly lucrative Can-Am series was made mid-season 1969 before the following year's tree-topping Le Mans win.

Porsche would provide the car, the driver would be Jo Siffert, plus a full support crew, while the new Porsche-Audi Division of Volkswagen of America would sponsor the entry. Once the contract was signed, it was then a matter of transforming the Group 5 917 coupé into a Group 7 Spyder. Porsche had recent form in the practice of turning coupés into spyders, such as the 906 and 910, and doing it quickly. Work began after Le Mans in June 1969, and the 917 PA (Porsche/Audi) arrived in the USA in August. The PA was a 917 shorn of its coupé top and fitted with a Spyder body inspired by the 908/2 Flounder prototype. The 100lb saved by the Flounder-style body was offset by the 56 litres of fuel required to run these Can-Am sprint races nonstop. The engine was a strictly stock 4.5-litre flat-12. Thus, on the grid for its first race at Mid-Ohio, the 917 PA gave away 3.0-litres, 200lb and 250bhp to the McLarens. By then, it had already missed five races, but in the six remaining, the 917 PA finished in all but one, and took 2nd place once, placing 4th overall in the '69 Can-Am Championship.

Naturally, Porsche was encouraged to get thoroughly committed, and a full Can-Am assault in 1972 with the Penske-run 917/10 and 917/10 Turbo stole the Can-Am laurels away from the McLarens, with George Follmer lifting the title. In 1973, the 917/30 followed, intimidating the opposition and demonstrating such dominance in the hands of Mark Donohue that the Can-Am series died due to a lack of competition.

As a postscript, the original 917 PA was acquired by collector and racer Vasek Polak, and converted into a full-on 917/10, fitted with an 1,100bhp turbocharged engine from the 917/30. In fact, the 917 PA raced in more Can-Am events than any other Group 7 car, and remained competitive until its retirement.

FAMOUS FLOUNDER

One of the REVS Institute's key exhibits: the 1969 Porsche 908/2 ex-works short-tail Flounder Spyder – one of the most extensively raced examples of Porsche's most successful sports racing line-up. In its inaugural season, chassis 908/02-018 was victorious with works pairing Jo Siffert and Brian Redman at the 1969 Watkins Glen 6 Hours – competing prolifically in successive decades right into modern times. Chassis 908/02-18 was constructed in May 1969 by the Porsche racing department, in short 'Flunder' form. The Flounder body was named after the 'sole' or 'flounder' flat fish, reflecting the new flatter surface design. Debuting at the 1969 Nürburgring 1,000kms, chassis 18 was entered by the works team and raced by Rolf Stommelen and Hans Herrmann, finishing 2nd as part of the famous 1, 2, 3, 4, 5 factory sweep. This result contributed to Porsche securing their first-ever victory in the 1969 Manufacturers' World Championship. After their victory at 1,000kms Nürburgring and retirement at Le Mans, driver pairing Jo Siffert and Brian Redman were enlisted to drive chassis 18. With three races to go, the Manufacturers' World Championship was already secured, so the win at Watkins Glen was the icing on the cake. The car was sold in October 1969 to privateer Karl von Wendt for his BG Racing Team, and appeared in 1970 at the 1970 Buenos Aires 1,000km and 200-mile races, and took 7th overall at the Nürburgring 1,000kms that year, in the hands of Willi Kauhsen and Herbert Schultze. From 1980 it was bought by Bill Bradley Racing, with a full restoration undertaken by ex-factory engineer Paddy O'Grady, including reinstating its original 908/2 Flunder bodywork. Later owners included Richard Attwood, who raced it in the 1980s in historic racing, also appearing at the Goodwood Revival, Le Mans Classic, Spa Classic and Mugello.

DRIVING THE 917: THE POWER AND THE GLORY

Most of us have a wish list of Porsches that we relish the prospect of having a go in, and for many of us that would include the 917 racing car. It's hot, it's loud, and it's cramped. And it goes without saying that it is also extremely powerful.

Well, one thing it is not, surprisingly, is difficult to drive. That writhing, snarling beast you thought you were going to have to wrestle with is… if not exactly a pussy cat, a massively over-engined classic Porsche. An overgrown 914/6, perhaps, characteristics multiplied tenfold. How did I come to this conclusion? Thanks to the guardian of #008, who let me loose in it at a select gathering at Donington Park.

Admittedly, to have driven a 917 at all is pretty amazing, but sampling two in a year is incredible. Okay, well, I will concede that the first one, the Icon 917, was a replica, but no less of an achievement on the part of its builders, Dave Eaton and John Hartland, who obtained IVA-type approval for it in 2019, and I helmed that on the broad, unencumbered sweeps of Bentwaters' runways near Woodbridge, a former US airbase from which Fairchild Republic 'Warthog' A10 Tankbusters flew missions. It was a taster, not so much of the power (which consisted, for economic reasons, of a tuned 964 flat-6 engine) and handling, but of the uncompromising confines of the 917 cockpit. Fast forward, then, to July 2019's Rennsport Collective meeting, centred on Castle Donington and the adjacent Donington Park racetrack, a sparkling event organised by Paul Geudon, featuring a wealth of high-end Porsches.

The gathering included plenty of the 'usual suspects', including racer John Fitzpatrick and collectors extraordinaire Johan Dirickx and Henry Pearman. And among the consignment of cars dispatched from the continent by Kobus Cantraine was the 917 #008, owned and raced in Historics by Claudio Roddaro of Monegasque company SAM Amstar, fresh from winning the curtain-raiser at the Hungaroring F1 Grand Prix the week before Donington Rennsport – imagine, a race half wet, half dry, on the same set of tyres.

Although it is presented as a short-tail KH car in Gulf livery, it is in fact a 1969 model, entered in WEC events that year by Porsche System – so it is a works car – and driven at Le Mans 1969 by superstars of the day Richard Attwood and Vic Elford. Given the car's main claim to fame is its one-off participation in the 1969 Le Mans 24-Hours, it is interesting to reflect on how it got on in that particular race. It all began reasonably auspiciously. Porsche had already won the 1969 World Sportscar Championship – the International Championship for Makes – with outright victories in the 1,000km races at Brands Hatch, Monza, Spa-Francorchamps and the Nürburgring, as well as the Targa Florio, and if winning the Championship had been their only interest they could justifiably have stayed away from Le Mans; but having yet to take the overall win at *La Sarthe,* the Porsche Racing Department were not about to miss out.

They had entered three long-tailed 908 coupés and a long-tail 908 Spyder, all powered by 3.0-litre flat-8s, and three new 917 coupés with 4.5-litre flat-12 engines. One was the first customer car, #005, for the ill-fated Woolfe Racing Team. John Woolfe – another race fans' favourite, due to his amiable personality in the paddock – lost his life on the first lap, and it is perhaps a salutary lesson that his original co-driver, the hugely experienced Herbert Linge, backed out, replaced at the last minute by Chevron B8 pilot Digby Martland who, thankfully for him, never got to drive it.

Blistering pace

Driving #007, Rolf Stommelen set a blistering pace in practice, 3min 22.9sec, 238.976km/h or 148.5mph, achieved through torque-induced acceleration rather than maximum speed, which was around 190mph. Stommelen, with co-driver Kurt Ahrens, was the initial leader, though slowed and finally halted after fifteen hours by oil leaks. After four hours' racing Vic Elford had taken the lead in #008. By 2.00am on the Sunday morning, with dense mist but dry roads, the lone 917 Porsche was well in the lead and taking things comparatively easy, comfortably four laps ahead of the 908 of Mitter/Schutz in 2nd place and five laps ahead of the 908 of Willy Kauhsen/Rudi Lins in 3rd. Two JW-Gulf Ford GT40s were 4th and 5th, but Jacky Ickx and Jackie Oliver were eight laps behind Elford and Attwood, so apparently not a serious challenge at that point. Fuel consumption was also a factor. Although the 917s were extremely fast they consumed petrol voraciously, needing to pit for refuelling just over every hour, while the GT40s could go an hour-and-a-half between stops. The 908s were somewhere in between in terms of thirst.

But, as Sunday morning wore on, the lead 917 #008 began to emit a trail of oil smoke, and it was clear that Elford and Attwood had backed off and were taking it easy. At 10.00am they still had six laps' lead over the 908 of Kauhsen/Lins and ten laps over the GT40 of Ickx/Oliver. But just an hour later, its transmission was finished, and its race was run. Despite this, even at the 21st hour, on distance covered it was still well in the lead, four laps ahead of the Ickx/Oliver Gulf GT40, and the mechanics were given an ovation by spectators as they pushed #008 over the line. The race result went right down to the wire, with Jacky Ickx in the Gulf GT40 outdriving Hans Herrmann's brake-deficient 908 to take the victory by a scant 100 yards – after 24 hours of racing.

Here's a bit of a reality check. At the time – 1969 – #008 had long-tailed *Lang heck* bodywork, painted white with blue frontal detailing, and although Quick Vic is name-checked, along with Richard Attwood, on the car's current Gulf-liveried manifestation, he never actually drove for John Wyer Automotive. Vic was always a works' Porsche Konstruktionen driver, while Richard triumphed at Le Mans the following year in 1970, also driving for Porsche Konstruktionen, although he was on the JW-Gulf driver roster for 1971. As Vic recalled:

> *I lobbied hard to drive the first 917 at Le Mans, and although Ferdinand Piëch and Helmuth Bott insisted the car was still very experimental and would only last six hours, we drove it with kid gloves and were leading by more than 50 miles when it broke, after 21 hours.*

With its switch from running Ford and Mirage GT40s to Porsche, JW Automotive acquired #008 in 1970, and it was then used extensively for aerodynamic testing at the Österreichring. It was the first 917 sporting the revised short-tail *Kurz heck* bodywork, which it has worn ever since. It ran in the Le Mans trials in April 1970 – coinciding, inconveniently, with the BOAC 1,000Kms at Brands Hatch – with Mike Hailwood on driving duty. Both long- and short-tail engine covers were tested, before Weissach agreed to produce a compromise version. As the car's current owner tells it, 'Steve McQueen was scouting for his movie, and he came to Le Mans in April 1970, and #008 was there, and we have pictures of Steve in the car and, two months later, when he came back to film the actual race for the movie, the car was still finished in white.' So, it was not yet in Gulf livery at that point, despite the short tail. The implication is that they were in no hurry to race it again, and JW Automotive retained it as a spare for the next two seasons. Checking race entries for those two seasons, 1970 and 1971, #008 does not show up at any international WSC event, not even as a T-car. When the new CSI (pre-FIA) regulations sidelined the 917 and its arch-rival the Ferrari 512 at the end of 1971, #008 ended up being stripped of its engine and gearbox and sold off as a rolling chassis to Porsche privateer Manfred Freisinger Snr. The car was rebuilt at Freisinger's Karlsruhe workshops and bought by Swiss racer Claude Haldi, and then between 1989 and 1991, Freisinger rebuilt it yet again for a private collection.

It passed into the hands of its current owners SAM Amstar in 2018. The business partners were offered the 917 #008 by its owner, French privateer Gérard Dantan Merlin, alias 'Gedehem', who raced 911s in the early 1970s partnering Claude Haldi, among others. The Amstar business partners bought the 917 because of its iconic status as well as it being a great investment, and, as Claudio Roddaro says, 'it's their mascot now, and they are not afraid of using it.'

When #008 was acquired in 2018, they had the chassis and componentry crack-tested, and discovered that magnesium does not last indefinitely: indeed, a life expectancy of 30 years seems about right, so yet more extensive renovation was carried out, back at Karlsruhe, this time by Manfred Freisinger Jnr, himself no slouch behind the wheel of an Interserie 917. Items such as the pedals, which were NOS and installed new during the previous restoration, along with hubs, were not in good shape, despite the car being unused. As the SAM Amstar mechanic says, 'when people talk about original matching components, they have no idea, because the material is 50 years old and you can't fix it, you have to make it new.' They raced #008 at 2018's Classic Le Mans, Monza and Dijon, plus Spa and the Hungaroring in 2019. 'This 917 is completely different to most racecars,' he says. 'It's a car that you race with your brain; you need to keep control of everything, because it's very easy to let the car get the better of you. But when you're used to the car then you can enjoy it.'

The author receives instructions on the controls of the 917 from Claudio Roddaro's obliging mechanic.

And now, at Donington, he's told me I can drive it too!

Possibly the most important piece of kit in the 917's tool-roll is something called 'the seat-of-the-pants' – because it is that kind of car. Indeed, Vic Elford said of its 1969 incarnation: 'the Mulsanne Straight wasn't wide enough to get the car to run straight!' But now, although it is a tad twitchy on Donington's two longish straights, it is perfectly controllable.

As you will have noted, I have had previous experience driving a 906 and a 910, forerunners of the 917, sure, but with 2.0-litre flat-6 power, as opposed to 4.5-litres of flat-12 rumbling away behind me.

In the Donington pit lane I clamber aboard: one foot on the broad sill, the other on the seat, then slide down under the large, thin-rim steering wheel. I am almost recumbent, and yet my helmet is right up against the roof bars. The five-speed shift pattern is conventional but the lever mechanism to my right would not disgrace a tractor. The mechanic fires it up: I blip the throttle to extinguish one of the two alternator lights. It's quick as I accelerate from the pits, sort of 993 quick, the pace I'm going, just to give you a comparison, but there again, I'm not pushing it one bit. You build up to these things gradually, of course, corner-by-corner and lap by lap.

But what I had expected would be a fairly daunting dragon-slaying prospect proves to be quite an easy car to drive. It helps to know what corner is coming up next – and Donington has several blind crests to be wary of – though the most amazing section is the Craner curves, where you can see right the way through the downhill set of bends and then up the other side. Once up to speed, I am doing most of it in 4th and 5th, and down to 2nd for tighter corners. With around 500bhp and an all-up weight of just over 2,000lb, its performance is unquestionably phenomenal. The massive torque is instantly apparent, and there is a huge amount of power available. Handling is flat and ride surprisingly soft, steering compliant, while turn-in is instant and inch-perfect, with almost no effort hauling on the vast, bus-sized wheel rim.

Here is what a lap of Donington Park consists of. No time for nerves; just drive at 75 per cent and not even 90 per cent, and we should be able to keep it on the asphalt. Hubris strikes the unwary. But, we are in a Le Mans car, and these machines do not take being mollycoddled well. Drive it like you mean it, I tell myself, but take your time to build the pace.

The 400-yards long Wheatcroft start-finish straight pitches the car into Redgate, an awkward right-hander with immediate apex, easing out left towards the Craner entry, a shallow right before plunging down to a tricky right-left including the Old Hairpin alongside the viaduct ruin to the

The 917 cockpit features the driver's bucket seat with six-point harness, smaller passenger seat, three-spoke steering wheel, right-hand shift lever, fuse box and pedals.

Possibly the most exhilarating aspect of the Donington Park racetrack is the Kraner Curves section, and powering a 917 through the flowing bends is one of life's greatest thrills.

Although liveried in Gulf blue and orange, 917 #008 never raced in these colours in-period. In fact, its one significant race back in the day was the 1969 Le Mans 24-Hours as a white long-tail, driven by Vic Elford and Richard Attwood, leading most of the race until the clutch failed in the 21st hour.

left; then power on to surge uphill on Starkey's Bridge to a tight-ish right, faced with a blind crest concealing McLean's, a sharp right that leads onto Coppice, a fast right, and the long 300-yard Starkey's Straight to the chicane-style Esses, running over the kerbs at each one. Then there is a medium-long straight and I drop down to 2nd for the tricky Melbourne hairpin.

Full on the throttle and the back-end squats for the dash behind the paddock to another hairpin, Goddard's, and it's power down in 2nd on the exit and go barrelling down the pits straight. Despite the weirdness of the recumbent driving position and constant contact of helmet against roof bars, I settle in reasonably quickly and go faster and faster. It's one of life's Nirvana experiences.

Indeed, it was a thrill and a privilege to have had a go in this 917 for twelve laps or so – I wasn't counting – not only having glimpsed what a practised driver can do with it, but also operating a car that Quick Vic Elford and Richard Attwood – not to mention Mike Hailwood – once handled. What's next on the bucket list? Chronologically, if I were to go backwards on the timeline, it would have to be the 908 Coupé, and that is my all-time favourite Porsche racing car.

A TASTE OF MARTINI

Ahead of the 1971 racing season, Porsche made a major announcement: to the effect that it would be cutting back its racing programme to devote more attention to producing road cars and selling them in the USA, which was in the throes of environmental legislation that affected cars such as the 911 and 914. As far as the Porsche factory was concerned, the 1970 endurance racing season had been ideal, and the results were more than satisfactory. But to the JW Automotive Gulf team, it was the reverse, for they had been conscious all season of the rival works-supported Porsche Salzburg Konstruktionen team giving them a hard time, especially with Elford in the number one car.

JW Automotive assumed that they had entered into a contract with Porsche to take over the factory racing, and were not amused at having to race against Porsche Konstruktionen Salzburg, as well as Ferrari, Matra, Alfa Romeo, Lola and Abarth. The consequence was that Porsche Salzburg was disbanded for 1971, and as it was to be the last year for 5.0-litre sports cars, the factory would pull back on development work on the 917. While the on-track battles raged between JW Automotive Gulf and Porsche Salzburg, there was a private German team not far behind, running 3.0-litre 908 Spyders, and often when one of the 5.0-litre 917s ran into trouble, it was one of these 908s that moved up into its place.

This was the Martini Racing team operated by Hans-Dieter Dechent, from Saarbrucken, who had done a lot of Porsche racing himself. He got financial sponsorship from Martini & Rossi, and had Gérard Larrousse, Rudi Lins, Helmut Marko and Gerald Pankl drive for him. When Dechent heard that the Salzburg team was to be disbanded, he made a bid for the three 917s, and also got Elford, Ahrens and Marko to come with them. Martini & Rossi agreed to continue their support, so that Dechent was able to set up an impressive programme for 1971 with the full support of the Porsche factory, plus support from Shell, Bosch, Firestone, Cibie

The Martini team's 917 #019, driven by Vic Elford and Brian Redman, is prepped for the BOAC 1,000km, 4 April 1971, in the Brands Hatch paddock. It failed to finish due to a fuel tank issue.

The Martini Racing 917 KH #053 of van Lennep/Marko is about to rejoin the race after a late pit stop in the 1971 Le Mans 24-Hours; the left-hand headlight assembly is damaged, but not deemed a necessary repair.

and Bilstein. The Martini Racing team had its trio of 917s painted silver-grey with the distinctive Martini International Club colours over the top and insignia writ large on each side and in front. The drivers would be Elford, Larrousse, Ahrens, Marko and van Lennep. Whereas the Martini Racing team's cars were prepared in the factory service department at Zuffenhausen by Dechent's mechanics, with the help of Porsche mechanics, the JW Automotive Gulf cars were prepared at the Slough factory.

THE 1971 SEASON

The opening round of the 1971 World Championship was staged on 10 January at the Autódromo de Buenos Aires Oscar y Juan Gálvez, Argentina, where the Group 5 entries comprised Porsche 917s and 908s and Ferrari 512s. JW Automotive despatched a pair of 917s for their new driver line-up, Jo Siffert and Derek Bell in #029, and Pedro Rodriguez and Jackie Oliver in #035,. The cars were fitted with works-made beryllium brake discs, and 5-speed gearboxes instead of 4-speeds.

Their strongest opposition came from Hans-Dieter Dechent's Martini International Team, fielding two cars for Vic Elford and Gérard Larrousse, and Helmut Marko and Gijs van Lennep, neither of which lasted the distance. These 917s were exactly as raced by Porsche Salzburg in 1970, except for having 4-speed gearboxes instead of 5-speed, and running 590bhp 5.0-litre engines. A trio of privately entered 4.5-litre 917s were driven by Dominique Martin and Pablo Bria, Reinhold Jöst (whose career peaked as head of the work's Audi Sport Team in the 2000s) and Angel Monguzzi, and Emerson Fittipaldi (then on the threshold of the F1 world title) and local hero Carlos Reutemann.

Bizarrely, the track was not only dusty, but a quantity of nails were found on it during practice, causing several punctures. Vic Elford led, swapping places with Rodriguez, though his car suffered from fuel starvation, causing its retirement. Tragically, this was also the event where Giunti was killed when his Ferrari hit Beltoise's Matra, which the Frenchman was pushing along the track, having run out of fuel. Indeed, all was not well with the lead car, because Siffert and Bell were coping with a slipping clutch, and needed to make an unscheduled fuel stop too. Rodriguez' car was not going as quickly as it might, because Jackie Oliver was driving with caution – call it prudence – rather than speed. But it still meant that JW Automotive-Gulf 917s came 1st and 2nd, with Alfa Romeo T33-3s 3rd and 4th and Ferrari 512 Ss 5th, 6th, 7th and 8th.

The Daytona 24-Hours was next on the calendar, and was another win for Rodriguez and Oliver in one of the JW Automotive 917s, despite losing over an hour in the pits when Oliver found it stuck in top gear. Elford's 917 had a puncture on the banking, throwing the car into the guard rail at the top of the banking, and he was subsequently hit by a wayward 911 that had itself been involved in an incident with Mark Donohue's Ferrari. Still in the USA Vic, with Gérard Larrousse, was victorious at the subsequent Sebring 12-Hours, with the JW Automotive cars 4th and 5th behind a couple of Alfa Romeos.

Come April, and the endurance retinue returned to Brands Hatch for the BOAC 1,000Kms. The entry was down to 24 cars, with JW Automotive presenting two 917s for Siffert/Bell and Rodriguez/Oliver, vying with Elford/Larrousse and van Lennep/Redman in the Martini 917s. A fifth 917 showed up, the Mannheim-based Auto Usdau car, driven by Reinhold Jöst and Willi Kauhsen. It was not especially one to remember for the Porsche fans: Siffert/Bell's 917 came 3rd behind an Alfa Romeo T33 (de Adamich/Pescarolo) and a Ferrari 312 PB (Ickx/Regazzoni), while Jöst/Kauhsen came 6th, van Lennep/Larrousse came 9th, and in the 2nd Auto Usdau car, Weigel/Spöerry were tenth in a 908/2 Flounder. Elford/Redman's 917 succumbed to a fuel tank issue, while Rodriguez/Oliver also went out with fuelling problems.

May 1971 was a packed calendar for the World Championship for Makes, with four events scheduled. On 9 May, the Royal Automobile Club of Spa organised the annual 1,000Kms race, still running on the old circuit. The outright lap record set by Rodriguez in a 917 in 1970 at

A trio of Martini Racing Team 917s undergoing preparation for the 1971 Le Mans race in the Garage Provost, Teloché, used by Porsche for 30 years. Two are LH and KH versions, with the one-off 'Pink Pig', #020, to the right. The anatomy of the flat-12 powerplants, chassis and running gear is revealed, plus the compulsory space-saver spare wheels.

Dusk falls at Sebring during the 1971 12-Hour race, with the Pedro Rodriguez/Jackie Oliver JW-Gulf 917 KH #009 heading for 4th place, 12 laps behind winners Elford/ Larrousse in 917 KH #020.

The Gulf- JW Automotive 917 #029 of Jo Siffert and Derek Bell finished 3rd overall in the 1971 BOAC 1,000Kms at Brands Hatch, behind a pair of Ferrari 512s, and 1st in the 5.0-litre Sports category.

approximately 160mph (258.32km/h) was much faster than a contemporary F1 car could achieve. This year there were two JW Automotive 5.0-litre 917s for Rodriguez/Oliver and Siffert/Bell, two similar Martini Racing 917s for Elford/ Larrousse and Marko/van Lennep. The Auto Usdau team brought along their yellow 4.5-litre 917 for Kauhsen and Jöst. Opposition consisted of a single Alfa Romeo T33-3 for Pescarolo and de Adamich, and a Ferrari 312 P for Ickx and Regazzoni. The Gulf 917s were using the earlier-style tails with no fins, but an adjustable centre aerofoil, while the Martini 917s and the Usdau car had the later tails with fins but no aerofoils. Amongst the GT cars there were seven 911s and two 914/6s along with sundry Corvettes and Chevrons. It was clear that no one was going to touch the Gulf 917s for outright speed, but the 3.0-litre Ferrari and Alfa Romeo were not going to need as many refuelling

Porsche experimented briefly with overhead air intakes along the lines of contemporary F1 cars but the idea was abandoned. Here, Dirk Sadlowski airs his 917 KH at Spa Francorchamps.

stops, placing an emphasis on the JW Automotive team's pit work.

A shower just before the start had many teams frantically busy swapping tyres over to wets, including the Martini cars, though JW-Gulf remained implacably on their intermediate Firestones. Elford stopped at the end of the first lap, unhappy with the high-speed handling of his 917, and had all the tyres changed, restarting almost a lap behind the leading 917s of Siffert and Rodriguez. Ickx in the Ferrari held third place ahead of Marko in the second Martini 917 and Kauhsen in the Usdau 917. In the final outcome, the winners were Rodriguez/Oliver, followed – just 0.5sec later – by Siffert/Bell in 2nd place, a perfect race for the Gulf JW team. The Alfa Romeo T33 was 4th, and Claude Ballot-Lena and Guy Chasseuil were 5th in their lurid yellow-and-green 'hippie' 908/2.

The 917 KH of Dirk Sadlowski in the old Spa-Francorchamps pitlane ahead of a test run in 2017.

Gijs van Lennep and Dr Helmut Marko finished 3rd in the 1971 Nürburgring 1,000Kms in their Martini Racing 908/3 #003, just 1min 44sec behind the winning sister 908/3 of Elford/Larousse.

Porsche tackled the 55th running of the Targa Florio on 16 May rather differently to what had become normal, in so far as the factory dispatched its own resident mechanics and technicians to look after the two 908/3s of JW Automotive as well as the pair of 908/3s of the Martini Racing team. This left the regular Gulf and Martini crews with not much to do, and it is a moot point whether or not this affected the result in any way, since none of these 908s finished the race. Noted for their low polar moment of inertia and the ability to change direction very quickly, the 908/3s should have been setting the pace, but a chaotic practice session put them on the back foot. Rodriguez was teamed for the event with Herbert Müller, and Siffert with Redman, and only one Martini 908/3 was delivered to Cerda, for Elford and Larrousse, so van Lennep and Kinnunen were loaned to Alfa Romeo to drive Tipo 33/3s. Both Siffert and Elford had crashes during practice, and Redman lost time with a puncture out on the circuit – which, at racing speeds, took the best part of 34 minutes to drive a lap. During the race, Rodriguez crashed in Collesano, and then Redman crashed. His car caught fire, and he was badly burned. Later on, Larrousse, who had led at the start and been going well, got a puncture, and then Elford, having set fastest lap, hit a kerb and was sidelined. The 911s that finished in 4th, 6th, 8th and 10th can be regarded as the model's burgeoning success in the GT category. The one that finished 6th, driven by Pucci/Schmid, was entered by an old Porsche stalwart, Paul Strähle.

Coming just two weeks after the Targa Florio debacle, the Porsche teams were still licking their wounds in the Nürburgring paddock ahead of the 1,000Kms, while morale at Alfa Romeo was in the ascendant. Both JW Automotive-Gulf and Martini International Racing were running 908/3s, but whereas the factory had been in charge in Sicily, the two separate organisations had independent control once more. JW Gulf had two brand-new 908/3s for

Few sights are more evocative of the thrill of endurance racing than a night shot of a 917 with lights ablaze, epitomised by Antony Fraser's evocative photo from Le Mans 2012.

Rodriguez/Oliver and Siffert/Bell, but when they arrived at the circuit, the cars were far from correctly set up for the Nordschleife. Throughout practice, they manifested niggling little faults that kept the mechanics busy and the drivers uneasy – like the gearbox sticking in 5th, the brakes lacking feel and erratic handling. The Martini team had two of the Targa Florio cars, one looking somewhat rough after its crash. These were driven at the Nürburgring by Elford/Larrousse and Marko/van Lennep, the latter substituting for Redman, who had not recovered from his Targa Florio accident. Martini also showed up with their own 908/2 for the Princes of Hohenzollern and Bayern to drive, but it got no further than the first practice session when Hohenzollern went off in it. One of the Martini 917s was entered but withdrawn before practice as van Lennep was given a seat in the 908/3. His co-driver Rudi Lins shared a 910 with Sepp Greger, the 56-year-old still driving as hard as ever. The teams had settled for the short and light 908/3, rather than the 917s, after carrying out comparative tests on the newly resurfaced Nürburgring circuit. Looking at period photographs now, the Brünnchen Curve (for example), so beloved at the N-24 by huge numbers of spectators, is unrecognisable in its austerity. Today's forests appear to have been freshly planted, which, five decades on, is a sobering thought.

Partisan crowd

By the second lap of the 44-lap race, the eight factory cars were out on their own, with Ickx in the Ferrari building up a lead of ten seconds a lap from the Alfa Romeo of Stommelen, which was being hounded by the 908/3s of Elford and Siffert, while van Lennep had dropped back to 7th, ahead of de Adamich and Rodriguez. The latter was not shining in the 908 in the way that he was wont to do in the 917. Confusingly for the partisan German crowd, the race was led by an Alfa Romeo driven by a German – but should they urge on the English driver in the German car in 2nd place, or settle for Siffert in 3rd? But then the tubular chassis of Siffert's car began to break up, and the gearbox and the engine parted company with the chassis. The Swiss was fortunate to be able to return to the pits, where broken engine mountings were diagnosed. Meanwhile, Ickx' Ferrari was suffering from a water leak, which left Stommelen in the Alfa and Elford in the 908 well out in front, while Rodriguez was 3rd, followed by de Adamich, van Lennep, and Ickx' Ferrari. At half distance, which was 22 laps, the Porsches came in to refuel. Elford took over the leading car, Rodriguez got back in the Gulf car, and van Lennep in the 3rd place car. The only other car on the same lap as these was the Alfa Romeo of de Adamich and Pescarolo. The three 908/3s now merely had to circulate and keep out of trouble, and no matter what their final finishing order was, this was going to clinch the Manufacturers' Championship. They were running to a regular schedule of eleven laps to the tank-full of fuel, and then, like London buses, all three pulled into the pits at the end of 33 laps. Larrousse took over the lead car, its Goodyear tyres being okay to run the remaining eleven laps, but when Rodriguez pulled in, it was noticed that his front Firestones would not go the distance. So, they were changed, and Siffert was prepared to take over again for the last session, but Rodriguez sat in the car, quite prepared to carry on. The second Martini car was refuelled, and the rear Goodyears were changed before Marko rejoined the race. Previously, Rodriguez had been holding the pace of Larrousse, but was now dropping back, obviously in some sort of trouble. The Martini team urged Marko on, as it looked as if he might be able to take 2nd place if only he could get by Rodriguez. Indeed, Rodriguez' 908/3 was in trouble as the chassis was breaking up at the front, and the left front wheel was leaning in, wearing the tyre out. And, since the Nordschleife is comprised almost entirely of corners, the handling became almost impossible. Larrousse brought the first Martini 908/3 over the line after 44 laps, and nearly two minutes later, Rodriguez arrived in 2nd place with Marko just behind to bag 3rd place for himself and van Lennep. Then came the two remaining Alfa Romeos, followed by the yellow and green 917 of Kauhsen and Jöst, which won the Group 5 Sports Car class. Throughout the race, the two private 3.0-litre flat-8 908/2s of Ballot-Lena/Chasseuil and Kraus/Basche had seldom been out of sight of each other, finishing 7th and 8th respectively.

Held over the weekend of 13 June, Le Mans 1971 was another outright success for Porsche, this time with the Martini 917 of Gijs van Lennep and Helmut Marko scoring the win. Another 917 KH, the Gulf car of Attwood and Müller was 2nd, though all the other four 917s retired.

THE WILLI KAUHSEN INTERVIEW

The author interviews a gesticulating Willi Kauhsen at his Aachen premises.

Willi Kauhsen rose through the touring car ranks to become a Porsche test driver, making a name for himself in sports prototypes and Interserie 917s.

'They thought I was some kind of desperado,' says Willi. 'Back in the late 1950s only beatniks and revolutionaries had beards.' Certainly not racing drivers. You can count the number with beards on one hand: Jo Bonnier, Henry Pescarolo, Peter Westbury, John Watson, Mike Wilds – and Willi Kauhsen. Back in the early 1970s when he raced Interserie 917s, he was not only a formidable driver, but he was also a formidable sight too. 'I've had my beard since May 1958 and in those days it wasn't easy. The police were always pulling me over to ask what I was doing, assuming I was up to no good.'

We are chatting in the showroom of an Aachen-based classic Porsche specialist, surrounded by the cars from Willi's salad days. He is jovial, rotund and still bearded, though it is silver fox now rather than black. The first time I saw him in action was as a lad at the 1969 BOAC 500 at Brands Hatch, though frankly there were so many works' Porsches in evidence that he could have been in any one of them. At any rate the 907 coupé he shared with Rudi Lins crashed out on lap 44 while Redman and Siffert went on to win from Elford and Attwood in 908 Spyders.

Kauhsen was still on his way up the Porsche racing ladder at that point. His father had a trucking business in Aachen, and he started off in the family Mercedes saloon, doing a few local rallies to earn his competition licence. His first proper race was a hillclimb at the Nürburgring driving his own 356 Super 90 Cabriolet, followed by a wet race at Trier airport, where he crashed while leading. The 356 went back to Zuffenhausen to be reconstructed as a race car. 'It was completely stripped out and it had a good strong engine,' he recalls. During the 356 rebuild he bought a Mini Cooper with a 1275cc Downton engine and clocked a practice time of 10m 51s around the Nürburgring, unheard of in a 1300cc car. It brought a protest from Broadspeed boss Ralph Broad, running similar cars for himself and John Fitzpatrick at the time, who doubted anyone could go round under 11 mins in a 1300. Kauhsen wagered an engine rebuild from Broadspeed if the engine was found to be legal, and he got it.

Good results with the 356 sportscar attracted the attention of Klaus Steinmetz at Abarth, and Willi got to drive one of the tiny 1000 TC tin-tops that made up the lower echelons of touring car grids all over Europe in the mid-1960s – typically buzzing around at the back of the pack, engine lid open. A drive followed in a Porsche 356 Carrera Abarth at the Nürburgring 500kms. 'I beat guys like Zanetti and Merzario, and the Abarth factory guy said, "you want to drive a World Championship car for us in '67?" and I said, "yes, why not," and he said, "we don't pay, but at the end of the year you get the car for free."'

In December 1967 at the end-of-season prize-giving in Milan, Willi met wealthy Porsche racer Baron Karl von Wendt, who made him an offer he could not refuse. Hired as co-driver for the 2.0-litre category of the European GT Championship with a Carrera 6, it was time to get serious. Concerned about his weight and fitness, Willi spent the winter of 1967–68 in the gym, getting in shape for the first race, the Monza 1,000kms. It went well:

> *...the old racetrack at Monza included the banking, and it was so bumpy I missed a gear, and the valves were damaged, but we won the 2.0-litre class. The Baron was very rich, and we had a lot of spare parts and spare engines, so it was OK.*

A week later came the Targa Florio, and Willi had an accident in the Carrera 6.

> *It was a very big step from a small saloon car with 85 horsepower to a Carrera 6, and I was too fast in a corner, and I went sideways. The car jumped three or four metres down into a garden, but I kept it going, looked for a way out and came back onto the track! It was a little bent but not too affected. It was ten laps or 750km, so I made it to the end.*

True enough; he and von Wendt came seventh overall amongst the works 907s and Alfa T33s – Elford/Maglioli won in a 907.

In typically wet Ardennes weather, von Wendt and Kauhsen tackled the 1968 Spa 1,000kms.

> *It was raining, raining, raining and we were 9th in practice in the Carrera 6, against the works 907s and 908s and the JW GT40s, and on Sunday I was 4th overall, a 2.0-litre car with a lot of 3.0-litre cars behind me. But then a front wheel bearing broke 20 laps from the end.*

They had had a comfortable class lead, and were classified 21st.

Porsche top brass were impressed, nevertheless. 'After the race Mr Bott from the factory came to me and said, "Mr Kauhsen, what are you doing next year? Do you want to drive for us?" And soon after that we signed a contract.' Meanwhile, Willi won the Spa 24-Hour race with Erwin Kremer and the 96-Hour Marathon de la Route on the Nürburgring Nordschleife, partnered by Herbert Linge and Dieter Glemser in a 2.0 911.

Willi's first job for Porsche was testing at Monza in preparation for the 1969 Daytona 24-Hours. After eighteen hours he had a huge shunt, and the car was destroyed. 'I was thinking, "that's it, before it starts, I've blown it," but Mr Steinemann (new competitions chief) said, "no, no, it's ok. You see and feel a lot of things on the car, and that's important to us so we can make changes and improvements". So, then I did testing with the 907s, the 908s, and with 917 coupés.' Paired with Rudi Lins, he was running 6th at Le Mans in a works 908 but retired after 22 hours with transmission trouble. That year brought some high placings though, including 4th on the Targa Florio, 5th at the Nürburgring 1,000kms, 6th in the Österreichring 1,000kms, all with von Wendt in a 908 Spyder, and not in the factory cars.

Hippie highlife

Highlight of 1970 for Kauhsen, and indeed of his whole career, was 2nd place in the Le Mans 24-Hours with Gérard Larrousse behind the winning 917 of Herrmann/Attwood.

> *The nicest race I did was with the Hippie car [so-called because of its psychedelic livery] in 1970 in Le Mans. We finished second but it was very nice. That was a long-tail car, and I had done a lot of work on this car, and everybody was laughing at me, 'why do we go with a long-tail, and why do I do so much testing with the long-tail?' But it worked very well at high speed.*

Though entered by Martini, the swirling-hued 917 was a works car, sibling of the Elford/Ahrens long-tail car, and it also won the Index of Thermal Efficiency despite ignition fluctuating in the wet.

Having bought Jo Siffert's 5.0-litre flat-12 917/10, Willi was set to partner the moustachioed Swiss driver in Can Am in North America, but sadly Siffert was killed in 1971's end-of-season non-title F1 race at Brands Hatch. Instead of going to the United States, another opportunity popped up for Willi closer to home: the Interserie Championship, which was founded in 1970 as a European version of the Can-Am series. A roll-call of the early contestants reads like a who's who of the racing galaxy: Niki Lauda, Vic Elford, Gérard Larrousse, Leo Kinnunen, Richard Attwood, Gijs van Lennep and Ronnie Peterson, to mention but a few, and Porsches mixed it with Ferrari 512s, McLaren M12s and Lola T70s. Jürgen Neuhaus won the inaugural series in a 917.

In the spirit of the age, the Martini Racing Team's 917 LH #043 was liveried in psychedelic swirls beloved of the Hippie generation; Gérard Larrousse and Willi Kauhsen came 2nd in the 1970 edition of the Le Mans 24-Hours.

'I started the 1971 Interserie Championship with my own 908/2,' remembers Willi. 'My first race was Hockenheim, and I came about 9th.' His laughing countenance goes sombre for a second: 'At the Nürburgring in September I had an accident when a Ferrari 512 came together with a McLaren as I was leaving the pits. I was leading, so when I came back onto the circuit maybe I was too early back to high speed before the tyres had warmed up. Or maybe my right rear tyre picked some up dirt, because it exploded on the fastest part of the circuit.' He wasn't hurt but the car was destroyed. 'I still had a contract with Porsche, so Mr Piëch asked me, "what do you want to do?" and I said, "my car has had a big accident," and he said, "you asked me for a new test car, so now I give you the old test car. You can paint it in Porsche colours and go to the States."' Willi did a couple of rounds of the Can-Am series and acquired another 917 Spyder with his mechanic Klaus Bischoff (now head of the Porsche Museum).

For three seasons, from 1972 to 1974, he and Finn Leo Kinnunen vied for the Interserie title. Both were well matched on circuits like Hockenheim and Silverstone, but on the Nürburgring Kauhsen was the master. At the season opener at the 'Ring, Willi was patently quicker than the Finn.

> *He [kinnunen] was a fast driver and at some race tracks he was very fast, but in the Nürburgring he was not fast enough. I was 30 seconds quicker than him in practice and he said to me, 'A 917 with 1,000 horsepower, it's crazy to do a race with that in the Nürburgring,' and I said, 'for me it's OK. I do a lot of testing with the 917 on the Nürburgring so it's just like a normal racetrack,' and he was very upset because I was that much quicker. Thirty seconds is an eternity, the difference between driving and not driving; he said to me, 'you are stupid, why do you drive here like that?' And I said, 'because I like it!' His was a very defeatist view, because you know you have got him beaten to start with.*

The needle match had started, and very soon the bile overflowed. At Silverstone there was a big coming together:

> *He gave me too much space at the last corner (old Woodcote), and I cut his nose off. He was in front, and I came from the inside, and I braked later, and it was a big accident. And then afterwards we had a fight, a big punch-up! It was very physical, and he was very upset. I said to him, 'why did you brake so early?' And he didn't like that!*

Interserie runner-up

Aside from Kinnunen, who beat him to the Interserie title three years running – 1971, 1972, 1973 – Willi reserves major respect for Mark Donohue. The American won the 1973 Can Am title, taking six out of eight rounds in the new 917/30 Spyder. The flat-12 was now up to 5.4-litres with twin turbos, its bodywork designed for maximum downforce, given that 200mph in a straight line was no problem. Lifting the throttle was like hitting the brakes on a normal car. 'I never saw a driver who was faster than Mark Donohue,' admits Willi. 'He was unbelievable, he would make it look like he had 300 horsepower rather than 1,000. It was a different way to drive, always sideways, not so easy with 1,000 horsepower. And this is a man who can win a TransAm championship with a Camaro and step into a 1,000 horsepower 917 and win with that.' Not without a little guidance from Willi though.

> *He came to the Nürburgring, and he asked Porsche, 'do you know someone who can show me the Ring?' and Porsche said, 'yes, Willi Kauhsen.' So, then I told him, 'You need at least four or five days.' He said, 'four or five days? I am a racing driver; I can't spare the time!' So, I said, 'when you come to the Nürburgring you will understand why.' 'No, no,' he went, 'it must be the same as Laguna Seca.' I said, 'you don't know what you are talking about, Laguna Seca is a*

Willi Kauhsen and Reinhold Jöst celebrate success with the Auto Usdau 917 KH in the 1971 Nürburgring 1,000Kms, placing 6th overall and 1st in the 5.0-litre Sports category.

small circuit, Nürburgring is ten times more than Laguna Seca.' And he came just three days before the Formula 1 race and asked me to show him the racetrack. He said, 'it's no problem, you go in front, and I'll follow you.' He lasted just two corners. But he was a very smart guy, and he agreed, 'after this I know why you asked me to come for four days!'

Their techniques were wildly different.

One time at Laguna Seca I stood by a corner and watched Mark in the 917/10, and every lap he braked so late and went sideways, and he changed from 2nd to 3rd mid-corner; I never saw a guy like this. My style was to brake a little earlier, go on the power and take the line and then give it more, and then you look to the last third of the corner and you can go sideways; but he brakes much, much later than me, goes sideways and goes also with the power, but you have problems with the tyres doing that. He warms up the tyres in half a lap, I do it in two laps. George Follmer was also faster than me over there; he was not the fastest guy, but he was more my style.

The 917 is Willi's favourite Porsche racer. He owns the Interserie Bosch 917/10 and a 908, which lives at his house at Marbella, plus a Silver Anniversary 3.2 Carrera from 1988 and a pair of 930s from the mid-1980s, cabriolet and coupé. He also imports wrecked 356s for his brother Heinz to restore. 'I drove every version of the 917, including the Pink Pig.' That was the wide-track, short-tail car with the cuts of pork drawn on the bodywork, shared at Le Mans with Reinhold Jöst, who crashed it in the night when running 5th.

But the 917/10 with 1,000 horsepower is the most exciting. We were at the Nürburgring testing in 1972 on the day the Israelis were massacred in Munich during the Olympic games. We had three cars, and I was the only driver and in one day I drove 43 laps, the equivalent of 1,000km, on my own and the slowest lap was 7m 43s and the fastest was 7m 07s and the Ferrari F1 car's lap record stood at 7m 13s, and we went 6 seconds quicker with a Can-Am car. It weighed 800 kilos because of the magnesium, titanium and aluminium parts, but you had a clutch with four plates, that's why nothing broke on the 917. It was over-engineered.

I was always the guy who changed something and made the car go faster, from 356 and Mini Cooper to Fiat-Abarth and Alfa Romeo, and all the Porsches of course, and we learned so much from racing that we were able to build a Formula 1 car. No one said to me, 'you have to stop,' so I went bankrupt. But I am happy, because if I hadn't done it, I would always be thinking, 'what if, why didn't I do Formula 1, because maybe I'd have been World Champion.' You don't know until you've tried.

Like beards, really.

The wide-track 'Pink Pig', AKA 917/20 #001, was driven by Willi Kauhsen and Reinhold Jöst in the 1971 Le Mans 24-Hours, but retired after Jöst crashed at Arnage in the 12th hour whilst running 5th.

THE HILLS ARE ALIVE

The Austrian 1,000 kilometres at the spectacular Österreichring on 27 June 1971 was the last round in Europe for the 5.0-litre Sports Car and 3.0-litre Prototype Championships, and in spite of Porsche having already won the 1971 title, a very good entry was received by the organisers. The JW Gulf team entered two 917s, while the Porsche factory produced a single car entered under the Martini team colours, but which was actually a full works entry, blessed with five spare factory engines and a full complement of factory mechanics to run it. Against them was a single 312P Ferrari flat-12 for Ickx and Regazzoni, and seven factory-backed Autodelta Alfa Romeo Tipo 33-3s. There had been a reshuffle in the JW Gulf team when Jackie Oliver opted out of his contract so he could go and drive Shadows in Can-Am, and his place was taken by Richard Attwood, who was by now a relatively old hand, as number two to Rodriguez. The second car was in the capable hands of Siffert and Bell, both of whom relished racing on the Österreichring. The team also had a training car, mostly driven by Attwood and Bell, which was fitted with a set of Girling double disc brakes, with bigger discs and a new type of caliper. It transpired that the real reason for the lone Porsche factory car, hurriedly painted in Martini livery, was also one of brakes, as this 917 was fitted with an electronic anti-lock braking system. Although the Porsche engineers were tight-lipped, it appeared to be a similar ABS system to that developed by Teldix of Heidelberg in conjunction with Mercedes-Benz. The drivers nominated for the factory car were Helmut Marko and Gérard Larrousse, neither of whom was especially enthusiastic, preferring the feel of a direct braking system. In the JW-Gulf Team pits, they changed the 917's rear bodywork from the newest 1971 pattern with vertical fins to the earlier type with no fins and an adjustable spoiler in the central valley behind the engine, and there was general approval from the drivers. Every time the Martini 917 stopped at the pits, a group of engineers and electronics experts crowded around the car. But when the training car of the JW Automotive team pitted, nobody seemed very interested in its double discs, except the lonely Girling rep.

On the front row of the 3-2-3 grid were Rodriguez and the Gulf 917, Ickx in the 312 P Ferrari and Marko in the Martini 917. Behind them were Siffert in the second Gulf 917 and Müller in the Ferrari 512S, and the third row consisted of the complete Alfa Romeo team in Tipo 33-3s. The rest of the field was largely made up of eleven privateer Porsches ranging from 906, 910, 911s and 914/6s. From the start, Rodriguez began to pull out a lead of nearly two seconds a lap, though Ickx was keeping him honest. Nobody else could stay with these two drivers, Siffert having become involved in a battle with Müller and Marko and the three Alfa Romeos. By lap 28, Rodriguez had a 25-second lead, and the JW-Automotive pit was beginning to prepare for the first refuelling stop, the filling-up time having been slowed by a regulation that limited gravity-feed towers to the height of the roof of the pits, which of course would not be the case today. A lap later, the 917's lead had dropped to 23 seconds, and it was heading for the pits instead of whizzing by at full speed. The fuel injection pressure had fallen dramatically, and the fault was traced to a flat battery, which was replaced, and Rodriguez rejoined in 7th place behind the Alfa Romeos and the Ferrari 312 P.

At this stage, it was obvious that neither Marko nor Siffert could challenge Ickx, and Rodriguez was apparently too far back to make a challenge, so all the Ferrari team had to do was to keep the 312 P lapping consistently. However, JW's Wyre and Yorke were still planning on winning the race, despite Siffert retiring with clutch failure. Considered race strategy in the JW pits gradually got Rodriguez within striking distance of the Alfa Romeos and Ferrari, and although Atwood did a short stint, Rodriguez was let loose once more to chase down the Ferrari, which was just 91 seconds ahead, with Regazzoni taking over the Ferrari from Ickx. At 145 laps, Rodriguez had the Ferrari in sight, and on the next lap, the two cars went past the pits side by side, the 917 getting onto the same lap as the Ferrari as they went up the hill at the end of the start-finish straight, drawing away as it did so, the 600bhp of the 917's 5.0-litres really telling on the hills. Rodriguez had got his lap time down to 1m 39.39s, a new circuit record, and with the fuel load going down, there was probably more to come. But then, on lap 148, the Ferrari suffered a suspension failure and Regazzoni crashed into the guardrail. Much against his better instincts, Rodriguez was given the appropriate 'Easy' sign from his pit, and he no doubt grudgingly slowed down to lap in 1m 50s to bring the 917 home in one piece to claim its final Manufacturers' Championship victory in Europe.

The winning JW Automotive Gulf 917 of Jo Siffert and Brian Redman has a narrow lead over the 4th placed Porsche Salzburg Konstruktionen 917 KH #023 of Vic Elford and Richard Attwood at the top of the hill after the start-finish straight at the new Österreichring circuit during the 1970 Zeltweg 1,000Kms.

END OF TERM

There was one counter left on the calendar, and the World Sportscar Championship cortege shipped over to Watkins Glen in Upper New York State for a last throw of the dice. There was actually little to play for in terms of the title, because Porsche had already grasped that – for the third year running – with eight out of eleven race victories. The Watkins Glen track had been lengthened and widened as part of a renovation scheme. The Martini Racing Team opted out, however, leaving the pair of Gulf-JW Automotive 917 sevens entered for Siffert and van Lennep and Bell and Attwood, with the concerted opposition in the shape of a trio of Alfa Romeo Tipo-33/3s for Pescarolo/Stommelen, Galli/Elford and de Adamich/Peterson, as well as the much-repaired Ferrari P312 for Jacky Ickx and Mario Andretti. There was also the sole privately-entered 917 of David Piper, driven by Mario Cabral and Tony Adamowicz while the rest of the pack consisted mainly of 911s, Corvettes and Lolas.

Two hours into the race, Bell parked his 917 on the start-finish line with a broken throttle pedal. It took some time for the JW mechanics to fix it, and he re-joined second from last, although he did prevent a complete rout by setting fastest time of the day at 1m 0.82s, 127.98mph. Van Lennep led for a while, but heavy rain affected the latter part of the race, taking out several key players. The winners were Peterson/de Adamich for Alfa Romeo – and it has to be said that Super-Swede Ronnie Peterson was very much on a charge as far as his race career was concerned. Next up came Siffert/van Lennep, two laps behind in their 917, and the Bell Atwood 917 finished 3rd, albeit ten laps down. This slight denouement for Porsche served to demonstrate that Alfa Romeo was in the ascendant – as Ferrari would be – in view of the upcoming sea change switch in the regulations from 5.0-litre Sports Cars to 3.0-litre Prototypes. And that is another story as far as Porsche racing history is concerned, focusing on turbocharged evolutions of the 911, 935 and 936.

A decade would pass before the all-conquering 956 and 962 dominated Group C in the 1980s.

Tragically, two of the heroes of the era, Jo Siffert and Pedro Rodriguez, would lose their lives before the year was out – Rodriguez in mid-July at the Norisring driving a Ferrari 512 in an Interserie race (that, like when Jim Clark perished at Hockenheim, was a race that really did not matter in the grand scheme of things), and Jo Siffert was killed in the end-of-season Victory Meeting at Brands Hatch when his F1 BRM P160 inexplicably hit the barriers, overturned and caught fire. Not wishing to end on a gloomy note, it is important to say that the majority of the cast went on to achieve major successes, some in Porsches, and several of them figure prominently today in demos at Historic events such as Goodwood, Nürburgring and Le Mans.

Back to the era encompassed by this book, and it is not far-fetched to claim that the 917 was surely the racing car of the decade, making 600bhp in its fully-fledged normally-aspirated 5.0-litre incarnation, with a 230mph potential top speed, enabling drivers to set lap records at all the fast circuits, including 162mph at Spa-Francorchamps, and 150mph at Monza and Le Mans. Porsche began this episode as sure-fire class winners – able to conquer outright ultimate road-racing challenges such as the Targa Florio as well as numerous long-distance endurance races and mountain-climbs, ultimately producing a colossus of a car that was never toppled from its plinth.

A marvellous line-up of 917s at the Porsche Museum, Zuffenhausen, representing each stage of the model's evolution.

ACKNOWLEDGEMENTS

We all have 'formative years' at some point in our lives, and mine, I reflect, coincided with the years covered in this book, the years when Porsche's fortunes in motor racing were very much on the up-and-up. That is my motivation here: to chart the rise of the marque from class winners and occasional victors to World Champions in the Sports-Prototype categories.

As with my six previous books on Porsche – including Carreras, Turbos and GT3s – I have been exceptionally fortunate to have the stalwart support of pals who have provided photos taken on test drives and when covering races and rallies. First up is super-snapper Antony Fraser, with whom I worked for the past 25 years doing that sort of stuff all over Europe, from the Nürburgring to Le Mans, Charade to Albi, Gaisberg to Schauinsland. We journeyed regularly to these semi-exotic locations before the Covid-19 lockdown torpedoed our kind of journalism, but the legacy is an amazing assortment of images showing Porsche sports racing cars in their natural habitat.

Next up is Roger Dixon, whom I have known since the Black and Gold JPS era when we would frequently bump into each other at European F1 Grands Prix in the early 1970s, he snapping racing cars, me touting ciggies and sundry John Player Special publicity material. Roger has very kindly supplied images of Porsches relevant to this book, taken in-period at Le Mans and Brands Hatch, especially on several occasions at the BOAC 500. Nowadays, we enjoy a coffee and a chat at Goodwood's Festival of Speed and the Revival meeting.

I followed the 2018 Le Mans Classic with photographer Sarah Hall, and between us we snapped the appropriate sports prototypes that were running. I have attended Le Mans Classic a number of times, including a couple with Antony Fraser, as well as Nürburgring Old Timer and Spa Six Hours, so you will see his (and my) photos from those events too. I have had the pleasure of working with Alex Denham, covering historic events, and there is something from her in here too. I met Sean Scott Smith in Connecticut whilst visiting racer Murray Smith; we toured local Porsche specialists and had lunch with Sean, who, some years down the road, has provided a selection of his photos from Lime Rock and RennSport Reunion at Laguna Seca racetracks. Other helpers on the photographic front are Marika Haapavaara, who visited the REVs Institute to check out their Porsche collection, and Verena Proebst, who provided photos and a career history of her dad Walter racing his 910 and 907 in the 1970s. From the annals, I have received and selected a large number of period images from the Porsche Museum collections at Zuffenhausen head office, via archivists Tobias Mauler and Jens Torner.

I also need to express gratitude to several famous racing drivers for giving interviews over the years, including Gijs van Lennep (who also penned the Foreword), Hans Herrmann, Herbert Linge, Richard Attwood, Vic Elford, Gérard Larrousse, Brian Redman and Willi Kauhsen, all of whom played a vital part in helping Porsche achieve superiority in the World Sportscar Championship chronicled here.

Over the years, I have been fortunate enough to have been let loose in three examples of the cars featured in the story: a 906, a 910 and a 917. So, I would like to credit the late Adrian Hamilton of Duncan Hamilton Motors (also hosting Roald Goethe's Gulf collection) for letting me loose in the Hampshire countryside in the ex-Mike D'Udy 906 #101, which involved Antony Fraser and my daughter Zoë crouching on the grass verge snapping my raucous progress through the rural idyll. We even took the car into Farnham town centre – just because you could with a 906, the last of the Porsche sports racers that could legitimately be used in this way.

I am also eternally grateful to Will Stone, then of race car auctioneers Fiskens, for enabling a session at Chobham test track – also known as Longcross – in Bill Bradley's former 910 #020. Once the province of military vehicles, Chobham replicates a B-road scenario but magically incorporates a shallow 90-degree banked corner and a mini-Nordschleife section known as The Snake. Untroubled by rival road testers, let alone any oncoming traffic, it is a marvellous location for putting a 910 through its paces.

With similar appreciation, I would like to offer heartfelt thanks to historic racer Claudio Roddaro for allowing me a dozen or so memorable laps of Donington Circuit in his 917 #037. The occasion was the RennSport Collective, and after a couple of laps with a bunch of 911s formed up behind me to augment the shoot, I was once again alone at the wheel of the epitome of Porsche's iconic sports prototypes, this time on a world-class racetrack.

APPENDIX: SPECIFICATIONS

TYPE 904 CARRERA GTS

In production:	1963–65
Chassis:	ladder chassis, fibreglass body
Wheelbase:	90.5in (2,300mm)
Track:	51.7in (1,310mm) front and rear
Height:	42in (1,100mm)
Ground clearance:	4.7in (120mm)
Engine:	flat-4, bore/stroke: 92.0 mm x 73.91 mm = 1966cc
Compression ratio:	9.8:1
Horsepower:	198bhp @ 7,800rpm
Drivetrain layout:	mid-engine, rear-drive
Transmission:	five-speed manual
Suspension:	coil springs, dampers, unequal-length A-arms
Wheels:	15in (380mm)
Brakes:	275mm (10.8in) discs front, 285mm (11.2in) rear
Drag coefficient:	cd0.34
Performance:	0–60mph (97 km/h): 6.0 seconds; top speed: 160mph (260 km/h)
Weight:	four-cylinder 904 = 1,443 pounds (655kg)
Numbers built:	109 Type 904/4; 7 Type 904 Bergspyder; 40 Type 904/6; 3 Type 904/8

TYPE 906 'CARRERA SIX'

In production:	1965–66
Chassis:	triangulated multi-tubular steel spaceframe, fibreglass body
Wheelbase:	2,300mm (90.5in)
Track:	1,338mm (52.7in) front, 1,402mm (55.2in) rear
Length:	4,113mm (161.9in)
Engine:	901/20, flat-6, bore/stroke: 80mm x 66mm = 1991cc
Compression ratio:	10.3:1
Horsepower:	210bhp @ 8,000rpm
Drivetrain layout:	mid-engine, rear-drive

Continued

Transmission:	five-speed manual
Suspension:	coil springs, dampers, unequal-length A-arms
Wheels:	15in (380mm)
Brakes:	275mm (10.8in) discs front, 285mm (11.2in) rear
Drag coefficient:	cd0.35
Performance:	0–60mph (97km/h): 6.0 seconds; top speed: 165mph (270km/h)
Weight:	620kg (1,367lb)
Numbers built:	73 Type 906/6; 8 Type 906/8, including 6 Bergspyders

TYPE 910

In production:	1966
Chassis:	triangulated multi-tubular steel spaceframe, fibreglass body
Wheelbase:	2,300mm (90.5in)
Track:	1,430mm (56.3in) / (54.3in) front, 1,380mm rear
Length:	4,113mm (161.9in)
Engine:	901/21, flat-6, bore/stroke: 80mm x 66mm = 1991cc
Compression ratio:	10.3:1
Horsepower:	220bhp @ 8,000rpm
Drivetrain layout:	mid-engine, rear-drive
Transmission:	five-speed manual
Suspension:	coil springs, dampers, unequal-length wishbones
Wheels:	13in
Brakes:	ventilated discs front and rear
Drag coefficient:	cd0.35
Performance:	0–60mph (97 km/h): 6.0 seconds; top speed: 165mph (270km/h)
Weight:	580kg (1,279lb)
Numbers built:	22 Type 910/6; 13 Type 910/8, including 6 Bergspyders

TYPE 907/8

In production:	1966–67
Chassis:	triangulated multi-tubular steel spaceframe (one in aluminium), fibreglass body
Wheelbase:	2,300mm (90.5in) coupé; 2,264mm (89.1in) Spyder
Track:	1,462mm (57.6in) front, 1,403mm (55.2in) rear
Length:	4,650mm (183.1in)
Engine:	aluminium 771/0, flat-8, bore/stroke: 76.0mm x 54.6mm = 1981cc
Compression ratio:	10.5:1

Horsepower:	260bhp @ 8,800rpm
Drivetrain layout:	mid-engine, rear-drive
Transmission:	five-speed manual
Suspension:	wishbones, coil springs, dampers, anti-roll bars
Wheels:	13in
Brakes:	ventilated discs front and rear
Drag coefficient:	cd0.27
Performance:	0–60mph (97km/h): 4.8 seconds; top speed: 183.3mph (294km/h)
Weight:	757kg (1,669lb)
Numbers built:	4 Type 907/6; 14 Type 907/8

TYPE 908

In production:	1968–75
Chassis:	triangulated multi-tubular aluminium spaceframe (17 in steel), fibreglass body
Wheelbase:	2,300mm (90.5in) Coupé; 2,264mm (89.1in) Spyder
Track:	1,462mm (57.6in) front, 1,454mm (57.2in) rear
Length:	4,020mm (158.3in)
Engine:	aluminium 771/0, flat-8, bore/stroke: 85.0mm x 66.0mm = 2997cc
Compression ratio:	10.4:1
Horsepower:	350bhp @ 8,400rpm
Drivetrain layout:	mid-engine, rear-drive
Transmission:	916 five-speed manual
Suspension:	wishbones, coil springs, dampers, anti-roll bars
Wheels:	13in
Brakes:	Ventilated discs front and rear
Drag coefficient:	cd0.27
Performance:	0–60mph (97km/h): 4.8 seconds; top speed: 183.3mph (260km/h)
Weight:	757kg (1,669lb)
Numbers built:	31 Type 908/1; 35 Type 908/2; 17 Type 908/3

TYPE 917

In production:	1969–73
Chassis:	triangulated multi-tubular gas-pressurised spaceframe (72 in steel, 34 in magnesium), fibre-glass body
Wheelbase:	2,300mm (90.5in)
Track:	1,564mm (61.6in) front, 1,584mm (62.4in) rear
Length:	4,149mm (163.3in)
Engine:	912/00, aluminium, flat-12, bore/stroke: 85.0mm x 66.0mm = 4494cc; 86.8mm x 70.4mm = 4999cc
Compression ratio:	10.5:1
Horsepower:	560bhp/600bhp @ 8,300rpm
Drivetrain layout:	mid-engine, rear-drive
Transmission:	917 five-speed manual
Suspension:	wishbones, coil springs, dampers, anti-roll bars
Wheels:	13in
Brakes:	ventilated discs front and rear
Drag coefficient:	cd0.27
Performance:	0–60mph (97km/h): 4.2 seconds; top speed: 224mph (360km/h)
Weight:	800kg (1,764lb)
Numbers built:	81 Type 917; 25 Type 917/10/30 Can-Am; 1 Kremer

The Goodwood Revival is a great event for seeing different generations of Porsche sports-racing cars – as here, with 904, 910 and RS60 in the paddock.

Vic Elford rounds Druids Hairpin at Brands Hatch in the1969 BOAC 500 in one of the works 908 KH, placing 2nd with Richard Attwood co-driving.

INDEX

First published in 2025 by
The Crowood Press Ltd
Ramsbury, Marlborough
Wiltshire SN8 2HR

enquiries@crowood.com
www.crowood.com

British Library Cataloguing-in-Publication Data
A catalogue record for this book is available from the British Library.

ISBN 978 0 7198 4459 1

Picture page 2: The 908 LH of Claudio Roddaro takes the chequered flag at the 2018 Le Mans Classic.

Page 4: The 906 could legitimately be used on road and track, and over the years many, such as this, running in the Dordogne in 2007, have featured on the Tour Auto Optic 2000.

Interview Dates
Richard Attwood: 2013 and 2016
Vic Elford: 2006, 2013 and 2016
Hans Herrmann: 2010 and 2013
Willi Kauhsen: 2012
Gérard Larrousse: 2009 and 2018
Gijs van Lennep: 2008, 2010, 2016 and 2024
Herbert Linge: 2008
Brian Redman: 2009 and 2023

Typeset by Simon and Sons
Cover design by Keith Woodcock
Printed and bound in India by Parksons Graphics Pvt Ltd

Photographic credits

Michael Baillie: p.193.

Alex Denham: p.32, p.61 (bottom right).

Roger Dixon: p.8, p.9 (bottom), p.14 (bottom), p.60 (top and bottom), p.62, p.80 (top right), p.81 (top left), p.82, p.85 (left), p.86 (top right), p.94, p.96 (top and bottom), p.97 (top), p.99, p.100 (top and bottom), p.105, p.106 (top), p.120 (top and bottom), p.123 (top and bottom), p.124, p.125, p.145, p.162, p.163, p.164, p.175, p.201 (top), p.206 (right).

Antony Fraser: p.4 (frontispiece), p.11, p.12 (left), p.14 (top), p.15 (top and bottom), p.23, p.28 (left and right), p.34 (top and bottom), p.37 (bottom right), p.43, p.48, p.49 (top), p.50 (top and bottom), p.51, p.52 (bottom), p.53 (top and bottom), p.64, p.65 (top and bottom), p.66, p.67 (top and bottom), p.69 (right), p.70 (bottom), p.72 (top left), p.74, p.76 (bottom), p.77 (top and bottom), p.78 (top and bottom), p.79 (top), p.85 (right), p.86 (left and bottom right), p.87, p.88 (top and bottom), p.90 (right), p.92 (left), p.106 (middle), p.113, p.127, p.129, p.131, p.134, p.141 (bottom), p.146 (top), p.147, p.153 (left and right), p.154 (top and bottom), p.155 (top), p.173, p.177, p.182, p.183, p.184 (top and bottom), p.189, p.190 (top), p.191, p.199, p.200, p.201 (bottom), p.202.

Marika Haapavaara: p.89, p.122.

Sarah Hall: p.2 (frontispiece), p.38 (top), p.136.

Albert Mensinga: p.19.

Porsche Photo Archive: p.9 (top), p.10 (bottom), p.12 (right), p.16 (top and bottom), p.18, p.20, p.21, p.24, p.25 (top and bottom), p.26, p.27 (top and bottom), p.29, p.30, p.31 (top and bottom), p.33, p.35, p.41, p.42, p.44, p.46, p.52(top), p.54, p.55 (top and bottom), p.56 top and bottom), p.58 (all), p.61 (top left), p.68 (top and bottom), p.69 (left), p.70 (top), p.71, p.72 (bottom left and top right), p.73, p.75 (top and bottom), p.76 (top), p.79 (bottom), p.80 (top left), p.80 (bottom), p.83, p.90 (top left and bottom left), p.97 (bottom), p.98, p.101 (top), p.102, p.103, p.106 (bottom), p.107, p.108, p.109 (left and right), p.110, p.111, p.112 (top and bottom), p.114, p.115 (top), p.116, p.117, p.118 (top and bottom), p.119 (top and bottom), p.121, p.126, p.135, p.137, p.138, p.142, p.143, p.146 (bottom), p.148, p.149, p.150, p.151 (top), p.156, p.157, p.158, p.159, p.160, p.161, p.166, p.167, p.168, p.169, p.170 (left and right), p.172, p.174, p.176, p.178, p.186, p.187, p.188 (top), p.190 (bottom), p.194, p.195, p.196, p.198.

Verena Proebst: p.91 (top and bottom), p.92 (right), p.93.

Johnny Tipler: p.6, p.10 (top), p.13, p.17, p.22 (top and bottom), p.36 (left and right), p.37 (top left and bottom left), p.38 (bottom), p.39 (all), p.40 (left and right), p.45 (top and bottom), p.47, p.49 (bottom), p.61 (middle left), p.61 (top right), p.81 (bottom left and top right), p.84, p.101 (bottom), p.115 (bottom), p.130, p.133, p.139, p.141 (top), p.151 (bottom), p.155 (bottom), p.171, p.179 (top and bottom), p.185, p.188 (bottom), p.206 (left).